Explorations in Information Space

Explorations in Information Space is an elegant book on the foundations of knowledge flow. Boisot and his co-authors have substantially extended his information space or *I-Space* theorizing to provide a rich framework of situated knowledge and agency. By taking knowledge to be an operator that acts on data to extract information from it, this framework enables a much more nuanced approach to knowledge based theories of the firm and to institutions more generally. This book will be a great resource for sociologists, economists and organizational theorists who are focused on understanding emerging information and institutional architectures of the 21st Century.

John Seely Brown
Former Chief Scientist, Xerox Corp
Co author of *The Social Life of Information* and *The Only Sustainable Edge*.

In a beautifully written collection of essays, Max Boisot develops his thinking on the intertwined concepts of space, time, and knowledge. He is one of those rare authors who can speak lucidly and authoritatively across disciplinary boundaries. His prose compels our attention and the content is far-reaching. Knowledge is more than mere information or data and all human societies have relied on its development. Nevertheless, recognizing the increasing importance of knowledge in modern economies, Boisot develops a challenging theoretical framework that provides invaluable insights about the world in which we live.

Geoffrey Hodgson, Research Professor in Business Studies at the University of Hertfordshire.

'Knowledge' has been all the rage in many, perhaps most, management fields over the last two decades. It is fair to speak of a 'knowledge movement' that cuts across traditional disciplinary and functional borderlines. Max Boisot has been one the primary thought leaders of the knowledge movement. His notion of the 'information space' and the theorizing underlying it have been among the most important innovations within the knowledge movement, and has been immensely helpful for thinking about knowledge processes within and between firms (and other social systems). In this important new collection of papers, Boisot and various co-authors further extend the knowledge-based view of the firm and expand on the theoretical underpinnings of the information space framework. Taken as a whole the papers build an impressive case for thinking of knowledge in organizations are value-creating processes rather than stand-alone resources.

Nicolai J Foss, Professor, Director, Center for Strategic Management and Globalization. Copenhagen Business School.

Few people can write in a way that is relevant to both scholars and practitioners, and Max Boisot is undoubtedly one of them. In this marvellous book, the inventor of I-space, along with his associates, seek to theorize organizational knowledge and show how it may be managed to yield competitive advantage. Theoretically sophisticated and empirically rich, this is a beautifully written account that moves beyond platitudes about the 'knowledge economy' to alert us to the complex nature of organizational knowledge and the conditions in which it may be cultivated. If there is nothing more practical than a good theory, this is a theory of organizational knowledge that resonates with practice precely because it takes the right theoretical distance from it.

Haridimos Tsoukas, The George D. Mavros Research Professor of Organization and Management, ALBA Greece and Professor of Organization Studies, University of Warwick, UK.

This book is essential for those who want to understand the knowledge economy. Using a powerful conceptual framework—I-Space—this book demonstrates that knowledge is deeply grounded in context, history and action. Anyone seeking to create value in the knowledge economy needs to understand the distinctions that this book develops so richly and so remarkably. Anyone looking for a research agenda to pursue will find that this book frames powerful questions that will occupy all of us for years to come. Whether you are a manager, entrepreneur or academic, this book is a compelling source of insight and analysis.

John Hagel, Chairman, Deloitte Center on Innovation.

Explorations in Information Space

Knowledge, Agents, and Organization

Max H. Boisot, Ian C. MacMillan, and
Kyeong Seok Han

OXFORD
UNIVERSITY PRESS

OXFORD

UNIVERSITY PRESS

Great Clarendon Street, Oxford OX2 6DP

Oxford University Press is a department of the University of Oxford.
It furthers the University's objective of excellence in research, scholarship,
and education by publishing worldwide in

Oxford New York

Auckland Cape Town Dar es Salaam Hong Kong Karachi
Kuala Lumpur Madrid Melbourne Mexico City Nairobi
New Delhi Shanghai Taipei Toronto

With offices in

Argentina Austria Brazil Chile Czech Republic France Greece
Guatemala Hungary Italy Japan Poland Portugal Singapore
South Korea Switzerland Thailand Turkey Ukraine Vietnam

Oxford is a registered trademark of Oxford University Press
in the UK and in certain other countries

Published in the United States
by Oxford University Press Inc., New York

© Max H. Boisot, Ian C. MacMillan, and Kyeong Seok Han 2007

The moral rights of the authors have been asserted
Database right Oxford University Press (maker)

First published 2007

British Library Cataloguing in Publication Data
Data available

Library of Congress Cataloging in Publication Data
Boisot, Max.
    Explorations in information science: knowledge, actors, and firms/Max H.
Boisot, Ian C. MacMillan, and Kyeong Seok Han.
        p.   cm.
    Includes bibliographical references and index.
    ISBN 978–0–19–925087–5 (alk. paper)
1. Knowledge management.   2. Intellectual capital.   3. Organizational
learning.   4. Information superhighway.   5. Intellectual property.
I. MacMillan, Ian C., 1940–   II. Han, Kyeong Seok.   III. Title.
    HD30.2.B638 2007
    658.4'038–dc22   2007020922

Typeset by SPI Publisher Services, Pondicherry, India
Printed in Great Britain
on acid-free paper by
Biddles Ltd., King's Lynn, Norfolk

ISBN 978–0–19–925087–5

1 3 5 7 9 10 8 6 4 2

Contents

Acknowledgements

Chapter 1: Reprinted from the *Journal of Evolutionary Economics*, Vol. 14, 2004, pp 43–67. Max Boisot and Agusti Canals, 'Data, Information and Knowledge: Have We Got It Right?'. © 2004. With kind permission of Springer Science and Business Media.

Chapter 2: Reprinted from *LRP Long Range Planning*, Vol. 37, 2004, pp 505–24. Max Boisot and Ian MacMillan, 'Crossing Epistemological Boundaries: Managerial and Entrepreneurial Approaches to Knowledge Management', © 2004. With permission from Elsevier.

Chapter 3: Reprinted from the *Journal of Bioeconomics*, Vol. 7, 2005, pp 309–34. Max Boisot and Yan Li, 'Codification, Abstraction and Firm Differences: A Cognitive Information-based Perspective', © 2005. With kind permission of Springer Science and Business Media.

Chapter 4: Reprinted from the *Journal of Bioeconomics*, Vol. 8, 2006, pp 219–51. Max Boisot and Yan Li, 'Organizational versus Market Knowledge: From Concrete Embodiment to Abstract Representation', © 2006. With kind permission of Springer Science and Business Media.

Chapter 5: Reprinted from the *Journal of Information Technology*, Vol. 21, 2006, pp 239–48, Max Boisot, 'Moving to the edge of chaos: bureaucracy, IT and the challenge of Complexity'. © 2006. Reproduced with permission of Palgrave MacMillan.

Chapter 6: Reprinted from the *Journal of Evolutionary Economics*, Vol. 17, No. 1, 2007, pp 63–93, Max Boisot, Ian MacMillan, and Kyeong Seok Han, 'Property Rights and Information Flows: A Simulation Approach' © 2007. With kind permission of Springer Science and Business Media.

List of Figures

List of Tables

Notes on Contributors

Max Boisot is Professor of Strategic Management at the Birmingham Business School, the University of Birmingham, Associate Fellow at Templeton College, Oxford University, and visiting scholar at the Snider Center for Entrepreneurial Research, The Wharton School, the University of Pennsylvania. Max Boisot has published in *Administrative Science Quarterly* in *Research Policy*, and in *Organization Science*. His book, *Knowledge Assets: Securing Competitive Advantage in the Information Economy* (Oxford University Press, 1998) was awarded the Ansoff Prize for the best book on strategy in 2000.

Dr. Agustí Canals is associate professor at the Universitat Oberta de Catalunya in Barcelona, and previously served on the faculties of the ESADE Business School and the Universitat Autònoma de Barcelona. He received his MBA and his PhD in Management Sciences from the ESADE Business School. He holds also a MSc in Physics from the Universitat Autònoma de Barcelona. He has been a Visiting Fellow of the Warwick Business School at the University of Warwick and a Visiting Scholar of the Sol C. Snider Entrepreneurial Research Center at the Wharton School, University of Pennsylvania. He has published several specialized and divulgation articles and the book, in Spanish, *Gestión del Conocimiento* ('Knowledge Management').

Dr. **Kyeong Seok Han** received his Ph.D. degree in MIS (Management Information Systems) at Purdue University in Indiana, USA. He was an assistant professor of University of Houston. He was a visiting scholar at The Snider Entrepreneurial Research Center, the Wharton School. He published research papers in well-known journals such as *International Journal of Electronic Commerce, Journal of Evolutionary Economics and Applied Economics*. Currently he is a professor of MIS, Soongsil University in Seoul, Korea. His e-mail address is kshan@ssu.ac.kr.

Yan Li is a doctoral candidate in economics at George Mason University. Prior to her doctoral studies she worked for Capital One, for Booz Allen &

Hamilton, and for Bain & Company in the U.S., and for Procter & Gamble in China. Yan Li received her BA from Tsinghua University in Beijing, and an MBA from the Wharton School, University of Pennsylvania.

Ian C. MacMillan is the Executive Director of the Sol C. Snider Entrepreneurial Center and Dhirubhai Ambani Professor of Entrepreneurial Management at the Wharton School, University of Pennsylvania. He received his BSc. from the University of Witwatersrand, and his M.B.A. and D.B.A. from the University of South Africa. He has published numerous articles and books on organizational politics, new ventures, and strategy formulation. His articles have appeared in the *Harvard Business Review*, *The Sloan Management Review*, *The Journal of Business Venturing,* and others. He is co-author with Rita McGrath of *The Entrepreneurial Mindset* and *MarketBusters*.

List of Abbreviations

AIC   algorithmic information complexity

CKOs   chief knowledge officers

EHMG   ethnically homogenous middleman group

ICTs   information and communication technologies

IPRs   intellectual property rights

CASs   complex adaptive systems

RBV   resource-based view

SOEs   state-owned enterprises

SLC   Social Learning Cycle

Introduction

Max H. Boisot

1. Background Issues

As humankind seeks to extend its spatiotemporal reach both on and beyond its planet, it is constantly being forced by a recalcitrant nature to renegotiate the terms of its covenant with her. In some cases, the bargaining gets tough and nature takes offence, gradually revealing her anger with the terms that humanity seeks to impose on her through rising temperatures and melting icecaps (Stern 2007). In other cases, where humanity shows some degree of respect for nature's laws—as they apply to inanimate things, living creatures, and, indeed, humanity itself—she can be cajoled into concessions of benefit to the species such as longer lifespans, healthier and more enjoyable lives, and greater security. Yet nature is coy about revealing her laws. Knowledge of these has to be painstakingly teased out of her, systematically in the case of science, less so in the case of other social and institutional practices.

Our constant need to undertake informed negotiations with nature in order to survive and prosper means that we have always lived in a knowledge society. If we have only just become aware of it, perhaps this is because it has only been in the past fifty years that mankind's collective claims on nature have begun to exceed what nature is currently prepared to deliver. Unfortunately, it now appears that we lack many of the skills needed to negotiate with nature and hence to move forward without offending her. The need for valid knowledge, then, has never been greater. Valid knowledge is the key to the generation and, through its transformation into capital, the exploitation of wealth. But valid for whom? In the Middle Ages, for example, the Church was the wealthiest single institution in Christendom (Baschet 2006) and the Church, through its control of education, largely determined what passed off as valid knowledge and what went against its teachings. The early Church had its doctors some 1,500 hundred years before the universities had their doctors in physics and chemistry. What passed off as valid knowledge for Saint Jerome or Saint Augustine would be unrecognizable as such to a modern scientist.

Although we have been discussing the problem of valid knowledge since Plato and probably before, it was only in the second half of the twentieth century that such knowledge came to be seen as an economic resource in its own right rather than as a support for the exploitation of other, more physical economic resources such as land, labor power, energy, etc. And even then, the conception of knowledge as an *economic* resource was largely confined to its technological and scientific manifestations. Only since the 1990s has the economic conception of knowledge broadened to incorporate other forms such as know how, organization competences, etc.

With the rise of the service economy and the decline of employment in manufacturing, there is a general feeling that the game has changed. The knowledge content of goods and services is going up relative to their material content. Economic value is increasingly seen to reside in the former—that is, in intangible assets—rather than in the latter. Yet the volatility experienced during the dot-com bubble of 2001 suggests a high degree of uncertainty with regard to how exactly knowledge relates to economic value. We are still attempting to force-fit intangible assets into schemes of representation—such as accounting, for example—designed for the tangible economy, only to discover that the asset-backing of the young dot-com 'stars' was more fragile than the balance sheet indicated. We want to turn knowledge into a thing with definite boundaries which can be measured, manipulated, and traded. In short, we want to *reify* knowledge.

It is becoming more difficult to do so. Consider the following example. Two years ago, one of us (MB) was invited by Markus Nordberg, the project manager of the Atlas Project at CERN, just outside Geneva, to spend a couple of days at the high-energy physics research institute looking at its installations. One of the machines, the size of a two-storey building, was designed to generate and weigh antihydrogen particles. MB asked the physicist in charge of the machine, Michael Doser, how sensitive the machine was. Imagine that the machine was weighing Mont Blanc, Michael Doser replied, and that a snow flake fell on the mountain. The machine would be able to register the difference in weight that the addition of the snowflake made to the mountain. Now, the knowledge required to achieve such levels of precision is distributed among thousands of highly trained specialists, it is also embedded in numerous measuring instruments, technical standards, manuals, formal and informal organizational procedures, etc. Most of the people involved may not actually know each other. If the machine has a glitch, a large network of people, objects, processes, and institutions needs to be mobilized. Knowing what procedures to follow, whom to contact, and in what organization is a valid and useful source of knowledge in such a case. How easy is it to contact them? Are they approachable? What then flows between these experts? A mixture of data, information, and knowledge. Two different types of asset are involved here. First there is the machine as a unique tangible asset, too specialized to have any market value in alternative uses—it is what economist would term a transaction-specific investment (Williamson 1985). Second, there is the organization that creates, operates, and maintains the machine. A unique intangible asset. Also a transaction-specific investment.

The economic concepts of goodwill and intellectual capital provide only a very crude measure of the value created by the way that such unique tangible and intangible assets come together. Indeed, in this particular case, given that CERN is not listed on the stock market, it can provide none at all—one of the reasons that CERN is funded by national governments rather than by the market. Here, the knowledge-as-a-thing model has to give way to the knowledge-in-people's heads model, an altogether more elusive concept.

History teaches us that knowledge is a delicate flower that only blossoms under very specific conditions (Landes 1998). Under most circumstances, many of which are political, religious, or ideological, it either never grows or it quickly withers. In many societies and organizations, only certain kinds of knowledge outputs are tolerated. What is more the right kind of incentive structure for creating new knowledge is often missing. What are the costs and benefits involved in first creating and then exploiting new knowledge? Who incurs the costs and who reaps the benefits? Incentive structures are linked to intellectual property rights (IPRs) issues. How effectively are ownership claims to new knowledge established? How credibly are they protected when made? Finally, a question currently being explored by the open source movement: when does sharing knowledge add value to a firm and when does it erode value?

One of the major achievements of the scientific revolution of the seventeenth century was to shift the terms of the cost–benefit calculation in favor of the creation of new knowledge at the expense of the protection of old knowledge. Old knowledge then survives only if it earns its keep. Otherwise it goes. The critical and rational habits of thought fostered by the scientific revolution gradually permeated Western cultures, spreading to all areas of social life. Today, new information and communication technologies (ICTs) are speeding up the 'metabolic rate' of knowledge production and destruction. For this reason, the political economy of the knowledge society will not look like that of the industrial economy from which it is emerging. The production and distribution of information and knowledge goods differ in important ways from that of physical goods, whether these are raw materials or industrial products. New habits of thought are therefore called for. The teenager who spends his evenings illegally downloading music on to his laptop without a second thought, for example, would not dream of trying to steal the chocolate sitting on the shelf of his local candy store. How should one account for such an ambivalent attitude to property rights? Imagine the average person's response to finding a $10 bill lying unclaimed in a deserted alleyway. Given the time cost involved in finding the bill's likely owner or in taking it to the police, the chances are that he or she would simply pocket it. An economist would say that the appropriability regime is weak and that in such a situation, property rights are weak and hard to enforce. This is what has been happening to the music business. Intellectual property rights in knowledge-based goods such as music and video—that is, the right to exclude others from use, the right to use, and the right to dispose of—have all been significantly weakened by the emergence of file sharing on the Internet.

In recent years, a new specialization has evolved to address some of the issues associated with the production and distribution of knowledge: it goes by the name of knowledge management. Its core tenets can be simply stated. Organizations do not make good use of their knowledge resources. They waste much valuable knowledge because they do not know that they know. Organizational knowledge needs to be articulated, recorded, and made readily available for reuse by selected others. Important efficiency gains are on offer if this can be achieved. Unsurprisingly, much of knowledge management—not all—is driven by an ICT perspective. Knowledge can be given contours, stored, accessed, and manipulated like an object. A key concern is how to get knowledge more widely shared between organizational actors without, at the same time, giving uncontrolled access to such knowledge to outsiders.

Yet the ICT-driven approach to knowledge management moves us further in the direction of reifying knowledge. It would not be able to capture all the different kinds of knowledge flows that underpin the performance of the antihydrogen machine at CERN and raises questions about the robustness of knowledge management as a nascent discipline. Modern chemistry took off with the atomic theory, modern physics with electromagnetism, relativity and the quantum theory, and modern biology with the reconciliation of Mendelian genetics with the Darwinian evolutionary paradigm in the 1930s. Now although there is no shortage of theory that finds its way into the practice of knowledge management, in contrast to the natural sciences, the field has no identifiable theoretical foundations as such. Can it then credibly qualify as an intellectual discipline? None of the terms and concepts that it draws from are as yet agreed upon by the majority of its practitioners, and there is little discussion of its epistemological foundations. In knowledge management, the focus is on practice and the application of tools. Much of the field's evolution has been driven by technology providers—that is, by product-push rather than by demand-pull; by solutions looking for problems rather than by problems looking for solutions. This is not a criticism. The birth of modern chemistry, after all, was preceded by centuries of searching in the dark and frequently blind alleys of alchemical practices (Hankins 1985). We merely point out that the field still lacks a founding theory focused on the nature of knowledge and knowledge flows.

There is no shortage of problems looking for solutions. Organizations, on the whole, *do* make poor use of their knowledge resources, broadly conceived. But the way that such problems are framed does not necessarily classify them as knowledge management issues—not, at least, as knowledge management is currently conceived. The challenge is to convince practical managers that most of the problems that they will encounter have a knowledge management dimension to them. But then, by implication, the tasks of knowledge management become coextensive with those of management itself. Is this not a tad hegemonistic? Not under a broader, less reified conception of knowledge, one less tethered to techniques of librarianship and data management, and more in tune with what it means to belong to a species, *homo sapiens*, that survives and prospers largely through its ability to collaborate and organize.

But if we associate the concept of the organization with that of the firm, we cannot have a credible theory of how to manage knowledge *in* the firm without first developing a knowledge-based theory *of* the firm. Such a theory, we believe, would effectively provide the underpinnings of management practice in the twenty-first century. The conceptual shift required by a knowledge-based theory of the firm would move us away from thinking of knowledge as a stand-alone *resource*—the ICT-centric view—and toward viewing it as a value-generating *process* (Spender 1996).

2. What We are Trying to do in this Book

Which brings us to the purpose of this book. It is primarily to provide some theoretical perspective on the nature of organizationally relevant knowledge and to indicate the kind of research that might generate empirically testable hypotheses and hence to further the development of a knowledge-based theory of the firm. We believe that the theoretical perspective we put forward, if accepted, would help to consolidate such a theory and provide a more credible basis for knowledge management practices. A good theory always points to a world beyond itself—that is, it can be generalized. How will we be able to tell whether we have achieved this? When the discipline is not just a recipient of theories coming in from outside—currently the situation with the knowledge-based theory of the firm—but also exerts a clear influence on the theorizing taking place in cognate fields. To draw from the natural sciences once more, modern chemistry had a significant impact on how physicists and biologists conceived of their own disciplines. Arguably, a theoretically informed, knowledge-based approach to the firm should exert its influence on economic theory, sociology, anthropology, etc. It is only when the balance of trade in theorizing begins to run in its favor that its status as an intellectual discipline will improve and that a theoretically grounded knowledge management practice will become a credible prospect. Until that happens knowledge management will lack a robust theoretical core and chief knowledge officers (CKOs) will spend much of their time scavenging in the gardens of neighboring disciplines, trying to fill their role with credible content—one which will vary from CKO to CKO.

In this book, we provide both some theory and a way of linking it to the real world. Our theorizing underpins a conceptual framework developed by one of the authors—the information-Space, or *I-Space*—by means of which we explore how knowledge first emerges, and then gets articulated, diffused, and absorbed by a population of agents (Boisot 1995, 1998). A few words on the I-Space will help to orient the reader.

In contrast to most models in knowledge management that start from what managers and workers in an organization actually do (Nonaka and

Takeuchi 1995), the I-Space adopts a more abstract point of departure, namely, the nature of information and knowledge flows in any system. Recasting Polanyi's well-known distinction (1958) between tacit and explicit knowledge in information theoretic terms, the I-Space exploits the idea that knowledge that can be articulated will diffuse more speedily and extensively within a given population of agents than knowledge that cannot be so articulated.

The speed and extent to which information diffuses within a population of agents is a function of how far that information has been structured. The structuring of information facilitates both information processing and information transmission. It is achieved through the joint activities of codification and abstraction. Codification establishes discernable differences between phenomena on the one hand, and between the categories to which these are to be assigned on the other. The idea is to make the process of categorization—that is, of assigning phenomena to categories—as speedy and as unproblematic as possible. Abstraction, by contrast, minimizes the use of categories by only drawing on those that are relevant for a given purpose. In order to adapt to phenomena in a timely way, one needs to apprehend them at an appropriate level of abstraction. What that level actually turns out to be will vary with circumstances. One apprehends a fifteen-foot wave in one way when one is attempting to surf it and in another when one is attempting to paint it.

The effective transmission of knowledge does not depend solely on whether information can reach the recipient. Information only becomes knowledge if it gets internalized and becomes part of the recipient's expectational structure—that is, if it affects the recipient's belief structure, taken as disposition to *act*. But action in this context can mean different things. On the basis of past statistical data, for example, I am 99.9999 per cent certain that the ticket I am buying would not win the lottery, but this would not stop me buying it and later checking up which number was drawn—just in case! On the other hand, I buy a put option on future wheat prices precisely because, although the meteorological data clearly points to a number of different possibilities, *I don't really know* which way the price will move in the next six weeks. Here, I know that I do not know and my purchase of the option reflects this.

The same data, however, will be internalized in different ways by different agents to produce different knowledge. Armed with same external data, my neighbor will refrain from buying either a lottery ticket or a put option. The data does not necessarily prompt her to action. She internalizes it differently and it does not modify her expectational structure in the same way. We share the same external data, but we are free to extract different patterns from the same data. For some, the patterns are banal and carry little information; for others, they lead to discontinuous insights—they are highly informative.

Action implies agency. What is an agent for our purposes? This is where our more abstract approach to theorizing achieves some generality. By abstracting from concrete organizational situations, the I-Space takes an agent to be any system that receives, processes, and transmits data with sufficient intelligence to allow *learning* to take place. This view of agency might exclude chemical agents and thermostats, but it would include ants and bacteria. This opens up new territory. An agent, for example, might be a neuron that receives inputs from other neurons, modifies its firing thresholds as a result, and emits outputs. Here, a network of neurons— biological or artificial—becomes a population of agents. When that neural network reaches a certain density and size, it can self-organize and exhibit agency at a new level—that of an animal or perhaps a human being. At the other extreme, an agent might be a firm—a population of human beings— or an organized configuration of firms such as a strategic alliance or an industry. Under certain conditions, even a nation-state can be considered an agent and in international relations it frequently is (Allison 1971). Thus, *whatever exhibits intelligent agency is an agent for our purposes.*

Thus because it operates with information and knowledge flows at an abstract level, the I-Space operates at a high degree of generality. A population of agents as we have defined it is *scalable* and does not limit us to what is going on at a single level such as that of the firm. For this reason, the conceptual framework can find applications at the levels of an individual and a whole society.

3. Structure of the Book

The chapters that follow present a set of papers most of which have been coauthored and published in various journals. Here they are placed in a coherent sequence so as to tell a story. The advantage of presenting papers as chapters is that each chapter can stand alone as a self-contained piece of work. The disadvantage is that of repetition. To the extent that the concepts presented are unfamiliar, however, some readers will welcome the inevitable redundancy. Taken together, the papers provide some of the foundational elements for the I-Space as a conceptual framework. All the papers but one—the last one—are of the theory-building variety. The final paper addresses the issue of theory testing. Unlike a theory, a conceptual framework is not directly testable as such; it can only be judged by its fruitfulness—its ability to generate new theories and hypotheses that are themselves testable. For this reason, the last paper does not actually test out the I-Space as a conceptual framework, but rather, through the use of simulation modeling, it generates a number of empirically testable hypotheses.

In Chapter 1, we look at how knowledge emerges out of data and information. If physicists have tended to ignore the distinction between data and information, economists, on the whole, have tended to go further and ignored the distinctions that can be made between data, information, and knowledge. As a result, they make the unarticulated assumption that information is something that stands apart from and is independent of the processor of information and its internal characteristics. For many purposes this makes sense, but not for all. In the quantum theory, the nature of the interaction between information and observer remains both intimate and mysterious (Nielsen and Chuang 2000). In this chapter, we argue that scholars need to revisit the distinction between data, information, and knowledge, one that is much discussed but little analyzed. Some scholars associate information with data, and others associate it with knowledge. But since none of them readily conflates data with knowledge, this suggests too loose a conceptualization of the term 'information'. We argue that the difference between data, information, and knowledge is in fact crucial. Information theory and the physics of information provide us with useful insights with which to build a political economy of information appropriate to the needs of the emerging information economy. In this chapter, we link information to expectations and beliefs—thus preparing the ground for our discussion of knowledge in Chapter 2—by representing an agent as an action system that extracts relevant information from incoming data in light of prior expectations—that is, prior knowledge and beliefs—to create new expectations. We then explore some of the theoretical implications of our analysis for the way that information is conceptualized in economics.

Chapter 2 examines different ways that the term 'knowledge' has been used. We identify two theories of knowledge that we respectively locate at the extreme points on a continuum between certain and uncertain knowledge. At the one end of the continuum, we have a demanding Platonic approach to knowledge that associates it with absolute certainty. At the other end of the continuum, we have a pragmatic approach that takes knowledge to be a belief that you hold and that you are willing to act upon—William James (2000) associates this with its cash value—whatever its degree of uncertainty. But, as our examples of lotteries and options suggest, acting here can mean many things. Options and insurance contracts, for example, are instruments of action that are useful under different conditions of ignorance. And since the feeling of certainty varies from person to person, what you would be willing to put your hand in the fire for might elicit little more than a cautious nod from me. So what kind of knowledge commands what action?

We identify two distinct yet complementary paths to the development of knowledge. The first one is holistic and field dependent and builds on the concept of *plausibility*; this path we associate with an entrepreneurial mindset (McGrath and MacMillan 2000). The second is more object-oriented—it deals with well-delimited states and outcomes—and builds on the concept of *probability*; this path we associate with the managerial mindset. We argue that both managerial and knowledge management practices have emphasized the second path at the expense of the first. To restore the balance, knowledge management needs to develop processes and tools—associated with scenarios and real options—that will allow it to credibly operate in both possible and plausible worlds, so as to extract value from the way they come together. We conclude the chapter by proposing a systems framework for thinking through the nature of such tools.

Chapter 3 moves down to the level of individual organizations and adopts a knowledge-based perspective to look at the nature of firms. The so-called resource-based view (RBV) of the firm shares with other perspectives on the firm—population ecology, organizational systematics, organizational cladistics, and institutional theory—a concern with why firms differ and with what keeps them different. The RBV attributes such firm-level heterogeneity to differences in the way that resources accumulate over time in individual firms and argues that in exploiting and maintaining such resource differences firms are able to build up sustainable competitive advantage. Questions related to sustainable firm heterogeneity, however, only have meaning if—as has been the case in the neoclassical theory of the firm—similarities between firms are taken as the default assumption. This chapter distinguishes between ontological heterogeneity—differences in the *world*—and epistemic heterogeneity—differences in the way that the world is *construed*. Focusing on the latter, it puts forward an argument for taking epistemic heterogeneity between firms—differences in their respective knowledge bases—as the default assumption rather than similarities. It starts with a general analysis of how living systems make sense of the world. It then goes on to identify the cognitive activities of codification and abstraction as key sources of epistemic heterogeneity. The findings are applied to those systems called firms where a dominant logic allows epistemic heterogeneity to persist. In some cases such persistence leads to competitive advantage, in others to a debilitating inertia. The implications for a knowledge-based theory of the firm are briefly explored.

Chapter 4 further explores the microeconomic and strategic assumptions that underpin current theorizing about the role of information and knowledge in firms. It relates the activities of codifying and abstracting knowledge developed in the previous chapter to the process of diffusing it, thus creating what we call an Information-Space or *I-Space*. In the space, knowledge flows faster and more extensively within a population of agents if it is more codified and abstract. However rapid diffusibility is only achieved at the expense of contextual richness. If, as argued in Chapter 3, organizations are epistemically heterogeneous, then this loss of contextual richness has consequences for a theory of markets that takes them to be epistemically identical. Thus, in contrast to the neoclassical economic presumption in favor of markets, we argue that organizations, not markets, should be taken as our default assumption. We do so on information processing grounds. We distinguish between Zen and market knowledge. The first type of knowledge is embodied and hard to articulate and the second type is abstract-symbolic. In human evolution, the first type of knowledge preceded the second type, and, on any pragmatic definition of knowledge, it still incorporates most of what we mean by the term. We take codification and abstraction as the two data-processing activities that facilitate the articulation of embodied knowledge first in a narrative form and then later in an abstract-symbolic form. We then develop the I-Space as a conceptual framework that relates the articulation of knowledge—its codification and abstraction—to the sharing of knowledge—its diffusion in a population of agents.

Whereas an unlimited and instantaneous sharing of information and knowledge leads to efficient market-oriented outcomes, a more limited sharing leads both to inefficient market outcomes *and* to organizational outcomes. The codification and abstraction of knowledge is a slow and uncertain business. The diffusion of knowledge is characterized by friction, data losses, ambiguity, and opportunistic behavior by agents. It follows that organizational outcomes based on limited knowledge sharing between agents who know and trust each other must have preceded market outcomes based on unlimited knowledge sharing between agents who, for the most part, never get to meet personally. A market-oriented economics has tended to look to physics for its models and thus assumed from the outset a friction-free universe in which knowledge flowed without restriction; the field of organization theory, by contrast, has tended to look to biology where friction is not only pervasive, but is actually a prerequisite for life. A more organization-oriented economics would follow Alfred Marshall's suggestion and thus look more to biology for its models.

Chapter 5 discusses the articulation and sharing of knowledge as generators of cultures and institutions. How knowledge is structured and how it flows within and between populations of agents establishes the cultural and institutional possibilities available to those populations. The I-Space allows us to distinguish four such possibilities: markets, bureaucracies, clans, and fiefs (Ouchi 1980). The chapter focuses on bureaucracies. Cast in a Weberian mold, whether of the state or corporate type, bureaucracies are rational–legal structures that are based on the controlled diffusion of well-codified and abstract knowledge and that are organized to deliver order, stability, and predictability. Early developments in ICTs appeared set to deliver such an outcome. Yet, by speeding up and extending the reach of knowledge flows within a given population, the new ICTs—the Internet, mobile telephony, etc.—generate a more 'distributed' cultural and institutional order than had originally been expected. What is the nature of the challenge that this poses for bureaucracies? Drawing on the I-Space as an institutional framework, the chapter examines what cultural and institutional challenges the new ICTs pose for both state and corporate bureaucracies.

We noted earlier that, as a broad conceptual framework, the I-Space does not lend itself to direct empirical testing. It operates at too high a level of generality. Its value resides in its ability to generate potentially fruitful and empirically testable theories. How is it going to do this? Chapter 6 presents an agent-based simulation model that implements some of the theoretical provisions of the I-Space—no attempt is made here to model the cultural and institutional issues discussed in Chapter 5—and that offers one way to approach to the challenge of validation and testability. It then applies the simulation model to a topical issue: IPRs. With the growth of the information economy, the proportion of knowledge-intensive goods to total goods is constantly increasing. At the one end of the spectrum of knowledge-creating businesses, we find media firms lamenting the loss of sales due to piracy and file sharing. At the other end, we find pharmaceutical firms being accused of profiteering on account of the way they exploit their knowledge base. Lawrence Lessig (2001) has argued that IPRs have now become too favorable to existing producers and that their 'winner-take-all' characteristics are constraining the creators of tomorrow. In this chapter, we look at how variations in IPRs regimes might affect the creation and social cost of new knowledge in economic systems. Drawing on the I-Space to explore how the uncontrollable diffusibility of knowledge relates to its degree of structure—its degree of codification and abstraction—we develop an agent-based simulation modeling approach to the issue of IPRs. We first take the ability to control the diffusibility of knowledge as a proxy measure for an ability to establish property rights in such knowledge. Second, we take the rate of obsolescence of knowledge as a proxy measure for the degree of turbulence induced by different regimes of technical change. Then we simulate the quantity and cost to society of new knowledge under different property right regimes. The chapter ends with a number of empirically testable propositions whose relevance extends beyond the IPR debate to touch both the knowledge-based theory of the firm and more practical knowledge management issues.

Chapter 7 is our concluding chapter. We first briefly recapitulate the main points made in the preceding chapters. Then, given that one of the tests of a good framework is the research that it makes possible, we briefly discuss the research perspective that the I-Space opens up as well as our own future research agenda. The research can move in a number of directions. At the end of the chapter, we extend an invitation to fellow travelers—in universities, firms, research institutions, or even interested individuals—to collaborate.

References

Allison, G. (1971). *The Essence of Decision: Explaining the Cuban Missile Crisis*. Boston, MA: Little Brown.

Baschet, J. (2006). *La Civilisation Féodale: De l'An Mil à la Colonisation de l'Amérique*. Paris: Flammarion.

Boisot, M. (1995). *Information Space: A Framework for Learning in Organizations, Institutions, and Cultures*. London: Routledge.

——(1998). *Knowledge Assets: Securing Competitive Advantage in the Information Economy*. Oxford: Oxford University Press.

Hankins, T. (1985). *Science and the Enlightenment*. Cambridge: Cambridge University Press.

James, W. (2000). *Pragmatism and Other Writings*. New York: Penguin Books.

Landes, D. (1998). *The Wealth and Poverty of Nations: Why Some Are So Rich and Some So Poor*. New York: W.W. Norton.

Lessig, L. (2001). *The Future of Ideas: The Fate of the Commons in a Connected World*. New York: Vintage Books.

McGrath, R. and MacMillan, I. (2000). *The Entrepreneurial Mindset: Strategies for Continuously Creating Opportunity in an Age of Uncertainty*. Boston, MA: Harvard Business School Press.

Nielsen, M. and Chuang, I. (2000). *Quantum Computation and Quantum Information*. Cambridge: Cambridge University Press.

Nonaka, I. and Takeuchi, H. (1995). *The Knowledge-Creating Company: How Japanese Companies Create the Dynamics of Innovation*. New York: Oxford University Press.

Ouchi, W. (1980). 'Markets, Bureaucracies and Clans', *Administrative Science Quarterly*, 25: 129–41.

Polanyi, M. (1958). *Personal Knowledge: Towards a Post-Critical Philosophy*. London: Routledge & Kegan Paul.

Spender, J. C. (1996). 'Making Knowledge the Basis of a Dynamic Theory of the Firm', *Strategic Management Journal*, Volume 17, December, Special Issue on Knowledge and the Firm.

Stern, N. (2007). *The Economics of Climate Change: The Stern Review*. Cambridge: Cambridge University Press.

Williamson, O. (1985). *The Economic Institutions of Capitalism: Firms, Markets, Relational Contracting*. New York: Free Press.

1

Data, Information, and Knowledge: Have We Got It Right?

Max H. Boisot and Agustí Canals

1.1. Introduction

Effective cryptography protects information as it flows around the world. Encryption, by developing algorithms that bury information deeply in data, provides 'the lock and keys' of the information age (Singh 1999: 293). Thus while the data itself can be made 'public' and hence freely available, only those in possession of the 'key' are in a position to extract information from it (Singh 1999). Cryptography, in effect, exploits the deep differences between data and information.

Knowledge and information are not the same thing, either. Imagine, for example, receiving an encrypted message for which you possess the key and from which you extract the following information: 'The cat is tired.' Unless you possess enough contextual background knowledge to realize that the message refers to something more than an exhausted cat—possibly a Mafia boss, for example—you may not be in a position to react in an adaptive way. To understand the sentence is not necessarily to understand the message. Only prior knowledge will allow a contextual understanding of the message itself, and the message, in turn will carry information that will modify that knowledge. Clearly, then, information and knowledge must also be distinguished from one another.

In everyday discourse, the distinction between data and information, on the one hand, and between information and knowledge, on the other, remains typically vague. At any given moment, the terms data and information will be used interchangeably; whereas at another, information will be conflated with knowledge. Although few people will argue that knowledge can ever be reduced to data, the two terms are unwittingly brought into a forced marriage by having the term information act as an informal go-between. The growing commercial interest in cryptography, however, suggests innumerable practical circumstances in which the need to distinguish between the three terms is becoming compelling. But if the distinction works in practice, does it work in theory? This is the question that our chapter addresses.

Beginning with the second half of the twentieth century, a number of economists—Koopmans, Marschak, Hurwicz, and Arrow—began to concern themselves with the nature of the economic agent as a 'rational information processor'. Since that time, information has become acknowledged as the key generator of wealth in postindustrial societies. We might therefore reasonably assume that, over the past fifty years, mainstream economists, concerned as they are with wealth creation, would have developed a conceptual approach to information that reflected its growing importance to their field.

In this chapter, we shall argue that they have some way to go. Both Stiglitz and Lamberton have noted how, even at the end of the twentieth century, the economic profession's conviction that there can be an 'economics of information' still has to reckon with the lack of any consensus as to what specifically it should cover (Lamberton 1998; Stiglitz 2000). As Arrow has commented, 'It has proved difficult to frame a general theory of information as an economic commodity, because different kinds of information have no common unit that has yet been identified' (Arrow 1974: iii). In fact, Arrow believed that such units were undefinable (Arrow 1996).[1] Economics, then, is still looking for a way of thinking about information that is adapted both to its own analytical needs and to the needs of the emerging information economy.

For this reason, we can support Lamberton's plea that we abandon a unitary and all-purpose concept of information and develop instead a taxonomy based on significant characteristics of information (Lamberton 1996: xx–xxii). However, descriptions will not, by themselves, build viable taxonomies. Only adequate theorizing will tell us what characteristics will be taxonomically significant. Here we initiate some necessary theorizing that takes as its focus the differences between data, information, and knowledge. We shall proceed as follows. First, in Section 1.2, we develop a simple conceptual scheme to inform our subsequent discussion. In

---

[1] James Boyle has analyzed the incoherence of information economics over a period of fifty years in his *Shamans, Software, and Spleens* (1996).

Section 1.3, we briefly look at how the economic and organizational sciences have dealt with these differences. Both have tended to conflate information and knowledge and to ignore the role of data. In Section 1.4, we examine what information theory adds to the picture. In Section 1.5, we broaden our analysis by introducing concepts from a new field, the physics of information. Here, the conflation has been of information with data rather than with knowledge—the 'observer' in physics needs to have no cognitive capacities as such, only a perceptual ability to distinguish between simple physical states. In Section 1.6, with the help of a simple diagram somewhat reminiscent of a production function, we briefly illustrate how the distinction between data, information, and knowledge might be exploited in economic theorizing. In Section 1.7, we explore the implications of our comparative analysis for an economics of information and put forward three propositions. A conclusion follows in Section 1.8.

1.2. Conceptualizing the Issue

Consider the way in which economists theorize about information in game theory. Game theory deals with a situation in which knowledge is either taken as being asymmetrically distributed or taken to be common knowledge (Aumann 1976; Hargreaves Heap and Varoufakis 1995), the Nash concept specifying both the game's information requirements and the conditions of its transmission (Kuhn 1952; Myerson 1999). These were hardly models of realism. Yet as game theory evolved in the 1980s and 1990s, it imposed ever-less plausible cognitive conditions on economic agents (Binmore 1990), reflecting its allegiance to neoclassical concepts of information, knowledge, and computability as well as to the Arrow–Debreu model of Walrasian general equilibrium (Mirowski 2002).

How, for example, does game theory deal with the situation in which repeated games unfold under dynamic conditions of information diffusion? Here, information is asymmetrically distributed when the first game takes place and is common knowledge by the time the last game occurs. This situation can also be made to work in reverse. Information can start off as common knowledge in a first game and become asymmetrically distributed by the time the last one occurs. Williamson takes this latter outcome as resulting from a 'fundamental transformation', wherein an initial large-numbers bargaining process by degrees gets transformed into a small-numbers bargaining process. Here, contract renegotiation involves an ever-decreasing number of players on account of asymmetrically distributed learning opportunities combined with the effects of information impactedness (Williamson 1985). This second situation might then count as an instance of repeated games in which information gets differentially 'impacted' (Williamson's term) among the different players according to their respective learning abilities as the games unfold to give them anything but 'common knowledge'.

How should data, information, and knowledge be conceptualized to account for this? Economists struggle. Or not: Hirschleifer and Riley, for example, in their widely read and popular text, *The Analytics of Uncertainty and Information* (1992), hardly deal with definitional issues at all. Taking information to be an input into decision-making, the authors identify the lack of objective information and the lack of information about the future as the key problems they wish to address. A third problem, the limitation of human understanding when dealing with information, the authors choose to ignore on the ground that their intention is to 'model economics, not psychology' (Hirshleifer and Riley 1992: 8). Clearly here, the unarticulated assumption—implicitly endorsed by Shannon's information theory (Mirowski 2002)—is that information is something that stands apart from and is independent of the processor of information and its internal characteristics. Information itself is loosely defined as either 'knowledge'—that is, as a 'stock'—or as an 'increment to the stock of knowledge'—that is, as 'news' or 'message'. Like information, knowledge and/or news are assumed to exist independently of a knower or a receiver of news. The tacit assumption that information and knowledge are 'things' is widely held. It is, however, a strong assumption, and therefore one that could only follow from an appropriate conceptualization of information, of knowledge, and of the ways in which they relate to each other. Yet nowhere in Hirschleifer and Riley's book is it possible to find a treatment of information and knowledge that is rigorous enough to serve as a basis for such an assumption and for the economic analysis that builds on it.

If Hirschleifer and Riley associate information with knowledge, two other economists, Shapiro and Varian, taking information to be anything that can be digitized, associate it with data (Shapiro and Varian 1999). Since data is 'thing-like', it follows that information is also 'thing-like', a shared property that allows these authors to claim that the new information economy can draw on the same economic laws as those that govern the energy economy. Here again, the way that data and information relate to one another is ignored. Yet, although data might be taken as thing-like and given—that is after all what the roots of the term *datum* (what is given) imply—what is taken to constitute information is always evolving to reflect the changing relationship between agents and data. Thus, whereas the analysis of data lends itself to the application of comparative statics and can be linearized, the analysis of information requires the examination of complex feedback loops and the application of nonlinear dynamics. The view that information is itself a thing rather than a relation points to the survival of essentialist thinking in economics, and of a concern with *being* rather than with *becoming* (Prigogine 1980).

Since the distinction between data, information, and knowledge is the focus of this chapter, we now briefly discuss how it might be approached.

Data can be treated as originating in discernible differences in physical states of the world—that is, states describable in terms of space, time, and energy. Anything that can be discerned at all is discerned on the basis of such differences (Rosen 1991) and is discerned by agents (Deleuze 1969; Derrida 1967). Agents are bombarded by stimuli from the physical world, not all of which are discernable by them and hence not all of which register as data for them. Much neural processing has to take place between the reception of a stimulus and its sensing as data by an agent (Kuhn 1974). It takes energy for a stimulus to register as data, the amount of energy being a function of the sensitivity of the agent's sensory apparatus (Crary 1999). *Information* constitutes those significant regularities residing in the data that agents attempt to extract from it. It is their inability to do so costlessly and reliably that gives encryption its power and that makes the distinction between data and information meaningful. For if data and information were the same thing, the effective encryption of messages—that is, the concealing of information in data in such a way that third party cannot extract it—would be impossible (Singh 1999).

What constitutes a *significant* regularity, however, can only be established with respect to the individual dispositions of the receiving agent. Information, in effect, sets up a *relation* between incoming data and a given agent. Only when what constitutes a significant regularity is established by *convention*, can information appear to be objective—and even then, only within the community regulated by the convention. Finally, knowledge is a set of expectations held by agents and modified by the arrival of information (Arrow 1984*a*, 1984*b*). These expectations embody the prior situated interactions between agents and the world—in short, the agent's prior learning. Such learning need not be limited—as required by the theory of rational expectations (Muth 1961)—to models specifically relevant to the expectations to which they give rise.

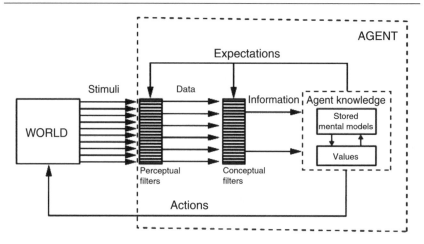

Figure 1.1. The Agent-in-the-World

To summarize, we might say that *information is an extraction from data that, by modifying the relevant probability distributions, has a capacity to perform useful work on an agent's knowledge base.* The essential relationships between data, information, and knowledge are depicted in Figure 1.1. The diagram indicates that agents operate two kinds of filters in converting incoming stimuli into information. Perceptual filters first orient the senses to certain types of stimuli that operate within a given physical range. Only stimuli passing through this initial filter get registered as data.[2] Conceptual filters then extract *information-bearing* data from what has been so registered. Both types of filters get 'tuned' by the agents' cognitive and affective expectations (Clark 1997; Damasio 1999), shaped as these are by prior knowledge, to act selectively on both stimuli and data.

The schema depicted in Figure 1.1 allows us to view data, information, and knowledge as distinct kinds of economic goods, each possessing a specific type of utility. The utility of data resides in the fact that it can carry information about the physical world; that of information, in the fact that it can modify an expectation or a state of knowledge;

---

[2] Roland Omnes, the philosopher of quantum mechanics, understands data thus: 'In order to understand what a measurement is, it would be helpful first to make a distinction between two notions that are frequently confused: an experiment's (concrete) data and its (meaningful) result. The data are for us a macroscopic classical fact: thus when we see the numeral I on the Geiger counter's screen, this is the *datum*. The *result* is something different, for it is a strictly quantum property, almost invariably pertaining only to the microscopic world, meaning that a radioactive nucleus disintegrated, for example, or providing a component of a particle's spin. The datum is a classical property concerning only the instrument; it is the expression of a fact. The result concerns a property of the quantum world. The datum is an essential intermediary for reaching a result' (Omnes 1999, author's italics).

finally, that of knowledge in the fact that it allows an agent to act in adaptive ways in and upon the physical world. Telephone books are paradigmatically data goods; specialized newsletters, being more selective, exemplify information goods; and brain surgery can be thought of as knowledge good. We shall not elaborate further on these different types of good.

1.3. Information, Individuals, and Organizations

Most of what modem economics has to say about knowledge and information originates in the tradition of methodological individualism (Hodgson 1988, 1993).[3] This tradition takes the individual human being, *Homo Economicus*, as the fundamental unit of analysis. The origins of methodological individualism are deeply rooted in the Anglo-Saxon political economy tradition that goes back to Hobbes and Locke (MacPherson 1962). The central challenge was to protect the rationality postulate inherited from the Enlightenment from the centrifugal tendencies at work when varied and complex individuals pursue their own interests in both markets and organizations. The socialist calculation controversy of the 1930s opposed those who believed that rationality was best preserved through a central planning mechanism—a metamorphosis of Walras's auctioneer—to those who believed in preserving it through a decentralized market mechanism. The concern with the computational efficiency of either mechanism placed the focus on the coordinating role of 'knowledge' and 'information' (Hayek 1999; Lange and Taylor 1938; Von Mises 1969) and on the computational characteristics of different types of economic agency—the state, the firm, and the individual. More recent attempts to deal with these threats to economic rationality have resulted in a kind of methodological 'cyborgism' (Mirowski 2002) that builds information structures both above and between agents.[4]

What are the computational requirements of the neoclassical rationality postulate? Most relevant from our perspective is the fact that, whatever the type of economic agent involved, it is not subject to communicative or data-processing limitations. The information environment in which

---

[3] The Marxist tradition in economics has an even less tenable position on information than does neoclassical economics. In the Marxist tradition, information asymmetries are deliberately created for the purposes of exploitation. Information goods are or should be, by their nature, free goods. See Marx (1970).

[4] We are indebted to a reviewer of this chapter for this observation.

it operates is free of noise and friction—well-structured information is instantaneously available in the form of prices and these fully capture the relevant attributes of trades into which the actor enters.[5] What does an individual economic agent actually do with information? He computes in order to take decisions (Arrow 1973; Hurwicz 1969; Marschak 1974). His computational abilities are unbounded, and it enjoys both infinite memory and infinite foresight (Stiglitz 1983). It follows, therefore, that such an agent does not need to learn much (Hodgson 1999). It is the frictionless ease with which the rational economic agent is able to compute and communicate that qualifies him as 'Newtonian'.

It is by now well established that *Homo Economicus* has not served neoclassical economics well as a model of the way in which real human beings process and transmit data. These agents are bounded in their rationality (Miller 1956; Simon 1957) and are subjected to systematic cognitive biases (Bruner 1974; Jung 1971; Kahneman 1994; Kahneman and Tversky 1982). It was a coming to terms with the cognitive limitations of individual and group processes that gradually turned economics into what Mirowski calls a 'Cyborg science', with Hayek as its prophet (Gottinger 1983; Hayek 1999; Lavoie 1985; Makowski and Ostroy 1993; Mirowski 2002; Smith 1991; Weimer and Palermo 1982).

Evolutionary economics has developed a more realistic—not to say 'naturalistic' (Quine 1969)—perspective on the role of knowledge in human affairs than has orthodox economics (Hamilton 1991; Hodgson 1993; Nelson 1994; Vromen 1995). The omniscience of agents is out! For Nelson and Winter (1982), for example, the routinization of firm activities is a response to information complexity. It is in rules and routines that a firm's knowledge is deemed to be stored. These then become the units of selection in an evolutionary process. Yet, as Fransman points out, the tight coupling of information and knowledge that is implied—with knowledge becoming little more than processed information—is unrealistic, since different agents may extract different knowledge from the same information (Fransman 1998). Indeed, the variety on which evolutionary selection is effectively predicated depends on it! Fransman himself goes on to associate information with data—a tight coupling in the other direction—and knowledge with belief.

If economists of different stripes have tended to conflate knowledge and information, sociologists, by contrast, have been more concerned

---

[5] As Koopmans put it 'The economies of information handling are secured free of charge' (Koopmans 1957).

with knowledge alone. Furthermore, sociology's point of departure is not the asocial atomized individual, but the embedded socialized actor (Granovetter 1985). Mead, for example, emphasized 'the temporal and logical preexistence of the social process to the self-conscious individual that arises in it' (Mead 1962: 186). Thus, in contrast with the methodological individualism of economics, sociology 'problematizes' the individual, often adopting a Vygotskian view that society should be the point of departure for looking at the evolution of human information processing capacities (Vygotsky 1986). Durkheim and Mauss (1963), for example, analyzed primitive classification schemes as *collective* forms of representation. Sociology, then, typically starts with a multiple-actor perspective and gradually homes in on the single actor.

Finally, the sociology of knowledge tradition emphasizes the way in which power shapes collective representations (Habermas 1987; Mannheim 1960). By viewing human rationality as socially bounded by power and institutions (DiMaggio and Powell 1983; Scott 1989), sociology avoids the requirements for hyperrationality that has plagued neoclassical economic thinking. Of course, since institutional economics borrows heavily from the sociology of institutions and organizations, issues both of bounded rationality and of power and influence have come to figure prominently in its analyzes. They also figure in agency theory and in theories of incomplete contracting (Grossman and Hart 1988; Hart 1995; Jensen and Meckling 1976).

The new institutional economics aspires to bridge the gap between neoclassical economics and organization theory (Furubotn and Richter 1998; Williamson 1985). Yet it remains weighed down by the neoclassical perspective on information. It acknowledges the existence of friction in the transactional processes that drive the economic system but offers little or no theorizing about it. At best, it can differentiate between markets—an external information environment in which data is well codified and can therefore flow freely—and hierarchies—an internal information environment in which the flow of data is viscous on account of the tacit nature of the knowledge involved. The first type of more analytically tractable environment has typically been the province of economists; the second, more qualitative environment has been left to organizational theorists.

Perhaps on account of its more qualitative material, organizational sociology has addressed the problem of knowledge in organizations, but not much that of data or information. Working in the interpretive tradition initiated by Weber, it has focused on sense-making, the process through which information is interpreted and converted by receivers into intelligible knowledge (Daft and Weick 1984; Gioia and Chittipeddi 1991; Weick 1995). But how the codes on which information is borne come into being in the first place is a question that needs to be addressed before one can progress on to sense-making. Habermas's theory of communicative action, for example, sees meaning as something to be freely negotiated between interacting agents (Habermas 1987). But can the idea of an open negotiation realistically apply to the codes that agents inherit and draw upon in their interactions? Such codes do much to shape the possible meanings that are up for negotiation. Some of the concepts that organizational sociologists apply to knowledge will also apply to information,[6] but for this to yield a credible result, they would have to explore the nature of data as well as that of information.

1.4. The Contribution of Information Theory

The discipline that comes closest to doing this is information theory. But, originating as it does in an engineering tradition, information theory concerns itself primarily with the challenge of information *transmission* rather than with problems of information *content* or *meaning* (Hartley 1928; Nyquist 1924; Shannon 1948). It is more abstract in its approach to information than is sociology, being concerned with the technical characteristics of communication channels independently of the nature of message sources, senders, receivers, or message destinations. It seeks to establish efficient encoding strategies for channels subject to noise.

By relating the definition of information to the freedom of choice we enjoy when we choose a particular message from among all the possible messages that we might transmit, it becomes possible to calculate the amount of information carried by that message. It turns out to be the inverse of its probability of appearance. Since within the framework provided by information theory, any message consists of a sequence of symbols drawn from a given repertoire of symbols, the theory allows one to assess the effectiveness of different coding schemes using

---

[6] Giddens's theory of structuration, for example, and his concepts of domination, signification, and legitimation (Giddens 1984) can be used to analyze the distribution of both knowledge *and* information in a social system, the nature and extent to which these are codified, and their normative status.

different symbolic repertoires in a channel. Shannon's *Mathematical Theory of Communication* (Shannon and Weaver [1949] 1963) yields a number of fundamental theorems which set theoretical limits to the amount of information that a channel of given capacity is able to transmit, in both the presence and absence of noise. Whether the limit is reached in a particular situation will turn on the choice of symbolic repertoires and syntactic rules, as well as on the choice of coding scheme.

The amount of information that can be transmitted, then, is a function of the size of the available repertoire of distinct symbols or states that is available, the relationships between symbols—that is, the syntax—as well as the degree of fidelity required given the amount of noise in the channel. Information theory is primarily concerned with maximizing the fidelity of transmission at an acceptable cost. Shannon and Weaver ([1949] 1963) refer to this as a technical level problem (level 1). As Shannon took pains to point out in his 1948 paper, information theory is not particularly concerned with what the symbols actually *mean*—a semantic level problem (level 2)—or with whether a given message has the desired effect on a given message destination—an effectiveness level problem (level 3). These he viewed as problems to be addressed by social scientists rather than engineers. Shannon thus sought to offer a clear line of demarcation between information and knowledge.

Crucially, information theory takes the repertoire of symbols to be transmitted as *a given*. It does not ask how the repertoire came into being, whence the distinctness of the symbol system came from, or whether the symbolic repertoire was established by prior convention or through a gradual process of discovery. Yet, before we are in a position to extract information from a symbol, we first need to extract the information *that it is indeed a symbol* and hence an acceptable candidate for further processing. It must, therefore, be distinguished from other stimuli that might register with an agent as data. In short, information theory ignores the question of data, of how a given repertoire of symbols—a preselected collection of states gets itself registered with an agent as a *data set* from which information can then be extracted.[7]

If, as we have argued, data is a discernible difference between two states, at a purely theoretical level, the limiting case of what constitutes

---

[7] Interestingly, Blackwell applied the precepts of information theory to states rather than symbols. These could then acquire the status of commodities in an Arrow-Debreu analytical framework. Blackwell's work was to influence game-theoretic and other work on the economics of information (Blackwell and Girshick 1954; Geanakoplos 1992; Lipman 1991; Plott and Sunder 1978; Rubinstein, 1998).

a difference is given by the calculus. It defines, in the limit, what can ever count as data. Perhaps the *physically* limiting case of data is given by Planck's constant, which defines the smallest discernable event that can pass off as a *state*. But for *us* as sentient beings, what counts as data is what we can actually discern. Our ability to discern differences between states only operates within a certain physiological range (Hargreaves Heap and Varoufakis 1995). Outside that range, we cannot be sure that the different states that constitute our data are orthogonal to each other and hence capable of yielding a viable repertoire, as required by Shannon.

Data, then, and the regularities that reside within the data, are properties of events and things 'out there' in the world—that is, physical processes and products that become available to us as sentient beings through our physiological apparatus, often amplified by instruments and other artifacts. Information, by contrast, is relational. As Bateson put it, it is 'the difference that makes a difference'—and that means making a difference *to someone* (Bateson 1971). Thus we might say that regularities within data, an objective property of events and things, convey more or less information to different individuals, depending on their respective circumstances, such as their individual histories, values and emotional makeup (Damasio 1999), mental models, and the specific state of their expectations at any given moment.

The early founders of modern information theory—Nyquist, Hartley, and Shannon—imported from thermodynamics the concept of entropy, which Shannon then associated with the amount of information H gained in a message. Building on the concept of entropy that information theory shares with thermodynamics, we would like to suggest that information-bearing data may be likened to free energy in a physical system. That is to say, data that carries information retains a capacity to do *work*—i.e., it can act on an agent's prior state of expectations and modify it. Data that carries no information may be likened to bound energy in physical systems: to the extent that it leaves an agent's state of expectations unmodified, it has performed no work on its expectational structure.

Note that we are dealing here with both an objective term—the quantity of information that can potentially be carried by a given data-set[8]—and a subjective term—the amount of information that can be extracted in practice from the data-set by a situated agent. When we claim that

---

[8] This quantity has been calculated for different states of physical matter by Seth Lloyd (Lloyd 2000).

information is relational, it is with respect to the second of these terms. This 'subjectivist' view of information, however, based as it is on an agent's *situated* expectations, confronts the 'objectivist' view of information developed by Shannon, one that is based on *conventionalized* expectations. The English language, for example, contains an objective amount of information based on the relative frequency of appearance of letters of the alphabet and of certain types of words, such as articles and pronouns. In Shannon's view, information content is set by the ratio of actual to possible events. In the examples that he gives, however, both the repertoire of possible events and their frequency are fixed a priori, so that the computation of information content is straightforward. Yet, to stay with the example of the English language, as soon as we move up to the level of sentences and paragraphs, the number of possible sentence constructions moves to infinity. Does this mean that information content moves to infinity? No, simply that the repertoire of possible sentences is now largely shaped by the circumstances in which any given sentence is likely to be uttered—that is, by its *context*. But *context varies in the extent to which it is shared across individuals*. Some contexts will be unique to individuals, while other contexts will be widely shared.[9]

Native English speakers, for example, will share almost identical expectations concerning the frequency of appearance of letters in English words. They will share somewhat similar expectations concerning the frequency of appearance of many classes of words in a well-constructed English sentence. They will share far fewer expectations, however, concerning the rate at which other words appear in the sentence, for these will depend on particular circumstances. The discourse that might take place in a biology laboratory, for example, will be meaningful to a much smaller group of people than the one taking place on a televized chat show. In sum, it is *shared context*, the generator of intersubjective objectivity (Popper [1959] 1980) that stops information content from ballooning to infinity and that renders discourse possible.

Shannon takes care of this difficulty largely by avoiding it. Given his focus, this was not unreasonable. As a communication engineer, he was concerned mainly with the objective and computable aspects of information and the requirements that these might impose on a communication

[9] Information in the objectivist view can be seen as the higher bound of the ensemble of all possible 'subjectivist' or 'intersubjectivist' interpretations that could be extracted from the data. Yet in any but the most simple contexts, the objectivist view confronts a Godelian 'undecidability' problem.

channel. Thus Shannon addressed what he called the level 1 or technical problem (Was the message received the same as the message sent?) and confined his analysis to well-defined and delimitable repertoires. What he called the level 2 or semantic problem (Is the received message understood?) was not his concern. This depended on whether the receiver possessed the relevant code—that is, some familiarity with the alphabet, the vocabulary and the syntactic rules of the English language, etc. Note that, even here, the repertoire was assumed by Shannon to be closed: the alphabet is limited in size as are both the vocabulary and the syntactic rules that have to be attended to. Finally, what Shannon called the level 3 or effectiveness problem (Does the message lead to the desired behavior?), was completely outside his purview. Both levels 2 and 3, we identify with knowledge.

It is clear that, where symbolic repertoires and syntactic structures are established by convention rather than by discovery, technical level (level 1) communication issues need not concern themselves with the idiosyncratic characteristics of communicating agents. However, the minute we move to the semantic level (level 2) or to the effectiveness level (level 3), the dispositional states of the agents—that is their prior knowledge—become relevant. Agents are *situated* processors and transmitters of data. The individual agent's *memories* as well as his preference orderings—and hence *values* and *emotional dispositions* (Damasio 1999)—therefore need to be reckoned with. It is at levels 2 and 3, then, that the idiosyncrasy and potential subjectivity of context become most manifest. Here, selection is constrained less by rules than by personal style and preference.

We can represent the issue that we are discussing with a diagram. In the rectangle of Figure 1.2, we variously mix expectations—and hence probabilities—based on agreed conventions concerning what constitutes an event, the number of recurrences of that event that constitute a fair sample, etc., with expectations based on personal experience. The first type of probability will lend itself to a frequency interpretation, whereas the second will lend itself to a Bayesian or subjectivist interpretation. We subdivide the rectangle into three zones and associate each zone with one of Shannon's three levels. We see that Shannon's level 1 problem—the technical problem—leaves little or no scope for the subjectivist approach to probability. It is also the level that is the most computationally tractable and the one to which Shannon himself decided to confine his analysis. His level 2 problem—the semantic problem—is one that offers somewhat more scope for subjective probabilities to kick in. In language,

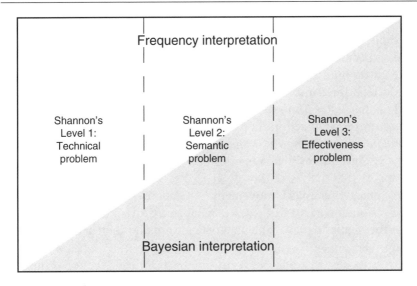

Figure 1.2. Frequency and Bayesian Interpretations in Communication

for example, syntactic constraints and word usage will conventionalize expectations to some extent, but personal idiosyncrasies and style will inject a strong subjective element into the communication process. Finally, Shannon's level 3 problem—the pragmatic problem—leaves little scope for the frequency perspective, since at this level, conventions hardly appear as anything other than subjectively experienced and highly variable constraints.

The implication of the above is that, whatever intrinsic regularities it contains, to the extent that data only carries information when it can modify an expectation, what constitutes data *tout court* for me, might turn out to be information-bearing data for you. How far we are aligned in our information-extraction strategies will depend on how far our respective expectations are shaped by conventions, that is, socially shared encoding rules and contextualizing procedures, or by idiosyncratic circumstances—codes and contexts that are not widely shared. The act of extracting information from data constitutes an *interpretation* of the data. It involves an assignment of the data to existing categories according to some set of preestablished schemas or models that shape expectations. For this to be possible, *such schemas or models must already exist in some form or other.*

But how do such schemas and models come into existence in the first place? They do so primarily through explicit or tacit rules of inference.

Explicit rules will for the most part be applied to codes; implicit rules will be applied primarily to context. Expectations and categories coevolve, with expectations shaping the categories that we create, and these, once created, in turn shape the evolution of subsequent expectations.[10] Our categories condition the dispositions that we adopt toward the world—that is, our knowledge, taken here in the Popperian sense of a disposition toward action (Popper 1992).[11] *Thus, data can only constitute information for an agent who is already knowledgeable.* Data can be viewed as a low energy system that acts informationally rather than mechanically (Boisot 1995), that is to say, it gives rise to *intentional* action rather than mere mechanical movement.[12] Guided by the structure of its expectations, an agent first extracts what constitutes information for him from the regularities available in a data stream and then acts upon it (see Figure 1.1).

Given its almost exclusive focus on the technical level of communication, the work of information theory has largely ignored such issues. These, occurring as they do at Shannon and Weaver's level 2 and their level 3—that is, at the level that we have identified with knowledge rather than information—have proved to be of more interest to interpretative sociology. In organizational sociology, the semantic problem shows up as a concern with sense-making (Weick 1995) or bounded rationality (Kahneman and Tversky 1982; Simon 1945), whereas the pragmatic problem shows up as a concern with power, values, and influence (Habermas 1987). Levels 2 and 3 problems are also of relevance to institutional theory (DiMaggio and Powell 1983; Scott 1989). It is clear, however, that at these levels, we are far removed from an economic world in which agents can be assumed to have common knowledge of rationality, a consistent alignment of beliefs, and rational expectations (Aumann 1976). But if information theory's concern with bits and bytes led it to shun the issue of knowledge, it also managed to sidestep the issue of data by assumption: for all intents and purposes, information and data were the same thing. Although it never explicitly claimed otherwise, almost unwittingly the new discipline of information physics has highlighted the issue.

---

[10] Kantians believe that the categories came first, while Lockeans believe that expectations came first and that these were shaped inductively by the recurrent features of our experiences. The debate continues; mercifully, we need not get involved.

[11] Kenneth Arrow has the same expectational view of information as Popper does. See Arrow (84).

[12] This is not to say that both informational and mechanical effects cannot be present at the same time. But where energy acts informationally, we can afford to ignore its mechanical effects on behavior. These are negligible.

1.5. The Physics of Information

According to the late Rolf Landauer, 'Information is physical' (Landauer 1999), and the most fundamental analysis of the nature of information so far carried out originates in physics. Within physics itself, since the most fundamental analysis of physical processes takes place at the quantum level, it is within the new field of quantum information theory that we confront the deepest level of analysis of information An important breakthrough for the development of quantum information theory was the discovery that quantum states could be treated *as if they were information* (Nielsen and Chuang 2000). Thus, if information is physical, *what is physical is also information* (Lloyd 2000). Quantum information theory, being broader in scope than classical information theory, operates at the most abstract level, quite removed from any social science conception of information. Can such a view of information have anything to offer the social sciences?

If information is physical, then, like any other physical process, it is subject to the second law of thermodynamics. The physical entropy involved here, however, must be distinguished from Shannon entropy, even though the two are closely related. One might, in effect, say that Shannon entropy is predicated upon thermodynamic entropy. In a closed system, both types of entropy-generating processes turn out to be irreversible.[13]

Although physicists have not much concerned themselves with it, the distinction that we are drawing between data, information, and knowledge is implicit in the work being done in the Physics of Information (Bennett 1999; Feynman 1996, 1999; Landauer 1999; Zurek 1990). If the bit is the fundamental unit of analysis in classical information theory, then the qubit is the fundamental unit of analysis in quantum information theory. Just as a classical bit is in one of two possible states, $|0\rangle$ or $|1\rangle$, so a qubit has two possible *eigenstates* $|0\rangle$ or $|1\rangle$, one difference between a bit and a qubit, however, is that the latter can also be in any well-defined linear combination of the two eigenstates, $|0\rangle$ or $|1\rangle$. Another difference is that, whereas we can directly examine a bit to determine what state it is in, we cannot directly examine a qubit to determine its quantum state without destroying that state. In short, *the eigenstates of the qubit are not available to us as data.*

---

[13] It turns out that, at the quantum level, not all computations are irreversible (Bennett 1999).

By the postulates of quantum mechanics, any measure that we perform on a qubit reduces it to one of its eigenstates. This dichotomy between the state of the qubit and what we can observe lies at the heart of quantum information and quantum computation. At the quantum scale, we can ask: how much information does a qubit represent in the absence of measurement? It turns out that nature holds a great deal of 'hidden information' in this way, and it grows exponentially with the number of qubits.[14]

In the classical world, we assume that we can distinguish, at least in principle, between different states, since this is what qualifies them as data. Yet in the quantum world, we have to abandon such an assumption, for, unless the orthogonality between two given states can be maintained, one can no longer readily distinguish between them and register such a distinction as data. Without data one cannot extract reliable information from the system concerning such states. It turns out that, below a certain scale known as the Planck scale, the orthogonality between two states can no longer be securely established. *There are thus physical limits to our access to data and hence to our ability reliably to extract information from data.*[15]

These limits first appeared in 1867 in the field of thermodynamics in the shape of Maxwell's demon, a microscopic creature that appeared to violate the second law by using information to distinguish between fast- and slow-moving particles and hence to throw dissipative processes into reverse (Leff and Rex 1990). To understand the nature of the thermo-dynamic limits on our access to data, we can revert to our earlier and perhaps somewhat oversimplifying analogy, taking data as correspond-ing to the general category of energy, and information-bearing data as corresponding to free energy—that is, it has a capacity to do work in the sense that it can modify our expectations, and, hence, the state of our knowledge. Noise would then correspond to bound energy: it either consists of data that carries no information for us and can therefore do no work, or it consists of states that cannot be distinguished from one another and that hence do not even graduate to the status of data for us. Noise cannot modify our expectations. Like bound energy, it can perform no work.

[14] Some, notably Penrose, have argued that quantum effects are also manifest in human cognitive processes (Green 2000; Penrose 1994). We cannot, however, observe each other's mental states directly without disturbing these states; we can only observe the behavioral outputs of these states.

[15] That there are *biological* limits to our access to data as well has been known since the work of Fechner in the nineteenth century.

Now, although knowledge itself is dispositional, it reveals itself in purposeful agent behaviors such as data processing, data transmission, and actions based on these. We hypothesize that data storage, on the one hand, and data processing, transmission, and purposeful action, on the other, can be respectively likened to the buildup of potential energy and to its subsequent exploitation as kinetic energy. As a disposition to act, then, knowledge corresponds to potential energy—a stock; and as purposeful action or behavior, knowledge corresponds to kinetic energy a flow.[16] In open systems, both the transformation of potential energy into kinetic energy and the transformation of the latter into work are subject to dissipation.

Landauer (1990) demonstrated that energy dissipation occurs both in the information storage process and in the information transmission process as a result of *information erasure.* No information is erased in a reversible computation, however, because the input can always be recovered from the output. When we say, therefore, that a computation is reversible, we are really saying that no information is erased during the computation. *Landauer's principle* provides the link between energy dissipation and irreversibility in computation, stating that, in order to erase information, it is necessary to dissipate energy. The principle can be stated thus (Landauer 1990):

If a computer erases a single bit of information, then the amount of energy dissipated into the environment will be *at least* $k_b T \ln 2$, where k_b is a universal constant known as *Boltzmann's constant,* and T is the environmental temperature of the computer.

The laws of thermodynamics also allow us to express Landauer's principle in terms of entropy rather than in terms of energy and dissipation (Landauer 1990):

If a computer erases a single bit of information, then the environmental entropy will increase by at least *at least* $k_b \ln 2$, where k_b is Boltzmann's constant.

It should be noted that Landauer's principle effectively provides us only with a lower bound on the amount of energy that must be dissipated to

---

[16] There are, of course, important differences between knowledge and potential energy, on the one hand, and behavior and kinetic energy, on the other. A stock of knowledge is not depleted in the way that a stock of potential energy might be. It can only be *dissipated,* in the sense that the information structures that constitute the stock are gradually eroded. Likewise, behaviors, through the mechanism of *learning,* can actually build up a knowledge stock rather than depleting it—which is what kinetic energy does to potential energy. Clearly, reasoning by analogy must know its limits.

erase information. Clearly, if all computational processes were reversible, then the principle would imply no lower bound on the amount of energy dissipated, since no bits would in fact be dissipated during computation (Nielsen and Chuang 2000).

Maxwell's demon is located at the meeting point of a physics of energy and information. Bolzmann's definition of entropy links the two types of physics. An informational limit is reached under two quite different conditions. The first occurs when the energy expenditure incurred by data capture and transmission activities required to distinguish between two states, and hence to create discernable data—often performed by specialized equipment—itself exerts a mechanical effect on those states, thus preventing them from stabilizing enough to get themselves detected—Heisenberg's uncertainly principle describes this condition. The mechanical effects of such energy expenditures then swamp and overwhelm their informational effects. The second occurs when the Demon needs to store transmitted data in memory for subsequent processing. Assuming that the Demon's memory is finite—that is, it is subject to bounded rationality (Simon 1945)—it will sooner or later confront the need to erase stored data in order to make way for new data. Landauer's principle tells us that at that moment data will be lost and entropy levels—both thermodynamic and informational—will increase. However, thermodynamic entropy and information entropy are quite distinct from one another. Although both draw on Boltzmann's formula, the first refers to the regularities or lack of them in discernible states of the world—that is, in data—whereas the second refers to the information that can be extracted from such states by a knowledgeable observer. In sum, if social scientists conflate information and knowledge, then physicists conflate data and information. In Section 1.6, by means of a simple diagram, we indicate why both types of conflation matter.

1.6. An Economic Interpretation of the Principle of Least Action

Any physical system is subject to the principle of *least action*, an integral variational principle initially put forward by Maupertuis in 1744 that establishes the difference between the actual motion of the system and all of its kinematically possible motions during a finite time interval (Barrow and Tipler 1986). According to Green, when the observables of the system, such as its energy, momentum, angular momentum, central vector, and certain other charges, have prescribed values on the boundary of any region of space and time, they will vary in such a way that the total action within the region has its minimum value (Green 2000). This will be as true of dissipative systems as it will be of Hamiltonian systems. To the extent that the system has a capacity for storing memories of earlier states—and this does not require that the system be intelligent or even alive—then it will be able to use data and information in such a way as to minimize the action.

Being universal in scope (Omnes 1999), the principle of least action implies that nature as a whole makes choices that are economic in their outcomes.[17] How might Maxwell's Demon apply the principle? In effect, it allows us to posit the existence of a trade-off between the Demon's consumption of energy and his consumption of data resources as it attempts to sort out fast-moving from slow-moving particles. Such a trade-off can usefully be represented by means of a scheme that is somewhat reminiscent of a production function, but the purpose of which is limited to illustrating the economic nature of the principle of least action.

A production function is a schedule showing the maximum amount of output that can be produced from any specified set of inputs (Fergusson 1969). In neoclassical production functions that take capital and labor as inputs, information, and knowledge are not explicitly represented as factors of production in their own right, although, in talking of capital and labor, we may take them to be implicitly present. The knowledge embedded in machinery and equipment, for instance, clearly forms part of the capital factor, and the labor factor clearly embodies the know-how and experience of employees. Given that in the so-called 'new economy' information and knowledge have clearly moved centerstage, some have claimed that they should therefore become critical productive factors in their own right alongside capital and labor (Bell 1973/1999; Romer 1986, 1990).[18]

Yet, given that information and knowledge are already implicitly embedded in traditional productive factors, this would result in double counting. As an alternative, therefore, one could move up to a more abstract and general level and bring together two different classes of productive factors: (a) purely physical factors such as space, time, and energy—these would be measured in physical units such as meters,

---

[17] In the nineteenth century, this was referred to as *the economy of nature*.

[18] By the term new economy, we mean more than an economy driven by the Internet phenomenon. We therefore avoid having to take sides in the current debate as to whether there is in fact a new economy.

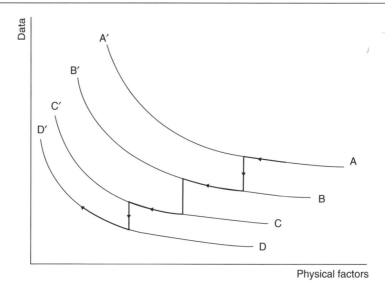

Figure 1.3. Data vs. Physical Factors Scheme

seconds, and joules and (*b*) data factors, being discernible differences in the states of the physical factors—these would be measured in bits (Boisot 1995, 1998). Note that, in this new scheme, information and knowledge are not taken as factors of production at all. According to our earlier arguments, information constitutes an extraction from the data factor that results in *economizing* on that factor and hence in a move toward the origin. Knowledge, likewise, economizes on data processing—and hence on the consumption of data inputs—more so in the case of abstract knowledge than of concrete knowledge.[19]

An example of the new scheme is shown in Figure 1.3. As will shortly be apparent, much as it may look like one, it is not actually a production function. In the diagram, we can distinguish two types of movement, one *along* isoquants and another *across* them. A move to the left along an isoquant represents a progressive substitution of data for physical factors, something that happens when, by gradually accumulating the data of experience, systems 'learn–by-doing', with less expenditure of time, space, and energy, in whatever task they are performing–manufacturing aircraft wings, miniaturizing electronic components, etc. Learning-by-doing can only work for systems that can store past states—that is, for systems

[19] Ernst Mach's 'Principles of the economy of thought' were an important source of inspiration for Hayek (Mirowski 2002).

that have *memory*. Some purely physical systems have memory and all living systems do. By implication, a move to the right along an isoquant can be interpreted either as forgetting, an erosion of memory, or as the workings of bounded rationality. Both rightward and leftward movements are possible. A downward vertical movement across isoquants and toward the origin in the diagram, by contrast, represents the generation of *insight*, the extraction of information from data to create new, more abstract knowledge concerning the structure underlying phenomena. This second movement—the joint effects of pattern recognition and computational activities—is discontinuous, reflecting the unpredictable nature of creative insights (Miller 1996). It makes it possible to reach the same output levels as before with less data processing and hence a lower consumption of data inputs. In addition to having memory, a system that has a capacity for insight must also be *intelligent*, that is, it must be capable of processing data in order to extract information from it in the form of patterns or structures.

Our scheme and the neoclassical production function have some similarities. For example, they both take movement along an isoquant as representing *technical change*—that is, a change in the mix of data and physical resources that generate a given output—and movement across isoquants toward the origin as representing *technical progress* (Boisot 1998)—that is, a reduction in the quantity of data and/or physical resources required to generate that output. Yet the two schemes differ in three important ways.

First, while the neoclassical production function offers no preferred direction for movements along an isoquant, the broad tendency to substitute data factors for physical factors in our scheme—a process of variation, selection, and retention that results in data accumulating in the form of memory—imparts a direction to technical change and to technical progress. Why? The clue resides not in the evolutionary nature of knowledge—although this is certainly a factor—but in the evolutionary nature of agents, individual or corporate (Metcalfe 1998). To the extent that evolution enhances both the memory and the data-processing capacity of agents—this can be achieved either via biological evolution or via the artifacts of cultural evolution (Boyd and Richerson 1985; Clark 1997)—they are able to make better use of whatever data accumulates over time, and this at a lower cost than that of using the physical resources available to them. Thus, if intelligence is selected for by evolution, intelligence, in turn, will demonstrate a selection bias in favor of data over physical resources

In effect, in contrast to the neoclassical production function in which movement along an isoquant is reversible, the arrow of time is at work in our scheme, allowing it to describe irreversible and hence path-dependent processes that, according to circumstances, might be characterized as being either evolutionary or as developmental. We must emphasize that the arrow of time manifests itself in global rather than local behaviors. The general tendency for a leftward movement up an isoquant is likely to have many local exceptions—brought about either by forgetting or by bounded rationality—that move it in the opposite direction.

Second, our scheme is able to account for technical progress. Although in both the neoclassical and our scheme, technical progress in described by a jump across isoquants toward the origin, in the neoclassical case, such a discontinuity cannot be explained; it had to be exogenously given. In our scheme, by contrast, a discontinuous jump from one isoquant to other is accounted for by a discontinuous jump in a living system's own learning processes—that is, it is accounted for by the discontinuous phenomenon of *insight*, the extraction of informative patterns or gestalts from data, and their subsequent conversion into knowledge.

Third, the data and physical factors that make up our scheme present quite distinct economic properties. While, in the neoclassical production function, purely physical factors are naturally subject to scarcity and hence appropriable, the data factors of our own scheme are not. While they may not always be immediately accessible—and in that sense they may be considered scarce—once one has secured them, they can often be replicated and distributed at almost zero-marginal cost. Providing it has found the right physical substrate, therefore, data will propagate rapidly and extensively. Scarcities will then only appear in the form of a living system's limited capacity to receive, store, process, and transmit data, not in the data factors themselves.[20] For this reason, data factors are much more difficult to appropriate and to subject to traditional forms of economic exchange than purely physical factors. They are hard to price, and this makes it hard to use price signals to guide a substitution of data

---

[20] We can see the logic of our new scheme at work in the way that organizations are today attempting to handle large amounts of transactional data. Data mining, for example, is the process of extracting information from data. People will not pay for data, but as information extraction becomes evermore difficult and user-specific—that is, customized—people will pay for information. To the extent that data can be turned into information that has relevance for someone, that someone will in principle be willing to pay for the data-processing and transmission economies on offer. What such economies offer is the possibility of reallocating a key data-processing resource possessed by all intelligent agents in finite quantities: *attention*. An information economy, by implication, has to be an attention economy as well.

factors for physical ones. Our scheme can illustrate such a substitution process; it cannot analyze it.

To summarize: except, perhaps, for the universe as a whole, there are no perfectly closed systems in the real world. Open systems are prey to unwanted interactions with their environment that get registered as noise when viewed informationally. Economics has tended to ignore the implications of the fundamental openness of the systems they study. Our scheme, by allowing the representation of the effects of time and entropy in the economic process, rectifies the situation. Once you admit learning, development, and evolution into the picture, you admit irreversible processes. But our scheme also suggests that the entropy concept is but one side of the coin when dealing with the second law of thermodynamics. Irreversible processes can lead to emergent, order-creating outcomes as well as to entropic ones, those that allow living things to jump across isoquants and move toward the origin in pursuit of factor savings (Brooks and Wiley 1986). Although we may agree with Shapiro and Varian when they observe in *Information Rules* (1999) that the information economy has not yet repealed the laws of economics, we feel that it poses explanatory challenges to economics—well captured by the way that novelty and new knowledge emerges in living systems and organizations—that the discipline has yet to take on board.

1.7. Implications

We can briefly summarize our discussion in the following three propositions:

1. Information is physical (Landauer 1999). It is a constituent element of all physical processes and hence cannot treated as something epiphenomenal to the economic process. It must be engaged with on its own terms.

2. Economic agents subject to the principles of least action and to the effects of the second law of thermodynamics aim to economize on their consumption of both physical *and* data resources by deploying effective cognitive and behavioral strategies.

3. Effective cognitive strategies extract information from data and then convert it into knowledge. Effective cognitive and behavioral strategies vary from agent to agent as a function of their situation, prior individual knowledge, values, and emotional dispositions.

1.7.1. *What Follows from Our Three Propositions?*

Developing further the difference between data, information and knowledge, data generates *thermodynamic* entropy, which we shall label *entropy* 1. It involves the erasure of differences between physical *states*. Information, by contrast, generates *Shannon* entropy, which we shall label *entropy* 2. It involves the erasure of differences between *symbols*. The difference between physical states might well be maintained, but the *form* given to such states no longer yield unambiguous symbols. Finally, knowledge generates *cognitive* entropy, which we shall label *entropy* 3. It involves the erasure of differences between the possible *contexts* required for the interpretation of either states or symbols.

All these different types of entropy constitute variations on Bolzmann's formula

$$N \sum P_i \log P_i' \quad \text{for} \quad i = 1, \ldots, n,$$

where n describes either the number of possible data states, the number of symbols in a repertoire, or the number of interpretative contexts that are compatible with a given set of states or symbols. N gives the message length, and we hypothesize that an inverse relationship exists between N and n. Efficient coding, however, should reduce both N and n to the extent that it builds on correlations between states, symbols, or interpretative contexts. Where such correlations are not given a priori, they must be discovered. In the absence of memory, however, an agent has no way of discovering such correlations so that, in effect, n can now potentially increase without limit. This makes Boltzmann's formula meaningless since it cannot be used as a basis for stable expectations.

Entropies 1 and 2 are to be found at Shannon's technical level. Entropy 3 is to be found at Shannon's semantic and effectiveness levels. At the semantic level, it can occur because the receiver does not know the codes or what, *specifically*, they refer to—this, in effect, is context narrowly defined—and at the pragmatic level it can occur because the receiver does not know how to embed the *message as a whole* into an appropriate context. Entropy 1 has the effect of increasing entropies 2 and 3. However, redundancy at the semantic and effectiveness levels can mitigate the effects of entropy 1.

Economics at best has only ever operated at Shannon's technical level. By largely ignoring problems of meaning and values, it has only scratched the surface of Shannon's semantic and effectiveness levels. Yet the implication of our analysis is that, strictly speaking, *there is no such thing as*

common knowledge and there is common information only to a limited extent.
Only data can ever be completely common between agents. As Metcalfe puts it,
agents may *live* in the same world, but they *see* different worlds (Metcalfe
1998). In its treatment of information, economics thus fell between
two stools. On the one hand, it eschewed the complexities of the 'soft'
approach to knowledge and information associated with the semantic
and effectiveness levels—and with the social and cognitive sciences as
a whole. On the other hand, it never really dug into the foundations
the way that physics did in order to distinguish entropies 1 and 2 from
one another.[21] It therefore allowed the concept of information to take
whatever form was needed to maintain analytical and computational
convenience.

1.8. Conclusion

From 'soft' sciences such as sociology right across to 'hard' sciences such as
physics, information has become a central concern. Economics, however,
has tended to treat information as something unproblematic, an auxil-
iary concept that can be left largely unanalyzed. Yet, in postindustrial
economies, information has now become the main focus of economic
transactions, and not merely a support for them. Economists, therefore,
cannot afford the luxury of neglecting the conceptual foundations of an
economics of information in this way.

Shapiro and Varian have argued that the laws of economics apply
to the information economy no less than to the energy economy that
preceded it. This is undoubtedly true and certainly needed to be said. The
issue, however, is not about the *applicability* of economic laws, but about
their *scope*. The physics of Newton was not displaced by that of Planck
and Einstein, rather it ended up having to share the stage with them.
Likewise, the physics of information neither falsifies the economic laws
of the energy economy, nor does it render them irrelevant. What it brings
out, however, is that, given their limited engagement with the concept
of information, such laws will have trouble dealing with many of the
phenomena associated with the evolution and growth of knowledge in
general and with the emergence of the new economy in particular. They
therefore need to be complemented with more encompassing and general

---

[21] Yet if the physics of information helped effectively, to distinguish entropy 1 from
entropy 2, this did not result in a distinction within the discipline between data and
information.

laws that take into account the pervasive roles played, respectively, by data and information in all physical processes, as well as that played by knowledge in biological ones. Such roles are distinct and complementary and in need of clear articulation. This chapter has attempted to provide some initial theoretical reflections on a task that still lies ahead.

References

Arrow, K. J. (1984*a*). *The Economics of Information*. Cambridge, MA: Belknap Press of Harvard University.

—— (1974). *The Limits of organization*, New York: W.W. Norton.

—— (1984*b*). 'On the Agenda of Organizations', in: K. J. Arrow (ed.), The Economics of Information, 1st edn. Cambridge, MA: Belknap Press of Harvard University, pp 167–84.

—— (1996). 'The Economics of Information: An Exposition', *Empirica*, 23: 119–28.

Aumann, R. J. (1976). 'Agreeing to Disagree', *Annals of Statistics*, 4: 1236–9.

Barrow, J. D. and Tipler, F. J. (1986). *The Anthropic Cosmological Principle*. Oxford: Oxford University Press.

Bateson, G. (1971). 'The Cybernetics of "self": A Theory of Alcoholism', *Psychiatry*, 34(1): 1–18.

Bell, D. (1973). The Coming of Post-industrial Society. New York: Basic Books.

Bennet, C. H. (1999). 'Quantum Information Theory', in A. J. G. Hey (ed.), *Feynman and Computation: Exploring the Limits of Computers*. Cambridge, MA: Perseus, pp 177–90.

Binmore, K. (1990). *Essays on the Foundations of Game Theory*. Oxford: Basil Blackwell.

Blackwell, D. and Girschik, M. A. (1954). *Theory of Games and Statistical Decisions*. New York: John Wiley & Sons.

Boisot, M. H. (1995). *Information Space: A Framework for Learning in Organizations, Institutions and Culture*. London: Routledge.

—— (1998). *Knowledge Assets: Securing Competitive Advantage in the Information Economy*. New York: Oxford University Press.

Boyd, R. and Richerson, P. J. (1985). *Culture and the Evolutionary Process*. Chicago, IL: University of Chicago Press.

Boyle, J. (1996). *Shamans, Software and Spleens: Law and the Construction of the Information Society*. Cambridge, MA: Harvard University Press.

Brooks, D. and Wiley, E. (1986). *Evolution as Entropy: Toward a Unified Theory of Biology*. Chicago, IL: University of Chicago Press.

Bruner, J. S. (1974). *Beyond the Information Given: Studies in the Psychology of Knowing*. London: Allen & Unwin.

Clark, A. (1997). *Being There: Putting Brain, Body, and World Together Again*. Cambridge, MA: MIT Press.

Crary, J. (1999). *Suspensions of Perception: Attention, Spectacle, and Modern Culture*. Cambridge, MA: MIT Press.

Daft, R. and Weick, K. E. (1984). 'Towards a Model of Organizations as Interpretation Systems', *Academy of Management Review*, 9(2): 284.

Damasio, A. R. (1999). *The Feeling of What Happens: Body and Emotion in the Making of Consciousness*. San Diego, CA: Hartcourt.

Deleuze, G. (1969). *Logique Du sens*. Paris: Les Editions de Minuit.

Derrida, J. (1967). *L'Ecriture et la difference*. Paris: Les Editions du Seuil.

DiMaggio, B. and Powell, W. W. (1983). 'The Iron Cage Revisited: Institutional Isomorphism and Collective Rationality in Organizational Fields', *American Sociological Review*, 48: 147–60.

Durkheim, E. and Mauss, M. (1963). *Primitive Classification*. London: Cohen and West.

Fergusson, C. E. (1969). *Microeconomic Theory*. Homewood, IL: Richard D. Irwin.

Feynman, R. P. (1996). *Feynman Lectures on Computation*. Reading, MA: Addison-Wesley.

—— (1999). 'There's plenty of room at the bottom', in: A. J. G. Hey (ed.), *Feynman and Computation: Exploring the Limits of Computers*. Cambridge, MA: Perseus, pp. 63–76.

Fransman, M. (1998). 'Information, Knowledge, Vision and Theories of the Firm', in: G. Dosi, D. J. Teece, and J. Chytry (eds.), *Technology, Organization, and Competitiveness: Perspectives on Industrial and Corporate Change*. New York: Oxford University Press, pp. 147–91.

Furubotn, E. and Richter, R. (1998). *Institutions and Economic Theory: The Contribution of the New Institutional Economics*. Ann Arbor, MI: University of Michigan Press.

Geanakoplos, J. (1992). 'Common Knowledge', *Journal of Economic Perspectives*, 6: 53–82.

Giddens, A. (1984). *The Constitution of Society: Outline of the Theory of Structuration*. Cambridge: Polity Press.

Gioia, D. and Chittipeddi, K. (1991). 'Sensemaking and Sensegiving in Strategic Change Initiatives', *Strategic Management Journal*, 12: 433–48.

Gottinger, H. W. (1983). *Coping with Complexity*, Boston, MA: Reidel.

Granovetter, M. (1985). 'Economic Action and Social Structure: The Problem of Embeddness', *American Journal of Sociology*, 91: 481–501.

Green, H. S. (2000). *Information Theory and Quantum Physics: Physical Foundations for Understanding the Conscious Process*. New York: Springer; Berlin: Heidelberg.

Grossman, S. and Hart, O. (1988). 'One Share-one Vote and the Market for Corporate Control', *Journal of Financial Economics*, 20: 175–202.

Habermas, J. (1987). *The Theory of Communicative Action I: The Critique of Functionalist Reason*. Cambridge: Polity Press.

Hamilton, D. B. (1991). *Evolutionary Economics: A Study of Change in Economic Thought*. New Brunswick, NJ: Transaction.

Hargreaves Heap, S. and Varoufakis, Y. (1995). *Game Theory: A Critical Introduction*. London: Routledge.

Hart, O. (1995). *Firms, Contracts, and Financial Structure*. New York: Oxford University Press.

Hartley, R. V. L. (1928). 'Transmission of Information', *Bell System Technical Journal*, 7: 535–63.

Hayek, F. A. (1999). '*The Use of Knowledge in Society*', in: J. W. Cortada and J. A. Woods (eds.), *The Knowledge Management Yearbook, 1999–2000*, 1st edn. Woburn, MA: Butterworth-Heinemann.

Hirshleifer J. and Riley, J. J. (1992). *The Analytics of Uncertainty and Information*. Cambridge, UK: Cambridge University Press.

Hodgson, G. (1988). *Economics and Institutions: A Manifesto for a Modern Institutional Economics*. Cambridge: Polity Press.

—— (1993). *Economics and Evolution: Bringing Life Back into Economics*. Cambridge: Polity Press.

—— (1999). *Economics and Utopia: Why the Learning Economy Is Not the End of the History*. London: Routledge.

Hurwicz, L. (1969). 'On the Concept and Possibility of Informational Decentralization', *American Economic Review*, 59: 513–34.

Jensen, M. and Meckling, W. (1976). 'Theory of the Firm, Managerial Behaviour, Agency Costs and Ownership Structure', *Journal of Financial Economics*, 3: 305–60.

Jung, C. G. (1971). Collected Works: vol. 6, Psychological Types. Princeton, NJ: Princeton University Press.

Kahneman, D. (1994). 'New Challenges to the Rationality Assumption', *Journal of Institutional and Theoretical Economics*, 150: 18–36.

—— and Tversky, A. (1982). 'Judgment under Uncertainty: Heuristic and Biases', in: D. Kahneman, P. Slovic and A. Tversky (eds.), *Judgment under Uncertainty: Heuristic and Biases*. Cambridge, UK: Cambridge, University Press, pp. 3–20.

Koopmans, T. (1957). *Three Essays on the State of Economic Science*. New York: Kelley.

Kuhn, H. (1952). *Lectures on the Theory of Games*. Issued as a report of the Logistics Research Project Office of Naval Research, Princeton University.

Kuhn, T. S. (1974). 'Second Thoughts on Paradigms', in F. Suppe (ed.), *The Structure of Scientific Theories*, Urbana, IL: University of Illinois Press.

Lamberton, D. M. (1996). *The Economics of Communication and Information*. Cheltenham, UK: Elgar.

—— (1998). 'Information Economics Research: Points of Departure', *Information Economics and Policy*, 10: 325–30.

Landauer, R. (1990). 'Irreversibility and Heat Generation in the Computing Process', in: H. S. Leff and A. F. Rex (eds.), *Maxwell's Demon: Entropy, Information,*

Computing. Bristol, UK: Adam Hilger, pp. 188–96. Originally in *IBM J Res Dev*, 5: 183–91 (1961).

—— (1999). 'Information is Inevitably Physical', in: A. J. G. Hey (ed.), *Feynman and Computation: Exploring the Limits of Computers*. Reading, MA: Perseus, pp. 77–92.

Lange, O. and Taylor, F. M. (1938). *On the Economic Theory of Socialism*. Minneapolis, MN: University of Minnesota Press.

Lavoie, D. (1985). Rivalry and Central Planning. Cambridge, UK: Cambridge University Press.

Leff, H. S. and Rex, A. F. (1990). *Maxwell's Demon: Entropy, Information, Computing*, Bristol, UK: Adam Hilger.

Lipman, B. L. (1991). 'How to Decide How to Decide How to ...', *Econometrica*, 59: 1105–25.

Lloyd, S. (2000). 'Ultimate Physical Limits to Computation', *Nature*, 406(31): 1047–54.

MacPherson, C. (1962). *The Political Theory of Possessive Individualism: Hobbes to Locke*. Oxford, UK: Oxford University Press.

Makowski, L. and Ostroy, J. (1993). 'General Equilibrium and Market Socialism', in P. Bardhan and J. Roemer (eds.), *Market Socialism: The CUlTent Debate*. New York: Oxford University Press.

Mannheim, K. (1960). *Ideology and Utopia*. London: Routledge & Kegan Paul.

Marschak, J. (1974). *Economic Information, Decision and Prediction: Selected Essays*, 3 vols. Dordrecht: Reidel.

Marx, K. (1970). *Capital: A Critique of Political Economy*. London: Lawrence & Wishart.

Mead, G. H. (1962). *Mind, Self and Society: From the Standpoint of a Social Behaviourist*. Chicago, IL: University of Chicago Press.

Metcalfe, J. S. (1998). *Evolutionary Economics and Creative Destruction*. London: Routledge.

Miller, A. I. (1996). *Insights of Genius: Imagery and Creativity in Science and Art*. Cambridge, MA: MIT Press.

Miller, G. A. (1956). 'The Magical Number Seven, Plus of Minus Two: Some Limits on Our Capacity for Processing Information', *Psychological Review*, 63(2): 81–96.

Mirowski, P. (2002). *Machine Dreams: Economics Becomes a Cyborg Science*, Cambridge, UK: Cambridge University Press.

Muth, J. F. (1961). 'Rational Expectations and the Theory of Price Movements', *Econometrica*, 29(3): 315.

Myerson, R. (1999). 'Nash Equilibrium and the History of Economic Theory', *Journal of Economic Literature*, 107: 1067–82.

Nelson, R. R. (1994). 'Economic Growth via the Co-Evolution of Technology and Institutions', in L. Leydesdorff and P. Van den Besselaar (eds.), *Evolutionary Economics and Chaos Theory: New Developments in Technology Studies*. London: Pinter.

—— and Winter, S. G. (1982). *An Evolutionary Theory of Economic Change*. Cambridge, MA: Belknap Press of Harvard University.

Nielsen, M. and Chuang I. (2000). *Quantum Computation and Quantum Information*. Cambridge, UK: Cambridge University Press.

Nyquist, H. (1924). 'Certain Factors Affecting Telegraph Speed', *Bell System Technical Journal*, April: 324–46.

Omnes, R. (1999). *Quantum Philosophy: Understanding and Interpreting Contemporary Science*. Princeton, NJ: Princeton University Press.

Penrose, R. (1994). Shadows of the Mind. Oxford, UK: Oxford University Press.

Plott, C. and Sunder, S. (1978). 'Rational Expectations and the Aggregation of Diverse Information in the Laboratory Security Markets', *Review of Economic Studies*, 45: 133–53.

Popper, K. R. ([1959] 1980). *The Logic of Scientific Discovery*. London: Routledge.

—— (1992). *Realism and the Aim of Science*. New York: Routledge.

Prigogine, I. (1980). *From Being to Becoming: Time and Complexity in the Physical Sciences*. New York: Freeman.

Quine, W. V. O. (1969). 'Naturalized Epistemology', in W. V. O. Quine (ed.), *Ontological Relativity and Other Essays*. New York: Columbia University Press.

Romer, P. M. (1986). 'Increasing Returns and Long-run Growth', *The Journal of Political Economy*, 94(5): 1002–37.

—— (1990). 'Are Nonconvexities Important for Understanding Growth?', *American Economic Review*, 80(2): 97.

Rosen, R. (1991). *Life Itself: A Comprehensive Inquiry into the Nature, Origin and Fabrication of Life*. New York: Columbia University Press.

Rubinstein, A. (1998). *Models of Bounded Rationality*. Cambridge, MA: MIT Press.

Scott, M. F. (1989). *A New View of Economic Growth*. Oxford: Oxford University Press.

Shannon, C. E. (1948). 'The Mathematical Theory of Communication', *Bell System Technical Journal*, 27: 379–423, 623–56.

—— and Weaver W. ([1949]1963). *The Mathematical Theory of Communication*. Urbana, IL: University of Illinois Press.

Shapiro, C. and Varian, H. R. (1999). *Information Rules: A Strategic Guide to the Network Economy*. Boston, MA: Harvard Business School Press.

Simon, H. A. (1957). *Administrative Behavior: A Study of Decision-Making Processes in Administrative Organizations*. New York: Free Press.

Singh, S. (1999). *The Evolution of Secrecy from Mary, Queen of Scots to Quantum Cryptography*. New York: Anchor Books.

Smith, J. A. (1991). *The Idea Brokers*. New York: Free Press.

Stiglitz, J. E. (1983). 'Information and Economic Analysis: A Perspective', *The Economic Journal*, 95: 21–41.

—— (2000). 'The Contributions of the Economics of Information to Twentieth Century Economics', *Quarterly Journal of Economics*, 140: 1441–78.

Von Mises, L. (1969). *Socialism: An Economic and Sociological Analysis*. London: Jonathan Cape.

Vromen, J. J. (1995). *Economic Evolution: An Enquiry into the Foundations of New Institutional Economics*. London: Routledge.

Vygotsky, L. S. (1986). *Thought and Language*. Cambridge, MA: MIT Press.

Weick, K. E. (1995). *Sensemaking in Organizations*. Thousand Oaks, CA: Sage.

Weimer, W. and Palermo D. (1982). *Cognition and Symbolic Processes*. Hillsdale, NJ: Erlbaum.

Williamson, O. E. (1985). *The Economic Institutions of Capitalism*. New York: Free Press.

Zurek, W. H. (1990). *Complexity, Entropy and the Physics of Information*. Reading, MA: Perseus.

2

Crossing Epistemological Boundaries: Managerial and Entrepreneurial Approaches to Knowledge Management

Max H. Boisot and Ian C. MacMillan

It is possible to identify two distinct yet complementary epistemological paths to knowledge development. The first one is holistic and field dependent and builds on the concept of plausibility, and we associate this path with an entrepreneurial mindset. The second is object-oriented and builds on the concept of probability; this path can be associated with the managerial mindset. We believe that both managerial and knowledge management practices have emphasized the second path at the expense of the first. To restore the balance, knowledge management needs to develop processes and tools associated with scenarios and real options—that will allow it to operate credibly in possible and plausible worlds, so as to extract value from them. We propose a systems framework for thinking through the nature of such tools.

2.1. Introduction

This chapter concerns the evolution of knowledge management as a subdiscipline of management. Specifically, we are concerned with how knowledge-bearing agents (individuals or groups of individuals with similar knowledge) develop and deploy their knowledge to create value for themselves: or in other words how they manage their knowledge.

Much of what passes for knowledge management today has its origins in practice, and qua practice, knowledge management has not much bothered with epistemological issues—that is, those related to the nature of knowledge and its justification. Yet without secure epistemological foundations, knowledge management is unlikely to evolve from a practice into an intellectual discipline. In this chapter, we argue that knowledge management is open to multiple epistemologies, which give access to alternative types of knowledge worlds, each with characteristic challenges and opportunities for knowledge management: possible worlds, plausible worlds, probable worlds, and actual worlds. Knowledge-bearing agents (hereinafter 'agents') use their knowledge in these worlds to take actions that secure future resources. The challenge for knowledge agents is to deploy their scarce resources in each of these knowledge worlds in such a way as to secure sustaining resources that exceed those committed. A key challenge for knowledge management is to understand the nature of, and the boundaries between, these worlds and, by implication, how and under what circumstances they can appropriately be crossed by knowledge agents. This chapter explores the nature and boundaries of these worlds and shows how they can be construed as sources of opportunities and of value for those who know how to move within and across them [a summary of other ways of thinking about boundaries can be found in the following: Dougherty and Takacs 2004; Grand et al. 2004; Karim and Mitchell 2004; Roos, Victor, and Statler 2004].

Consider the following investment events:

- During the Internet bubble of the mid-1990s, large numbers of small firms raised huge sums of venture capital. Many came to market with little or no track record to speak of and never having made a profit. Investors placed their money in these firms on the strength of what their rudimentary business plans promised and of a blind faith in the future of the Internet. The bubble burst in 2000 and the irrational exuberance of the market for these online companies, even ones with real potential, vanished with it.

- One day, before going on a trip to the United States, Masaru Ibuka (then Honorary Chairman of Sony) asked Norio Ohga (then Executive Deputy President) for a simple, playback-only stereo version of the 'Pressman', the small, monaural tape recorder that Sony had launched in 1977. He wanted to be able to take something light and portable with him on his travels. In 1979, Sony launched the 'Sound-about', a personal stereo that was later relabelled the 'Walkman'. It

49

was developed on the basis of nothing more than a strong personal hunch. Sony expected to sell 5,000 Walkmans a month. Within two months of the product launch it was selling ten times that amount and the 'Walkman' has since become a cultural icon.

- Inside large organizations, innovative managers approach their board with meticulously drawn up business plans and a mixture of objective statistical facts and estimates to justify these plans. The managers proposing these plans know—and often, the members of the board know—that these highly uncertain estimates are tentative and thus very likely to change as events unfold. Nevertheless, based on the evidence provided by the figures, the board will decide whether investment in these proposals is justified. Entrepreneurs persuade venture capitalists to invest with perhaps even more uncertain business plans.

- To be sure that they can meet their obligations, pension funds are required to place a significant proportion of their resources in risk-free investments. For this reason they invest part of their cash in money market instruments of proven reliability. This is a highly liquid form of investment that yields low returns but is certain to give back the cash originally invested.

In pursuit of an appropriate knowledge management perspective, in what follows we conceive of knowledge as comprising a set of beliefs which informs decisions by agents to take actions that consume the agent's (scarce) resources. With this conception of knowledge, each of the above cases involves deploying knowledge: that is, it involves taking action that consumes the resources of agents on the basis of sets of beliefs that they hold individually or collectively. In the first example, the beliefs were vague and carried little or no justification and the risk was significant. In the last example, the justification is well established and the degree of certainty is high. In the second example, what mattered was the strength with which the belief was personally held by a powerful decision-maker, irrespective of whether it could be justified to outsiders. And in the third example the key requirement is to justify the belief to members of the board, whether one holds it oneself. In each of the above examples, action is a commitment of resources to belief in a perceived opportunity. In the four cases, beliefs are more or less strongly held, and more or less capable of being justified to outsiders. The opportunity is characterized by high or low levels of uncertainty that gets eliminated with the passage of time. In a world characterized by complexity, variety, and uncertainty, the challenge is to take actions that are appropriate to the nature of the belief that is held, and to match the latter to the level of uncertainty inherent in a given situation.

Such a matching exercise illustrates Ross Ashby's law of requisite variety. This states that the variety of stimuli impinging upon a system must be countered by the variety of responses that the system can muster. As Ashby put it, only variety can destroy variety (Ashby 1956). Yet some variety only constitutes 'noise' for the system, and therefore calls for no response by the system save that of filtering it out. A system that is incapable of filtering out noise from the set of stimuli that it responds to is condemned to dissipating its scarce resources unproductively as it overreacts by attempting to respond to every opportunity or threat, real or imagined. Variety reduction then becomes necessary in order to filter out stimuli that do not give rise to actionable beliefs—that is, to a form of knowledge. However, in intelligent systems—that is, systems capable of forging meaningful representations of the states of the world that they respond to—what constitutes noise and what constitutes information for them will itself be a function of their models of the world; that is, the prior beliefs that they apply to the interpretation of stimuli (Boisot 1998). And the larger the number of models that the system can choose from, the wider the range of possible interpretations of stimuli available to it. Also, by implication, the larger the number of models that the system can choose from, the more tentative and uncertain becomes the application of filtering processes that distinguish information from noise.

The law of requisite variety is a call to action, and knowledge is an essential ingredient of effective action (Clark 1997). But what is likely to constitute sufficient knowledge to take action? How do the different types of belief that an agent is willing to act upon relate to each other? And how do they increase in certainty? Furthermore, intelligent action is action that can handle variety adaptively within a given time frame—requisite variety has a time dimension. How, then, to zero in on the relevant models and appropriate beliefs in a timely fashion?

Getting answers to questions such as these is likely to grow in importance in the coming years. The questions can be subsumed under a broader one: how might we economically manage our scarce knowledge resources under conditions of uncertainty? The burgeoning field of knowledge management has hardly ever framed its challenges—let alone attempted to answer them—in these terms. Why so? We argue that to be able to answer such questions, knowledge management will need to develop its epistemology—for our purpose, the question of what constitutes valid knowledge for who and under what circumstances. Epistemology provides the basis for action and thus serves as a foundation for the institutionalization of practice. In the absence of a credible epistemology, knowledge management is playing Hamlet without the Prince, condemned to remain a loose collection of empirical practices rather than evolving into a full-fledged intellectual discipline.

Epistemology, however, is not physics. Its principles and its application will vary according to time and place. There is therefore a need to identify the different circumstances—social, technological, economic, etc.—in which knowledge is considered valid and actionable. In this chapter, we unpack the Platonic view of knowledge as 'justified' true belief, into combinations of its different components. We argue that different mindsets will emphasize different combinations of the components 'belief,' 'truth' and 'justification'.

The chapter is structured as follows. In Section 2.2, we introduce some of the epistemological issue that confront knowledge management and put forward a simple scheme for relating these to each other. We then provide a brief overview of the current state of knowledge management as well as of its antecedents in the institutions of science, following which we show the relevance of our interpretive scheme for the current challenges that confront knowledge management. Our conclusion offers implications for both theorists and practitioners.

2.2. Defining Epistemological Boundaries

Epistemology—further discussed in our appendix—is the study of the nature of knowledge and justification (Audi 1995). Plato, aiming at the attainment of certainty, an infallible state of mind, (Ayer 1956) took knowledge and uncertainty to be antithetical to each other. In the Meno and the Theaetetus (c.400 BC) he defined knowledge to be justified true belief. This definition identifies three individually necessary and jointly sufficient components of what counts as infallible propositional knowledge: a truth condition, a justification condition, and a belief condition.

While it is appropriate for philosophical debate, when it comes to resource allocation decisions such a definition of knowledge is too restrictive. More crass than Plato, we are interested in knowledge that informs agent action. We suggest that it is beliefs that underpin agent action—so an agent can have justified true beliefs; justified beliefs; true beliefs and unconstrained beliefs. Thus different kinds of knowledge are possible, not all of which can be expressed propositionally, and not all of which require the presence of all the three components for action-based knowledge. We do not require the presence of all the three Platonic components for action-based knowledge to be possible.

The naturalistic perspective on knowledge, for example, concerns itself with possibilities for action in which knowledge, as well as being representational, can be tacit (Polanyi 1958) or embodied in skills and know-how—what the Greeks termed 'techne' (Thelen and Smith 1994). From this perspective, one drops the truth condition and settles for justified belief as a ground for action—if it is tacit or embodied, such belief may not take an explicitly propositional form and nor will its justification. If, on the other hand, one drops the justification condition, an agent may settle for true belief alone—that is an agent may be willing to act on beliefs that square with its own prior experience without seeking to justify such beliefs to others. Finally, an agent may settle for belief *tout court* and act on a 'hunch' where neither truth nor justification are involved. In the last two cases, however, a price is paid in the form of a loss of social legitimation of the belief in question. Agents who 'have the courage of their beliefs', however, are often willing to pay such a price.

As outlined earlier, the challenge for an agent is to deploy scarce resources in each of the knowledge worlds in such a way that the agent secures sustaining resources that exceed the resources committed. Such sustaining resources are only secured in actual worlds—that is, those characterized by certainty. In worlds characterized by varying degrees of uncertainty, however, there is some advantage in being able to develop appropriate forms of knowledge and to be able to migrate from one world to another in line with changing levels of uncertainty.

Thus, we can take the three components of justified true beliefs as representing different types of constraints on our definition of knowledge and then go on to rank different epistemologies by the degree of constraint that they impose upon us. Clearly, the most demanding constraints on our beliefs are that they should be both justified and true. As we go about our daily business, few of our beliefs are ever actually called upon to pass this demanding test and, indeed, few, if any, of our daily actions are based upon such epistemologically demanding conditions. We can greatly expand what we will count as valid knowledge, therefore, by dropping the truth condition and settling for a justification condition on its own. That is the strategy adopted by science. It is constrained by the requirements of justification—an essentially social process based on the authority of sensory evidence and logic rather than on charismatic or institutional authority—but no more than this.

Alternatively, we can drop the justification condition, acting solely on the basis of true belief a strategy that gives more scope to personal intuition, conviction, and experience. Of course (as Polanyi noted) this type of knowledge often being highly subjective: we may be unable to get others to accept it and we may then end up acting alone. Finally, we can have a large number of beliefs that are unconstrained by either a truth or a justification requirement but that we are still willing to act upon, albeit in a more cautious and tentative fashion—that is, we hedge our bets.

We represent our constraint-relaxation model in the form of a Venn diagram (see Figure 2.1). The larger circle, 1, represents the full range of what we can take to be knowledge—that is beliefs that to some degree we are willing to act upon. The two intersecting circles, 2 and 3, represent the more restricted views of knowledge, that is, those that either meet the truth condition, the justification condition, or both. Clearly, the most

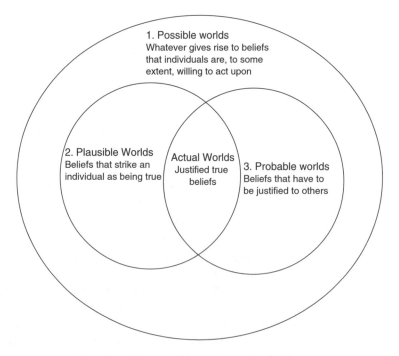

Figure 2.1. Possible, Plausible, Probable, and Actual Worlds

constraining condition is to be found in the area given by the intersection of circles 2 and 3. The least constraining one is given by belief on its own—that is circle 1 minus circles 2 and 3. We briefly discuss each condition in turn:

- Circle 1 minus circles 2 and 3 describes beliefs that are constrained neither by truth nor justification requirements. Here, 'anything goes' providing that it does not contradict the laws of logic or of physics—that is, providing that it is not actually impossible (Feyerabend 1970). Such unconstrained beliefs give us possible worlds. These worlds are characterized by phenomena to which no probabilities can (yet) be attached. This has two origins. The first is that a given phenomenon may not give rise to discernible events that are amenable to measurement—i.e., the phenomenon will not be identifiable and hence it will not be possible to distinguish an event from a nonevent. The second is that even if an event is so discernible, it may not be repeatable within an empirically relevant time frame and hence cannot give rise to a probability distribution (Borel 1937). This has reproducibility as a core requirement. In short, possible worlds lack both the clarity and the regularity that underpin the formation of rational expectations. Here, neither memory, nor perhaps even perception, has much purchase. At the height of the Dotcom boom, a good number of start-up firms were sustained by little more than the possible worlds that they had identified for over-gullible or overly optimistic and greedy investors.

- Circle 2 describes beliefs that are constrained by a truth requirement but not by a justification requirement. Like justification, truth requires both coherence and correspondence with the facts. Yet in the absence of an external reference group, whatever strikes one as coherent and in correspondence with the facts—that is as being true—will remain personal and subjective rather than intersubjectively validated. It may be based on deep intuitions and extensive personal experience but, unless an agent possesses a strong charismatic authority, it may prove hard to convince others of a truth without providing sharable evidence that would be acceptable to them. We are here in a plausible world, one which individuals might reasonably act upon but which lacks the objective (or intersubjective) justification for collective action. It was inside such a subjectively derived plausible world that Masaru Ibuka of Sony initiated the design of what was to become the Sony Walkman. The decision could be justified on the basis neither of reasoned arguments nor of observed regularities. Ibuka was able to act on the strength of entrepreneurial hunch alone.

- Circle 3 removes the constraint imposed by a requirement for truth and accommodates beliefs that have been justified. Where justification is not based on revelation or authority—we will not deal with these here—but rather on objectively demonstrable coherence and correspondence with the facts, such beliefs access probable worlds. These are worlds in which rational expectations can be developed and shared on the basis of the discernible regularities that reside in past experiences. They are accessible to probabilistic and statistical analysis, and allow action to be based on calculable risk. For this reason probable worlds can be justified to others. In our earlier examples, managers and entrepreneurs who lacked the resources to back their own hunches in the way that Ibuka did at Sony, had to justify their beliefs to board members or venture capitalists by presenting carefully analyzed technical and financial data as evidence. We noted that they themselves did not have to believe in the truth of this evidence in order to put it forward as justification.

- The intersection of circles 2 and 3 accommodates Plato's definition of knowledge, that is justified true belief. Such beliefs, justified to others either directly by the evidence provided by the senses or by the inferences that these allow, access actual worlds in which experience has immediacy and is indubitable. I do not doubt the existence of the laptop computer on which I am typing this chapter; it is here, before my very eyes. Nor, typically, do I doubt the veracity of my bank statement, when it credits my account with a cheque that I paid in yesterday. The truth of my own experience squares with the justification provided by the bank statement to reinforce my belief that my account has just been topped up by an amount corresponding to the value of the cheque. It is this kind of certainty that pension funds pursue in their investment strategies.

Each of the regions in the Venn diagram offers a distinct epistemological perspective that, to paraphrase Abraham Lincoln, will have validity to all of the players some of the time and to some of the players all of the time. One geometrical consequence of our Venn diagram is that both the number of plausible and of probable worlds is larger than the number of actual worlds, and that the number of possible worlds, in turn, exceeds the number of plausible and probable worlds. Actual worlds can be represented as singular outcomes that can be intersubjectively agreed upon; plausible worlds contain singular outcomes that will not necessarily command intersubjective agreement; probable worlds can be represented as a probability distribution of outcomes defined over a given range; possible worlds can be represented as a range of outcomes over which no probability distribution can be specified.

Each region in the diagram yields some kind of actionable knowledge, even though only the intersection of circles 2 and 3 inside circle 1 yields the kind of knowledge that would have been acceptable to Plato or Kant. The knowledge in each region, therefore, has some value for action, but, typically, any action in the real world will to some extent draw its epistemic resources from all regions simultaneously. Furthermore, action, by generating new knowledge, will shift epistemic resources from one circle to another in both the inward and the outward direction. How, specifically, might we establish the value-for-action of these different kinds of knowledge?

In Figure 2.2 we take action as requiring some kind of a resource commitment that varies according to the world that an agent finds itself in. Taking each world in turn:

Possible worlds are characterized by unconstrained beliefs. An undiscriminating commitment to all possibilities would quickly deplete the agent's resources. Resource commitments to action therefore must be highly tentative and can only be based on the option value of a selected set of possibilities. Framed in terms of action, an agent might—just—get what it pays for. Scenario thinking in organizations exemplifies the kind of thinking required in possible worlds. Over time, some subsets of possible scenarios may acquire plausibility on account of their coherence; other subsets, with accumulating empirical evidence, may come to seem probable. In this way, from possible worlds an agent can gradually move either toward plausible worlds, toward probable worlds, or toward both simultaneously. The knowledge inherent in possible worlds is generative of value, but it remains provisional. In possible worlds anything is possible—knowledge in this space comprises beliefs in possibilities— hints and hunches about what linkages among beliefs might be. However there is not yet any coherence of linkage among these hints, nor with the insight or experience of the agent. Furthermore, there is no history or evidence by which to corroborate and justify these hunches. The challenge for the agent is to recognize the potential for forging value from some subset of these possibilities by taking out options to exploit the value of whatever hunches can be navigated, either through plausible worlds or

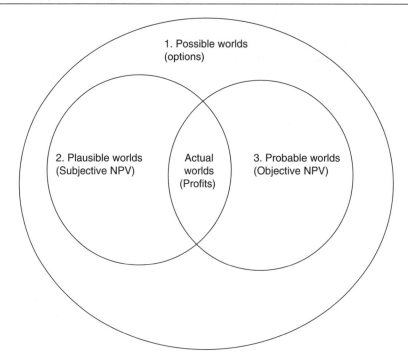

Figure 2.2. The Value of Different Worlds

probable worlds (where profit potentials are created)—into actual worlds, where value is captured.

Plausible worlds: Knowledge here also has value, but now only for the agent (individuals or groups with common belief) holding the belief. In plausible worlds knowledge is true for the agent (but not necessarily for other agents) in the sense that the linkages among beliefs held by the agent have coherence with one another and with the agent's experience, in other words the set of beliefs is plausible to that agent. The challenge for the agent is to recognize the potential for creating value from some subset of plausibilities by making 'speculative' investments in these opportunities unseen by others. The agent thereby creates the potential to capture abnormal profits in the form of Knightian rents derived from the agent's idiosyncratic insights. Expectations are sufficiently coherent and grounded in the agent's experience to justify applying an agent-specific discount rate. The subjective net present value that results will reflect the application of the agent's idiosyncratic insight—rather than objective criteria. In a plausible world an agent may strongly believe that it will get what it pays for, but, in the absence either of objective evidence to justify such a belief, or of a strong personal charisma, the agent will not easily persuade other agents to pay along with it.

Probable worlds: In probable space knowledge is justified in that the linkages among the set of beliefs can be corroborated by external evidence. Through empirical testing and replication the outcomes can be replicated and a probability distribution assigned, thus creating socially justifiable probabilities. The challenge for the agent is to recognize the potential for creating value from some subset of probabilities by making risk-adjusted investments which create the potential for normal profits. The kind of replicable empirical knowledge available in probable worlds allows for the application of a socially derived discount rate; it thus has an objective net present value. Framed in terms of action, an agent will probably get what it pays for. Much scientific knowledge is of this type, not indubitable, but, on account of systematically recorded repetitions and replicated tests, highly corroborated and hence, highly probable.

Actual worlds: In actual worlds knowledge comprises true, justified belief—either the agent is in a spot market where cash flows immediately out of spot contract or the emergent successes of agents' investments in options, speculations, or projects are cashed out. We argue, as William James did, that the certain knowledge available in such worlds to any agent which has direct or indirect access to the sensory evidence, has cash value (James 2000). Framed in terms of action, the agent will certainly get what it pays for, and so will those who pay with it.

The diagram highlights the fact that an agent has two quite distinct paths for navigating from possible to actual worlds:

- via plausible worlds—an agent starts off building coherence into its beliefs thus moving from the possible to the plausible, and then seeks to establish a correspondence between these coherent beliefs and the real world in order to justify them.

- via probable worlds—an agent first looks for justificatory phenomena in the real world that might correspond to its beliefs and then gradually builds up a coherent and plausible interpretation of this correspondence.

Plausibility and probability constitute alternative yet complementary bases for action. Whereas the first bases action on the coherence of an experience—does it make sense?—the second bases action on the robustness of the experience's replication—that is on its reliable correspondence to some recurring state of the world. Both help to underpin action, but each may kick in at a different moment on the journey from belief to action. In the early stages of any innovative process, for example, replication is hard to come by, if not impossible. For this reason entrepreneurial mindsets are more likely to look for plausibility and coherence before acting than managerial mindsets. The managerial mindset will look mainly to probability and correspondence to justify its actions. As experience accumulates over time and repeats, plausibility gradually gives way to probability as a basis for action.

If we think of a 'mindset' as the embedded epistemology that an agent employs to navigate a path from possible worlds to actual worlds, there are two basic types of navigating mindsets. We will call the navigating strategy using the path through plausible worlds the entrepreneurial mindset. An entrepreneurial epistemology seeks to extract real world value by enacting plausibilities. On the other hand, the navigating strategy that uses the path through probable worlds employs what we will call a managerial mindset. An embedded managerial epistemology seeks to extract real world value by enacting probabilities.

Entrepreneurial and managerial mindsets will each draw on their respective epistemologies as a basis for action. Whereas the managerial mindset seeks evidence and uses probabilities to justify its actions to others—stakeholders, shareholders, etc.—typically, the entrepreneurial mindset need not. By contrast, whereas the entrepreneurial mindset has to have the courage of its conviction in its beliefs—after all, it typically has to 'put its money where its mouth is'—the managerial mindset can afford to be more tentative in its beliefs before acting on them as long as it can justify them.

Now, as the uncertainties associated with the process of innovation are gradually removed or converted into measurable risk, and as the number of stakeholders associated with the process increases, the entrepreneurial mindset is required to cross the boundary between entrepreneurial and managerial epistemologies. Likewise, as firms experience the need to change and renew themselves—and hence to behave more entrepreneurially—the managerial mindset is required to cross the boundary in the other direction. There are costs and benefits, both personal and institutional, associated with such boundary crossing. Not everyone can make it.

These alternative mindsets and their associated navigation paths have profound implications for knowledge management. After a brief review of the current state of knowledge management we will look at these implications.

2.3. Knowledge Management

2.3.1. *Between the Possible, the Plausible, the Probable, and the Actual*

As is often the case with emerging fields of professionalization, much of what today passes for knowledge management has its origins in practice—and in particular, in the spread of ICTs (Castells 1996). And, as elsewhere, practitioners of knowledge management have not to date been much troubled by epistemological or foundational issues. This uncertain progression from a casual and empirical stance to a more theoretically informed one is a well-established phenomenon (Copp and Zanella 1993). Steel-making in the nineteenth century, for example, was largely a matter of empirical trial and error that preceded the development of metallurgy as a science (Derry and Williams 1960). Steel making, then, was understood empirically long before it was understood theoretically. But the kind of concrete knowledge embodied in such empirically derived practices was highly local and hard to replicate in a controlled manner. It lacked any capacity for leveraging, for getting extensively applied beyond the local context. The potential for leveraging is the great advantage that abstract science-based knowledge enjoys over more empirical practices, rooted as they often are in the vagaries of craft traditions (Cardwell 1994). Such knowledge can have relevance and can be applied over a much wider and more diverse range of circumstances. The gradual application of science-based knowledge to steel making helps to explain why the total world output for steel grew from 500,000 tons in 1870 to a total of 28 million tons by the turn of the century (Derry and Williams 1960).

However, to date, much of the knowledge that has been of interest to knowledge management has tended to be concrete and local in nature. It consists of rules of thumb, anecdotes, and best practices assembled and deployed within one organization and/or its related network, but not beyond it. Knowledge management thereby contributes to making better use of the knowledge that an organization already possesses. 'Knowing what it knows' spares an organization the expense of 'reinventing the wheel'. There is typically no intention of leveraging such knowledge beyond the confines of a single organization or network of linked organizations. The resulting knowledge 'makes sense'—it gives the right gut feeling to those who directly share the relevant experiences. But because the knowledge is local, replication, and dissemination is a problem. Such knowledge is plausible, but only to those who directly experience it or to those who can take such experiencing on trust. However, if knowledge is to move from small local populations to larger and more distant ones, access to the direct experiences that gave rise to such knowledge becomes increasingly problematic. How is another agent to trust such knowledge? How is a claim of having knowledge to be justified? To be justified, claims of having knowledge require independent and replicable testing. The results of such testing create knowledge patterns that follow distributions, and thereby allow resulting claims of knowledge to rest on probabilities.

Contemporary knowledge management to date has contributed even less to the creation of significant new knowledge. We say 'contemporary' because there is one form of knowledge management that has been outstandingly successful in this respect. We refer to the practices of the scientific community (Ziman 1968). This kind of knowledge management has been around for some time. But the creation of knowledge by the scientific community does not follow the 'logic' of knowledge creation as practiced in a corporate environment or, indeed, that advocated by knowledge management practitioners. The different 'logics' show up as differences in emphasis. In all three cases the key concern has been with control of the diffusion of new knowledge. Yet whereas the scientific community's primary concern has been with the epistemological validity of the newly created knowledge, that of the corporate community has been with the economic utility of such knowledge.

The philosophy of science has a subbranch—methodology—that takes the validity of knowledge as its central concern (Audi 1995). It attempts to endow the practice of science with solid epistemological foundations. The more solid those foundations, the greater is the potential for leveraging scientific knowledge, both existing and new, and reliably extending its application to new fields. Arguably, it is precisely the absence of solid epistemological foundations that is undermining the numerous attempts at leveraging corporate knowledge creation both within and across organizations. Yet because its primary concern has been with the utility rather than with the validity of knowledge beyond the boundaries of the firm, knowledge management as practiced by corporations has not so far felt any pressing need to secure its epistemological foundations. One plausible explanation for this, perhaps, is the daunting nature of the task: a two-and-a-half-thousand-year old debate on the nature of knowledge that goes back to Plato has not so far made those foundations any more secure. Drawing a boundary between useful and useless knowledge, therefore, may be easier for a corporation to do than drawing a boundary between valid and invalid knowledge.

So far we have argued that entrepreneurial and managerial mindsets arise in different circumstances and tend to draw on different epistemologies. As circumstances change, however, these mindsets not only need to cross epistemological boundaries, but they also need to be aware that they have crossed them. In Section 2.4, we briefly explore the nature of these boundaries and to show how they can be construed as sources of opportunities for those who know when and how to move across them.

2.4. Epistemology and Knowledge Management

From an epistemological perspective, the key skill in knowledge management involves understanding the basis on which an agent can move the products of its thoughts across the epistemological boundaries represented by the circles of our Venn diagram—that from one type of world to the other. Both the worlds of the plausible and of the probable, for example, are sources of potentially fruitful hypotheses. If carefully analyzed and reflected upon, such hypotheses gradually gain in plausibility. On the other hand, if repeatedly corroborated through testing, they become more probable. In both cases they improve their epistemic status. Yet the world of the possible is large relative to the worlds either of the probable or of the plausible, and when it comes to hypothesis selection, it offers an excessive amount of choice. An agent needs a good reason for selecting one hypothesis rather than another for further development and testing, since such activities consume scarce resources—after all, even options have a carrying cost.

In the world of the possible, if no prior distribution is available, no expectation can be built on the basis of recurrence. It must therefore be built on the coherence of the expectation relative to our other beliefs that act to constrain it (Thagard 1999). This is a theory-driven, sense-making activity that gives plausibility to an expectation and reduces subjective feelings of uncertainty. If, in contrast, phenomena exhibit recurrence and prior distributions are therefore available, an agent can subordinate the need for making sense of things to establishing a correspondence between prior beliefs and recurrent phenomena. Thus it will be the states of the world that suggest the appropriate trajectory to follow in moving from a possible to an actual world.

Given the lack of replicable precedents under conditions of innovation, the entrepreneurial mindset will tend to favor an initial move from possible to plausible worlds. It will then enact for itself the replications that

63

will lead them into the region of Figure 2.1 where the plausible intersects the probable. It will do so by constantly testing prior assumptions against accumulating empirical evidence in a process known as discovery-driven planning (R. McGrath and MacMillan 2000) The managerial mindset, by contrast, focused as it is on the need to justify its epistemic stance, is generally more disposed to move into actual worlds via probable ones, and to build its theories on the basis of available empirical evidence rather than seeking out evidence in support of a priori theories that have been subjectively derived.

Society has a large say in establishing what gets placed within each of our worlds and what gets excluded, what constitutes legitimate moves across epistemological boundaries and what does not (Douglas 1966), and what gets emphasized or played down. French culture, for example is more likely to stress coherence than Anglo-Saxon culture, which is more drawn to an empirical approach, and hence to correspondence. Chinese culture on the other hand will stress the complexity and multicausal nature of phenomena in contrast to Western cultures operating on the principle of Occam's razor and the quest for simple explanations (Nisbett 2003). Chinese culture is thus likely to draw the boundaries more loosely around our worlds than cultures reared in the Western scientific tradition.

Firms will often take their cues from established social practice in drawing boundaries. And for them as for other institutions, the issue will be one of balance. Draw the boundaries too tightly and you stifle innovative moves; draw them too loosely and scarce resources are squandered. The issue of balance leads us back to the question raised by Ashby's law of requisite variety. How much variety is actually requisite? Does every instance of variety call for a response? We can illustrate the nature of the issue by means of a diagram that presents Ashby's law in a graphic form (see Figure 2.3). The vertical axis of the diagram measures the variety of the stimuli to which a system is subjected. The horizontal axis measures the variety of the responses available to the system. Ashby's law locates adaptive responses on or below the diagonal in the diagram—that is the variety of a response at least matches the variety of the stimulus that provoked it. Yet, as we saw earlier, in a regime of high-variety stimuli, the sheer variety of responses that appears to be required might well lead to the disintegration of the system. At the other extreme, a system with little on no variety in its responses eventually fossilizes or gets selected out.

The challenge for any living system, then, is to navigate between the twin threats of disintegration and unresponsiveness. Living systems

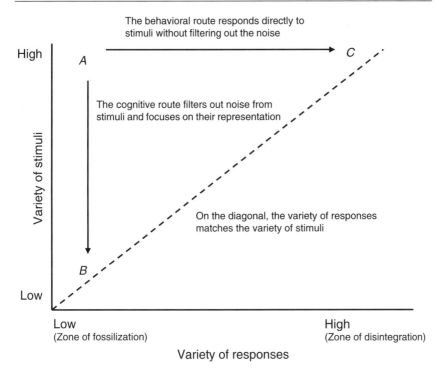

Figure 2.3. Ashby's Law of Requisite Variety

endowed with cognitive capacities, however, have successfully evolved responses to representations triggered by the stimuli rather than to the stimuli themselves, that is, they draw on prior knowledge of the stimuli to filter out those elements of stimulus variety that constitute noise, concentrating their response on the much smaller variety of information-bearing stimuli that remain. In Figure 2.3 this more 'cognitive' strategy is indicated by the arrow AB. In contrast with the horizontal arrow AC, it does not attempt to match the variety of a given set of stimuli on a one-to-one basis with a given set of responses. Rather, through a filtering and interpretive process, it reduces the variety of the response called for by reducing the number of stimuli that it actually needs to respond to. The epistemological challenge for knowledge management may well be to help us decide how far down the scale we can legitimately move and still be responding to valid knowledge.

Applying this thinking now to Figure 2.1, it is clear that moving toward the rim of the outer circle, 1, is a variety-seeking strategy that moves us up the vertical scale of Figure 2.3, whereas moving toward the intersection of circles 2 and 3 in the figure is a variety-reducing one that moves us down the vertical scale.

Looking at it another way, moving inward in the diagram from circle 1 to the intersection of circles 2 and 3 involves exercising options that already exist. Moving outward from the intersection to circle 1, by contrast, involves creating new options. The movement inward, toward the intersection of circles 2 and 3, reduces uncertainty and renders knowledge more reliable and usable. Since it represents a movement toward increasing constraint, it will be incremental in nature. It can be associated with a process of exploitation, one that builds up and consolidates existing knowledge. The movement outward, by contrast, broadens the horizons of awareness and can sometimes lead to a radical restructuring of what has already accumulated in the inner regions. It can be associated with a process of exploration, the creation of new knowledge (Holland 1975). Exploitation, then, is likely to stabilize and consolidate the existing knowledge base whereas exploration is likely to destabilize it and make it contingent. In Kuhnian terms, we might say that inward movement entails puzzle solving whereas outward movement will often look more like paradigm creation (Kuhn, 1962).

Our analysis suggests that an effective knowledge management process would not only attempt to strike a balance respectively between outward and inward movements in Figure 2.1—that is between variety-seeking exploration and variety-reducing exploitation—but it would also establish which of the different regions of the Venn diagram it was operating in at any given moment so as to match the behavioral strategy required to the epistemic resources available. Thus it would align the relevant mindset— in our case, entrepreneurial or managerial—to the nature of the task and the knowledge available.

The foregoing has implications for the way we think about the process of innovation. Schumpeter placed innovation at the heart of the process of economic development. He viewed it not as the fruit of rational planning, but rather as the unleashing of 'gales of creative destruction' (Schumpeter [1934] 1961). Innovation, then, offers benefits to society, but it comes with a cost to some individual firms. A parallel problem exists for firms: new products and processes can disruptively supplant the firm's established order. Innovation thus produces growth, but it also produces losers as well as winners. Many agents inside firms would prefer not to risk being losers. They thus tend to favor reinforcing incumbency rather than encouraging innovation—that is, the managerial rather than the entrepreneurial mindset—and for this reason are skewed toward a trajectory that favors probable over plausible worlds—that, is circle 3 over circle 2 in Figure 2.1. Small wonder that a managerial mindset dominates managerial practice, and thereby knowledge management practice and even managerial education today.

Can we reduce the costs of firm-level creative destruction to the losers? Indeed, do they have to be cast as losers at all? When viewed from an evolutionary perspective, one of epistemology's key insights was that 'hypotheses could die in our stead' (Popper 1972). Embodied in appropriate policies, this insight should increase our tolerance for higher levels of uncertainty, and encourage us to aim for bolder hypotheses, hypotheses that strike us as plausible on the basis of their innate coherence rather than of their initial correspondence with the facts. To repeat: correspondence with the facts is typically not on offer in the early phases of a genuine innovation. The facts do not yet exist.

We can summarize the above points by means of Table 2.1, in which the cognitive inputs required by the different types of worlds that we have been discussing are each associated with specific kinds of knowledge management tools and where each creates a specific kind of value as an output.

Table 2.1 lays out in a systems format the challenges that confront the practice of knowledge management: inputs required, actions required, outputs expected, and criteria for investment decisions. These will vary depending on the epistemological space you are operating in. We progress

Table 2.1. Knowable Worlds and Their Tools

World	Knowledge Inputs	Actions	Outputs	Investment Criterion	Knowledge Management Processing Tools
Possibilities	Hunches	Real option investments	Real option potential	Real option value	Brainstorming and scenario analysis
Plausibilities	Speculations	Speculative investments	Knightian rent potential (potential entrepreneurial profits)	Subjective NPV	Pattern generation and recognition tools
Probabilities	Estimates	Risk-adjusted investments	Profits (normal or abnormal)	Objective NPV	Statistical processing and analysis tools
Actualities	Calculations	Contracts	Profits (normal or abnormal)	Optimal solution	Optimization techniques

from possibilities toward actualities as we move down the table. Note that profits are an output only in an actual world; in all other worlds profits remain potential, and with different degrees of likelihood.

The spaces in which knowledge management practices are currently the least developed, and therefore the least effective, are those describing possible worlds and plausible worlds—especially possible worlds, for which in our view, few really successful practices have been created. Yet, in the absence of credible and powerful knowledge management methodologies that can identify hunches and evaluate the option potential of hunches, identify speculative investments, and assess their Knightian rent potential, managers will naturally gravitate to risk-adjusted investments, with their more certain and therefore normal, as opposed to abnormal, profit potential.

Confining our epistemologies to a managerial mindset focused on the worlds of probabilities and actualities in the bottom two rows of the table thus denies us access both to the rent potential of option values and to Knightian rent potential.

In a world of pure possibilities, for example, we can invest in low-cost real options based on hunches derived from vaguely linked beliefs, which if successful, create real option potential that has option value. In this world, knowledge management can build on and improve brainstorming and scenario generation processes with a view to helping the firm to surface more and better possibilities and assess them as option candidates. One reason why scenario planning has had difficulty establishing itself is because it has not articulated an explicit relationship between its epistemology and the process of creating option values. Evaluation of such opportunities calls for knowledge management tools that identify those options opportunities with superior properties: upside potential, potential control of downside, and potential sustainability (McGrath 1997).

On the plausibility front, knowledge management tools that enhance pattern generation and recognition need to be developed that will encourage searches for patterns of coherence and thereby more aggressive generation and exploration of plausible opportunities to commit resources to speculative investments that the firm alone can see. Much more aggressive development of discourse analysis and text-based pattern recognition methodologies would be a major place to start.

In conclusion, by highlighting the extent to which knowledge management has been concentrating on the bottom two rows of Table 2.1, we can begin to appreciate both how far it has been underselling itself as well as the scope that it has for broadening its agenda. Knowledge management can and should restore epistemic legitimacy to an entrepreneurial mindset that is primarily located in the top two rows of the table. This is partly a matter of cognitive style but partly also a matter of education. We keep teaching people that there are right and wrong answers to be derived by analysis. In some areas, to be sure, there will be; in others, however, we ourselves create the right answers by enacting them, thus converting a possible or a plausible prospect into a probable or an actual one. Reduce the social, organizational, and personal costs of operating in possible or in plausible worlds, improve the payoff for doing so, and more people will start behaving entrepreneurially. But to take on this task, knowledge management needs to come to grips with epistemological issues.

2.5. Conclusion

In this chapter, we have made four points:

1. The managerial and entrepreneurial mindsets operate with different epistemologies that reflect differences in their respective circumstances. The entrepreneurial mindset operates under conditions of novelty and uncertainty, where prior probability distributions, being nonexistent, can offer little guidance, and in which coherence is the epistemological underpinning. The managerial mindset, by contrast, is constrained to seek justification from probability distributions and thus cannot operate in their absence, so that correspondence is its epistemological underpinning.

2. Within each mindset the agent navigates from a world of possibilities to one of actualities, but through a different trajectory. The entrepreneurial mindset attempts to enact bold yet plausible hypotheses that create their own reality; the managerial mindset acts on the basis of objectively verifiable facts and constraints from which it derives hypotheses with a high degree of probability. The first epistemic strategy will be appropriate under conditions of novelty and uncertainty. The second will be appropriate where accumulated and objectively verifiable experience is available.

3. Current institutional practice is heavily skewed in favor of the managerial mindset. Knowledge management could help to redress the balance, but only if it becomes more epistemologically aware.

4. In particular there is a need for knowledge management tools that allow agents to develop and explore possibilities—especially to generate and process possibilities—and also to develop and explore plausibilities—especially to generate more and bolder ones. Seed tools already exist but need more epistemologically oriented development. These are brainstorming and scenario planning for possibilities, and pattern recognition tools like text-based processing and analysis for plausibilities.

The above has implications for theory. Much of modern management thinking has been inspired by the success of large established enterprises that operate on the basis of well-tested routines, well-documented facts, and hence articulable probability distributions. Starting with the Scientific Management movement at the beginning of the twentieth century, therefore, the managerial mindset has come to dominate both management education and management practice. As a result, the entrepreneurial mindset has got crowded out.

Yet the entrepreneurial mindset, it turns out, may have a broader scope than what is offered by purely entrepreneurial settings. As the level of uncertainty goes up in many walks of life, the entrepreneurial approach to the management of knowledge will surely grow in importance. When should we use it and when should we have recourse to a more traditional epistemological stance? Answers to this question have important implications for the way we select governance mechanisms appropriate to different mixes of risk and uncertainty. In a regime of multiple and complementary epistemologies, a 'one size fits all' approach to the problem of corporate governance cannot deliver convincingly. Yet the near-total absence of any knowledge management contribution to the debates provoked by the recent Enron, WordCom, and other scandals suggests that the discipline has not begun to address the challenges that it faces at the level of governance.

Our findings also have implication for practice. We have stressed that we are dealing with mindsets and not with particular individuals. Large corporations are as much in need of entrepreneurial mindsets as they are of managerial ones. However, building an entrepreneurial mindset will require the explicit development of internal organizational procedures that both counterbalance and complement existing managerial mindsets. Corporate venturing activities, for example, have often suffered when submitted to internal evaluation procedures that reflect the predominance of the managerial mindset.

New procedures need to be put in place in organizations that aspire to entrepreneurial behavior, procedures that acknowledge the contingent nature of the epistemologies under which organizations operate. The procedures will vary from firm to firm, but we believe that at a minimum they should observe the following principles:

- Develop systematic procedures for distinguishing between risk and uncertainty. Is the situation repetitive and hence amenable to probabilistic thinking, or is it so novel that little or no prior data can really guide a decision?

- Separate out the management of uncertainty from that of risk. They are not the same. If a proposed venture is uncertain rather than risky—that is, neither the full range of possible outcomes nor their respective likelihood can be identified—do not submit it to the quantification requirements of a risk situation;

- In order to manage uncertainty, develop skills in creating and linking together options that can be exercised in different sequences as the states of nature become known;

- Establish in which of the different worlds—possible, plausible, probable, actual—a venture proposal is currently located, and for each develop systematic evaluation criteria that are appropriate both to what can reasonably be known and to the chosen trajectory from one world to another. As suggested above, for example, do not ask for quantified estimates in possible or plausible worlds where none are to be had. In plausible worlds, focus on the coherence of a proposal and on the consistency of its underlying assumptions rather than on their likelihood;

- When dealing with entrepreneurial proposals, move away from the analytically oriented business plan questions of 'how do you know that this will happen?' This is the possible-to-probable-world trajectory of managers. Instead, move toward the more action-oriented entrepreneurial question of 'what actions will you undertake to make this happen?' This is the possible-to-plausible-world trajectory of entrepreneurs. In order to evaluate entrepreneurial proposals, insist on the construction of scenarios for the possible outcomes of such actions together with the identification of the options available should something like the scenario come to pass; until there is a cadre of internal people with an entrepreneurial mindset, choose outside entrepreneurs to carry out the evaluation of plausible and possible proposals rather than managers;

- Avoid procedures that filter out entrepreneurial proposals prematurely. Allow such ideas to ferment during the evaluation phase. If they are radically new, they may need getting used to.

Questions of epistemology may strike practicing managers as somewhat remote from their practical day-to-day concerns. But, as the psychologist Kurt Lewin once observed, 'there is nothing as practical as a good theory'. We hope that these principles will bring out the practical value to managers of taking a theoretical subject like epistemology seriously.

Appendix: Epistemological Issues

Since Plato, we have assumed that knowledge has a truth condition—that is a proposition either corresponds with the facts, is coherent with a wider system of propositions, or has pragmatic cognitive value. It can, of course have all of these. Also, knowledge implies belief but the converse is not generally held to be true.[1] A belief is a dispositional psychological state and a belief can be false. To satisfy the belief condition for knowledge, such satisfaction must be 'appropriately related' to the satisfaction of its truth condition. A proposition is epistemically permissible if consistent with a given set of epistemic rules of evidence (Chisolm 1988); it is epistemically good if based on adequate grounds. Less normative, perhaps, is the demand that the justification of a proposition be based on evidential support. A contextualist view of justification that is endorsed, for example, by Dewey, Wittgenstein, and Thomas Kuhn, holds that all justified beliefs depend for their evidential support on some unjustified beliefs that themselves need no justification. These will vary from context to context and from social group to social group (Kuhn 1962). Yet whatever one's approach, questions of justification attract the lion's share of attention in contemporary epistemology. Epistemology concerns itself with the limits of knowledge—and by implication with its scope.

The more restrictively we draw the boundaries around what we take to be knowledge, the more sceptical we are. The most extreme forms of scepticism hold that we are not actually justified in believing anything at all! (Unger 1971). But should the justification of beliefs be based on their predictive performance or on

---

[1] Here, we leave aside the issue raised by the so-called Gettier problem. In a highly influential paper published in 1963, Edmund Gettier challenged the equation between justified true belief and knowledge. Given that Gettier raises issues that are both beyond the scope of our discussion and not particularly relevant to it, we shall take that equation as an anchoring point for our discussion.

the understanding they give rise to? If on the first, then the quantum theory must be counted an outstandingly successful instance of justification—after all, the whole of modern electronics is based on it. If on the second, then it must be recognized that the theory remains highly problematic (Miller 2000). Feynman famously remarked that, whatever they might claim, no one really understands the quantum theory (Omnes 1999).

In recent decades, justification has been progressively 'naturalized' (Quine 1969). In contrast to theories of justified beliefs that concentrate on probabilistic or logical relations between a hypothesis and the evidence for it, the naturalized approach looks at the psychological processes at work in developing the belief. Alvin Goldman, for one, holds that one can only justify a belief if one can show that it has been produced by a reliable belief-forming process (Goldman 1967). But where, exactly, should we locate such a 'belief-forming process'? Dretske, for example, adopts an information-theoretic approach that has the possibilities for knowledge dependent on the physical capacity of instruments, gauges, neurons, etc., to pick up and process signals from the environment, extracting the relevant information from them (Dretske 1981). And almost as a natural extension of such an approach, naturalistic epistemology has been linked both to artificial intelligence and to the history of science (Laudan 1977). Inspired by models of population biology and economics, naturalistic epistemology has also been analyzed from a social perspective in which both power and authority relations can shape beliefs (Hull 1988).

Given these trends, we will not be surprised to discover that naturalistic epistemology had developed an affinity with evolutionary epistemology, a term coined by the social psychologist Donald Campbell to describe a theory of knowledge that is both inspired by and derived from organic evolutionary processes. One variant of such a theory that goes back to 'Darwin's bulldog', T.H. Huxley, sees the growth of knowledge—particularly scientific knowledge—as analogous to the transformation of organisms through processes of variation, selection and retention (Campbell 1974). Another variant, which was espoused by Darwin himself, sees the process as literal, with our thinking capacities being channelled in certain directions by the biological selection processes that we are subject to (Barkow, Comides, and Tooby 1992). Some supporters of the latter variant identify with Quine's naturalistic epistemology. A naturalistic epistemology takes the human subject as a natural phenomenon and studies its epistemic activity empirically. Quine argued that epistemology should be a branch of psychology, a study of how organisms take sensory stimulations as inputs and use them to output theories of the three-dimensional world. It is descriptive rather than normative, although it could be made normative according to Quine.

Naturalistic epistemology, recognizing that in the real world certainty is rarely, if ever, on offer, has pragmatic aims. In line with a proposal originally put forward by the philosopher of probability, F. P. Ramsey, it is happy to take as knowledge whatever subsets of an organism's beliefs it is willing to act upon providing that these contribute to its survival and—in the case of human organisms to its prosperity (Ramsey 1931). A requirement for justification and objectivity in this scheme merely translates into a requirement for intersubjective agreement. A requirement for truth translates into a good fit between an agent's beliefs and his or her stock of prior experiences rather than between such beliefs and some 'God's eye' view of the states of the world. As Lackoff and Putnam have each shown, such an approach to knowledge, by linking it to the conditions under which action is possible, opens up the field to multiple, nonexclusive epistemologies (Lackoff 1987; Putnam 1975). If the wilder forms of relativism are to be avoided, however, it poses the challenge of understanding the nature of the boundaries that might help one to distinguish one epistemology from the other, and by implication, the circumstances under which each can validly be drawn upon.

References

Ashby, R. W. (1956). *An Introduction to Cybernetics*. London: Methuen.

Audi, R. (1995). *The Cambridge Dictionary of Philosophy*. Cambridge: Cambridge University Press.

Ayer, A. (1956). *The Problem of Knowledge*. London: MacMillan.

Barkow, J., Comides, L., and Tooby, J. (1992). *The Adaptive Mind: Evolutionary Psychology and the Generation of Culture*. Oxford: Oxford University Press.

Boisot, M. (1998). *Knowledge Assets. Securing Competitive Advantage in the Information Economy*. New York: Oxford University Press.

Borel, E. (1937). *Valeur Pratique et Philosophie des Probabilites*. Paris: Gauthier-Villars.

Campbell, D. (1974). 'Evolutionary Epistemology', in P. A. Schlipp (ed.), *The Philosophy of Karl Popper*. La Salle, IL: Open Court, pp. 413–63.

Cardwell, D. (1994). *The Fontana History of Technology*. London: Fontana Press.

Castells, M. (1996). *The Rise of the Network Society*. Oxford: Blackwell.

Chisolm, R. (1988). 'The Indispensability of Internal Justification', *Syntheses*, 74: 285–96.

Clark, A. (1997). *Being There: Putting Brain, Body, and World Together Again*. Cambridge, MA: MIT Press.

Copp, N. and Zanella, A. (1993). *Discovery, Innovation, and Risk: Case Studies in Science and Technology*. Cambridge, MA: MIT Press.

Derry, T. and Williams, T. (1960). *A Short History of Technology: From the Earliest Times to* A.D. *1900*. Oxford: Oxford University Press.

Dougherty, D. and Takacs, C. H. (2004). 'Team Play: Heedful Interrelating as the Boundaries for Innovation', *Long Range Planning*, 37(6) (Special Issue on Boundaries for Innovation): 569–90.

Douglas, M. (1966). *Purity and Danger: An Analysis of the Concepts of Pollution and Taboo*. London: Routledge & Kegan Paul.

Dretske, F. (1981). *Knowledge and the Flow of Information*. Cambridge, MA: MIT Press.

Feyerabend, P. K. (1970). 'Against Method', *Minnesota Studies for the Philosophy of Science*. 4; Minnesota, MN: University of Minnesota Press.

Goldman, A. (1967). 'A Causal Theory of Knowing', *The Journal of Philosophy*, 64: 357–72.

Grand, S. et al. (2004). 'Resource Allocation Beyond Firm Boundaries: A Multi-Level Model for Open Source Innovation', *Long Range Planning*, 37(6) (Special Issue on Boundaries and Innovation): 599–610.

Holland, J. (1975). *Adaptation in Natural and Artificial Systems: An Introductory Analysis with Applications to Biology, Control, and Artificial Intelligence*. Cambridge, MA: MIT Press.

Hull, D. (1988). *Science as a Process: An Evolutionary Account of the Social and Conceptual Development of Science*. Chicago, IL: University of Chicago Press.

James, W. (2000). *Pragmatism (1907)*. New York: Penguin Books.

Karim, S. and Mitchell, W. (2004). 'Innovating through Acquisition and Internal Development: A Quarter-Century of Boundary Evolution at Johnson & Johnson', *Long Range Planning*, 37(6) (Special Issue on Boundaries and Innovation): 525–47.

Kuhn, T. (1962). *The Structure of Scientific Revolutions*. Chicago, IL: University of Chicago Press.

Lackoff, G. (1987). *Women, Fire, and Dangerous Things: What Categories Reveal about the Mind*. Chicago, IL: University of Chicago Press.

Laudan, L. (1977). *Progress and its Problems: Towards a Theory of Scientific Growth*. Berkeley, CA: University of California Press.

McGrath, R. N. (1997). 'A Real Options Logic for Initiating Technology Positioning Investments', *Academy of Management Review*, 22: 974–96.

McGrath, R. and MacMillan, I. (2000). *The Entrepreneurial Mindset: Strategies for Continuously Creating Opportunity in an Age of Uncertainty*. Boston, MA: Harvard Business School Press.

Miller, A. (2000). *Insights of Genius: Imagery and Creativity in Science and Art*. Cambridge, MA: MIT Press.

Nisbett, R. E. (2003). *The Geography of Thought: How Asians and Westerners Think Differently . . . and Why*. New York: Free Press.

Omnes, R. (1999). *Quantum Philosophy: Understanding and Interpreting Contemporary Science*. Princeton, NJ: Princeton University Press.

Polanyi, M. (1958). *Personal Knowledge: Towards a Post-Critical Philosophy*. London: Routledge & Kegan Paul.

Popper, K. R. (1972). *Objective Knowledge: An Evolutionary Approach*. Oxford: Clarendon Press.

Putnam, H. (1975). *Mind, Language and Reality, Philosophical Papers, 2*. Cambridge: Cambridge University Press.

Quine, W. (1969). *'Naturalized Epistemology'*, in *Ontological Relativity and other Essays*. New York: Columbia University Press, pp. 69–90.

Ramsey, F. (1931). 'Truth and Probability (1926)', in F. Ramsey (ed.), *The Foundations of Mathematics and Other Logical Essays* London: Routledge & Kegan Paul.

Roos, J., Victor, B., and Statler, M. (2004). 'Playing Seriously with Strategy', *Long Range Planning*, 37(6) (Special Issue on Boundaries and Innovation): 549–68.

Schumpeter, J. ([1934] 1961). *The Theory of Economic Development: An Inquiry into Profits, Capital, Credit, Interest and the Business Cycle*. London: Oxford University Press.

Thagard, P. (1999). *Coherence in Thought and Action*. Cambridge, MA: MIT Press.

Thelen, E. and Smith, L. (1994). *A Dynamic Systems Approach to the Development of Cognition and Action*. Cambridge, MA: MIT Press.

Unger, P. (1971). 'A defense of Skepticism', *Philosophical Review*, 80: 198–219.

Ziman, J. (1968). *Public Knowledge: The Social Dimension of Science*. Cambridge: Cambridge University Press.

3

Codification, Abstraction, and Firm Differences: A Cognitive Information-based Perspective

Max H. Boisot and Yan Li

3.1. Introduction

Much contemporary strategy thinking has been in the tradition of industrial economics (Bain 1959; Caves 1982; Porter 1980), a discipline that in its neoclassical variant—still today the dominant one—drew its inspiration from nineteenth-century physics (Mirowski 2002; Schumpeter 1961; Walras 1874). Nineteenth-century physics was primarily concerned with the problem of energy. Two new and deeply interrelated problems, however, came to confront physics in the twentieth century:

1. The second law of thermodynamics and the arrow of time—that is, the problems of a system's history, its path dependency, and the irreversibility of its processes. In short the problem of *change*.

2. The role of information and communication in physical systems—a problem at the core of the quantum theory (Feynman 1996; Nielsen and Chuang 2000).

Both are problems that neoclassical economics has had difficulty dealing with satisfactorily. Alfred Marshall (1920) had a sense that physics might not be the best source of inspiration for economics, arguing that its mecca lay in biology. Biology has had to grapple both with the second law—and hence with history, evolution, and development—and with information and its transmission.

In recent years, the field of evolutionary economics has built on the biological analogy (Aldrich 1999; Hannan and Freeman 1989; Hodgson 1993; McCarthy et al. 2000; McKelvey 1978; Nelson and Winter 1982; Vromen 1995). Yet in spite of its aspiration to achieve the same status as the natural sciences, economics remains a *social* science and thus confronts both the problem of knowledge, interpretation, and meaning, within and across social actors and the problem of information (Boisot and Canals 2004).

In pursuit of its natural science status, economists adopted a number of simplifying assumptions concerning the nature of information and knowledge in social systems that allowed it to maintain a mechanistic orientation when confronted with the complexities of social and economic exchange—tastes are stable, firms employ identical technologies, economic actors all have instant access to price information, they construe such information in the same way, exhibit synoptic rationality, etc. Such assumptions of homogeneity and linearity facilitated the use of mathematics. As in mechanics, all minor variation in a distribution was treated as noise; the relevant information was to be found in the mean. Such assumptions deliver computable equilibria. Unfortunately, social systems are complex adaptive systems (CASs) that operate far-from-equilibrium. The CASs do not require synoptic rationality either at the agent or at the systems level, and although they are subject to the physical laws of mechanics and constrained by them, the nature of their operations cannot be reduced to mechanics (Prigogine 1980).

The field of strategy—tethered as it has been for much of its existence to the neoclassical paradigm—paid a price for the failure of economics to credibly handle the problems of information and knowledge in social systems. This has become apparent in the way that strategy has conceived of the firm. Until quite recently economists gave the firm pretty short shrift, reducing it to a dot on a production function that transforms inputs into outputs within a framework of known and readily shared technologies and tastes. What actually went on inside a firm did not much interest them (Leibenstein 1987). The firm was treated as a unitary actor responding in a rational and hence predictable way to market forces. If they were to survive the competitive processes of selection, rational firms placed in similar positions would thus be led to respond in similar ways. Oversimplifying somewhat, competitive advantage could be secured either by making the best of one's position, or by changing it (Porter 1980). The resource-based view (RBV) of the firm challenged this environmental determinism. In an organizational variant of the nurture-versus-nature debate, it argued that firms were not just products of their external circumstances. Because of their history and the path-dependent choices made by their managers, they were intrinsically heterogeneous (Child 1972; Penrose 1959; Porter 1991). The RBV claimed that competitive advantage originated inside the firm and took the form of valuable, rare, hard to imitate, and heterogeneous resources that it had accumulated over time in path-dependent ways (Barney 1986a, 1986b, 1991; Dierickx and Cool 1989; Peteraf 1993; Wernerfelt 1984). Such resources, it was argued, could systematically give rise to superior performance—that is, above average returns (Hoopes, Madsen, and Walker 2003; Lippman and Rumelt 2003; Schoemaker 1990). Competitive advantage would only be sustainable, however, if the firm could maintain the scarcity of its resource set. If these could easily be replicated or imitated by others then both heterogeneity and, by implication, competitive advantage would erode. Sustainable heterogeneity, then, was the key to securing competitive advantage. The two questions put forward by the RBV were: (a) What makes firms different from each other? and (b) What keeps them different from each other?

These two questions implicitly take the similarity of firms, the core premise bequeathed by neoclassical economics to strategy, as their default assumption. Recently, however, the view has been gaining ground that heterogeneity and diversity rather than homogeneity and similarity prevail in the natural world (Mainzer 1994; Prigogine 1980). Could this be true of firms as well? If interfirm heterogeneity rather than homogeneity were to become the default assumption, then the fundamental mission of strategy and the RBV would shift from explaining how diversity arises in a sea of homogeneity to explaining how coherence of purpose and coordinated rent-generating activities by human economic agents—*intra*-firm homogeneity—can emerge in a sea of heterogeneity.

In this chapter, building on the work of McKelvey (1978) on organizational systematics, McCarthy et al. (2000) on organizational cladistics, Hannan and Freeman (1989) and Aldrich (1999) on organizational evolution in general, we argue for interfirm heterogeneity as the default assumption. In addition, we partly relocate the sources of heterogeneity in the cognitive processes of individual human agents. We take firm similarities and differences as residing as much in the eye of the beholder as in the external world. Such a cognitive approach, focused as it is on the data-processing strategies of agents, is one that is more appropriate to the emerging knowledge-based view of the firm (Spender 2002). However, it involves exploring the nature of heterogeneity at a more general level than that of firms or, indeed, of economics in general.

We proceed as follows. In Section 3.2, we start with a brief discussion of the RBV. In Section 3.3, we move to a higher level of generality and look at how living systems substitute data processing for energy resources in their struggle for survival and how they then seek to economize on data-processing resources. In using the term 'living systems' we shall follow Miller (1995) to include systems of living things such as organizations. In Section 3.4 we show how processes of codification and abstraction, the twin pillars of any classification activity, generate cognitive heterogeneity while economizing on data processing. We develop the implications of this finding for how we think of resources in Section 3.5. A conclusion follows in Section 3.6.

3.2. The Resource-Based View (RBV)

The RBV has served as the dominant explanation of firm differences in the strategy literature (Hoopes, Madsen, and Walker 2003). At first sight, this focus on the heterogeneity of firms is puzzling. Why would firm differences need explaining at all? After all, what is the evolutionary perspective on firms, with its focus on variation, if not a presumption in favor of heterogeneity (Weeks and Galunic 2003)? And as Tsoukas (1996: 22) points out, 'From a research point of view, what needs to be explained is not so much "why firms differ" (Nelson 1991) (they inevitably do), as what are the processes that make them similar.' Arguably, the RBV was reacting to an earlier presumption of firm similarity held by microeconomists. Johnson and Hoopes (2003), for example, point out that in economics the assumption endures that differences in beliefs and technologies are not sustainable in competitive situations. Interfirm homogeneity thus becomes a natural corollary of efficient markets, the default assumption made by microeconomists, for whom what then has to be explained is heterogeneity and not homogeneity.

That said, there is something faintly tautological in the way that the RBV has conceptualized heterogeneous resources (Bromiley and Fleming 2002; Foss, Knudsen, and Montgomery 1995; Hoopes, Madsen, and Walker 2003; Priem and Butler 2001). Resources are anything that can be *construed* as increasing revenue (Lippman and Rumelt 2003). But then revenue increases are used as a guide to identify resources *ex post* so that everything and anything can be made to count as a potential resource.

Managers, then in effect, become *bricoleurs*, opportunistically converting whatever is at hand—inside or outside the firm—into a resource. Unsurprisingly, it has proved difficult to falsify the RBV in any systematic way (Hoopes, Madsen, and Walker 2003; Priem and Butler 2001).

Yet if resources turn out to be what one makes of them, then perhaps exploring the processes through which resources get construed offers a more fruitful line of investigation than establishing what resources actually consist of. Such a cognitive approach is not without some justification. After all, RBV theorists themselves have persuasively argued that competitive advantage results from a combination of superior knowledge and luck (Barney 1986a; Dierickx and Cool 1989; Priem and Butler 2001; Rumelt 1984). This has been the line pursued by the knowledge-based view of the firm. By putting the emphasis on the epistemic dimension of resources, the knowledge-based view emerges almost naturally out of the RBV (Conner and Prahalad 1996; Grant 1996; Kogut and Zander 1992). Independently of whether resources exist in any objective way or not, from a knowledge-based perspective resources are now what are construed to be resources (Tsoukas 1996), and a superior ability to identify a resource—whether located inside the firm or merely accessible to the firm on an exclusive basis—becomes itself viewed as a resource (Lippman and Rumelt 1982).

Clearly, whether resources are really heterogeneous—*ontological* heterogeneity—is one thing, and whether we all construe such resources, heterogeneous or not, in the same way—*epistemic* heterogeneity—is another. Ontological heterogeneity reflects the workings of complexity and diversity in nature. Whatever similarities appear at a given level above that of elementary particles—the quantum theory, for example, teaches us that electrons are identical and display no variation whatever (Pesic 2002)—reflect the influence of law-like constraints upon phenomena that limit their degrees of freedom. High degrees of freedom open the door to complexity and hence to ontological heterogeneity (Wolfram 2002). Epistemic heterogeneity, by contrast, arises when the complexity and variety of the phenomenal world become perceptually and conceptually accessible to us as observers. Such accessibility, however, varies as a function of our respective situations, interests, and cognitive capacities— that is, our ability to distinguish between different states of nature. In short, if we take epistemology to be *observer-dependent* then epistemic heterogeneity reflects the diversity of situations that observers find themselves in as well as differences in their respective abilities to capture such situations.

What we set out to do in this chapter is to strengthen the theoretical underpinnings of the knowledge-based view of the firm by first arguing for a new default assumption based on epistemic heterogeneity and then exploring some of the implications of doing so. We make no assumptions with respect to ontological heterogeneity: two firms' physical resources could well be identical but still be construed differently by different observers. The questions we address thus differ somewhat from those posed by the RBV. We ask: (*a*) Are firms epistemically different from each other? (*b*) If so, what sustains such epistemic differences in the face of any pressure toward ontological homogeneity? and (*c*) Can sustainable epistemic differences be a source of competitive advantage?

To credibly establish epistemic heterogeneity as a default assumption we need to show that it characterizes any organized cognitive system receiving, processing, and transmitting data. Answers to the above three questions, therefore, will initially be sought at a general level. In Section 3.3, we look at how living systems process the data of experience. In Section 3.4, we identify two key drivers of this activity in more detail.

3.3. Energy, Data, Information, and Knowledge

All living systems have to deal with Ashby's law of requisite variety. The law—perhaps the most discipline-free presumption in favor of heterogeneity—states that 'only variety can destroy variety' (Ashby 1956: 207). If living systems prove unresponsive to the variety that impinges on them, they fail to secure the resources needed to survive and are either selected out or eventually fossilize. However, if they overrespond to variety, they waste scarce energy resources and are threatened with disintegration. To be effective, living systems have to be *selective and parsimonious* in the variety that they respond to (David et al. 2002). They must be able to distinguish between variety that is significant and variety that is 'noisy'. That is to say, they must first be able to extract useful information from the data impinging on them—whether this originates in their own behavior or in their environment—and secondly they must be able to convert some of this information into meaningful representations of that environment that they can subsequently act upon—that is, knowledge. The process is illustrated in Figure 3.1.

Figure 3.1 highlights the fact that data are physical properties of the world, a set of physically distinguishable states that are discernable by a living system—that is, an *agent*—and from which useful information can

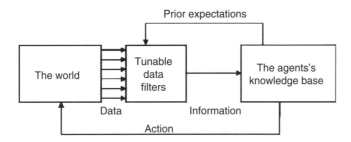

Figure 3.1. The Relationship between Data, Information, and Knowledge

Source: Boisot and Canals (2004).

be extracted. It further indicates that agents deploy expectations derived from their prior knowledge and experience to tune a set of perceptual and conceptual filters by means of which information is extracted from the data (Clark 1997). Accessing such data and converting it into information is thus an *active* process: the tunable filters are brought into play by *behaviors*(Cotterill 1998). As the diagram indicates, agents themselves also act directly upon the world, thereby modifying the source of the incoming data that they will subsequently be filtering in a way that is situation-specific (Weick 1995). As indicated in Figure 3.1, the blending of new agent-filtered information with the agents' own path-dependent prior knowledge and 'situated' experiences (Suchman 1987), brings out the essentially heterogeneous nature of agent knowledge. The coherence that results and the options for action that suggest themselves are specific to a given agent. The diagram, however, is scalable. It applies at the level of an individual, a group, an organization, or an institution—that is, to any complex entity that exhibits agency and computational capacity and that manipulates data structures (Boisot and Canals 2004; Frawley 1997).

To the extent that data deal with discernable differences in states of the world—temperature differences being the most basic—they rest on an energy substrate. Energy, then, acts on us in two quite distinct yet complementary ways: it acts *mechanically* in the sense that it translates into mechanical forces or energy differentials that directly affect our bodily states; or it acts *informationally* in the sense that having physically registered as data—that is, energy differentials—within our sensory apparatus, the subsequent information extraction processes go on to affect our cognitive orientation (Boisot 1995). The first type of action is broadly linear; the second broadly nonlinear. The evolution of living systems toward higher levels of complexity can be described as a process in which the linear mechanical action of energy is gradually replaced by the nonlinear informational action of energy. Over evolutionary time, for example, the phenomenon of vision comes to complement that of photosynthesis as a biological activity. The former treats light as a source of information that saves on the energy costs of a blind exploration for food sources whereas the latter treats it solely as a source of energy. Such informational action allows disembodied forms of knowledge, based on representations of objects and events that are more distant in space and time, to be either correlated or to coexist with the more embodied forms of knowledge through which proximal events are handled (Clark 1997). In this way, the spatiotemporal reach of a living system is extended, enhancing its access to physical resources and hence its survival prospects.

Furthermore, to the extent that living systems have memory they can learn from experience, accumulating, and storing data over time in the form of knowledge that is either embodied in behaviors and physical skills or in representations—in both cases, a by-product of activity. In other words, just as they can store energy in fat and have it available for the future performance of work, so they can store the data of path-dependent experiences in memory for various information extraction operations that they might need to perform in the future. As indicated in Figure 3.1, they are thus able to draw on a growing stock of embodied knowledge and/or stored representations in responding to environmental contingencies. By correlating these with incoming data, they can then become more selective about which of these they need to adapt to and which they can afford to ignore—as reflected in how they tune their perceptual and conceptual filters. In effect, they are substituting data stored in memory for energy in an attempt to reduce the amount of variety that they need to respond to in order to survive.

But for any level or mix of energy and information—atoms and bits—that living systems consume, entropy processes constantly kick in to deplete both their energy and their data-processing budgets (Vermeij 2004). We hypothesize that this dynamic drives a logic of economizing that requires two steps. Such systems, being open, first face a race between the rate at which the production of entropy erodes their energy budgets and the rate at which, through a learning process, they are able to substitute data for energy. Yet economizing on energy consumption alone cannot be the end of the story. As they substitute it for energy, living systems engage in an ever-larger consumption of data. Sooner or later they then confront a problem of data overload (Boisot and Canals 2004). Beyond a certain level, they can no longer store and process all the data that they accumulate and still remain within their data-processing budget. They will then either need to erase data—and as Bennett (1999) and Landauer (1982) have both shown, the erasure of data is an entropy-increasing activity—or, in a second step that McKelvey (2004) has labelled *order-creation*, they will need to economize on their data processing as well as on their energy processing activities. Boisot (1995) has argued that such economizing on energy and data by living systems is a biological manifestation of the *principle of least action*, a variational principle initially formulated by Maupertuis in the eighteenth century that underpins much of modern physics (Barrow and Tipler 1986; Green 2000; Hilderbrandt and Tromba 1996; Yourgrau and Mandelstam 1968).

Insofar as living systems exhibit cognitive capacities—and Popper (1972), for one, has argued that cognitive capacities are present in such systems from the amoeba to Einstein—they economize on data processing, and hence on entropy production, by classifying phenomena so as to respond to them in a discriminating way—in other words, they create order out of the 'blooming, buzzing confusion' (the expression is William James's) that surrounds them. The construction and deployment of effective classification schemes is then an essential requirement for any knowledge system taken as a structured set of expectations and capacities for action as indicated in Figure 3.1 (Arrow 1984; Popper 1972; Thelen and Smith 1994). Classification schemes economize on data-processing activities by devising appropriate strategies for extracting useful information from data and shedding irrelevant data as noise. For living systems, these schemes are generators of order and predictability.

Creating and using categories, however, are data-processing activities that are both time- and energy-consuming. A concern to economize on scarce data-processing resources, therefore, prompts two questions: (*a*) How clear and robust do the categories created by living systems or the phenomena that they assign to them need to be to allow them to distinguish different categories or phenomena from each other? This is a problem of *differentiation*. (*b*) How many categories do living systems actually need to relate to each other for the purposes of achieving a representation that is adequate for a given purpose? This is a problem of *integration*.

Answers to these two questions will tell us what data processing and transmission costs living systems face when confronted with a given phenomenon or a given task. Although these are likely to be largely context-specific, where cognitive tasks are demanding, living systems will be able to economize both on data-processing and on data-transmission costs, firstly by keeping the categories they create for themselves well differentiated, and secondly by minimizing the number of categories that they need to draw upon and integrate in constructing any given representation. Keeping such categories distinct and differentiated is something that living systems achieve through a process of *codification*. Keeping such categories to a well-integrated minimum is something that they achieve through a process of *abstraction* (Boisot 1995). Many modern organizational routines and technologies act in support of these basic processes (Lawrence and Lorsch 1967), as did some of the commercial practices such as the classification system—based on Confucian code of ethnics—used by Chinese merchants in Southeast Asia to rank trading partners on the basis of trust (Landa 1981). In Section 3.4, we shall examine codification and abstraction—potential sources of heterogeneity—in more detail.

Living systems collaborate and compete with each other in the struggle for survival (Michod 1999). Both activities require a measure of cognitive alignment. The question is: how much? Both perceptual and conceptual filters are tuned by an agent's prior beliefs and expectations. These globally constrain its thinking, limiting it to what is relevant to its interests, and even defining what is relevant. Prior beliefs and expectations thus constitute a *frame* that helps to shape an agent's systems of representation—its schemata (Norman 1976)—and maps out the cognitive territory within which it will operate (Haugeland 1987). A frame corresponds to what Prahalad and Bettis (1986, 1995), in an organizational context, have termed a *dominant logic*. An organization's dominant logic, just like a frame, acts upon its tunable filters, attempting to achieve economy and coherence by securing some minimum cognitive alignment across organizational members. The diagram used by Prahalad and Bettis to illustrate the workings of the dominant logic is similar to our Figure 3.1. But whereas they focus specifically on the firm and hence on the organizational level, we deal with cognitive systems at a more general and abstract level.

But how far do the schemata of individual agents have to be aligned to deliver a dominant logic—that is, a shared frame? Micro-diversity, for example, is built into the very fabric of human cognitive systems so that agents might share the data of experience without necessarily interpreting it in the same way (Rosch 1975). Figure 3.1, however, suggests—and the facts of psychology demonstrate—that through the action of the agent's perceptual and conceptual filters, external data is transformed and recoded into something that is emergent, individualized and often idiosyncratic (Frawley 1997). Both within and across groups, therefore, agents will be drawn to different frames and hence to competing logics.

Where a dominant logic does emerge we get something like unitary behavior and can thus speak of intelligent agency at whatever level such logic manifests itself. Where it does not, however, we get bargaining and an erosion of intelligent agency (Cyert and March 1963). Imparting a measure of epistemic homogeneity across agents must therefore be viewed as an *achievement* rather than as something that can be taken for granted. This much has been acknowledged by the Austrian economists (Hayek 1945; Kirzner 1979) as well as by some of the organizational literature on managerial coordination (Child 1972), even though it has yet to gain widespread acceptance in mainstream economics (Mirowski 2002).

We now turn to the role played by codification and abstraction in generating an agent's system of representations.

3.4. Codification and Abstraction: Economizing on Information Processing

Codification and abstraction are the two data-structuring activities through which living systems endowed with memory and intelligence economize on data processing and transmission costs (Boisot 1995, 1998). That codification and abstraction play an important role in such processes was first recognized by William James in his analysis of brain function. James accorded primacy to two key faculties: *discrimination* and *association* (Cotterill 1998; James 1890). Modern learning theories also frame their issues in terms of stimulus discrimination and stimulus generalization (Hahn and Chater 1998). In each case the first term corresponds to codification and the second to abstraction. In intelligent organisms like ourselves, discrimination and association have gradually evolved and become respectively institutionalized into the statistical activities of hypothesis testing and of correlation—the two basic strategies available to us for systematically extracting information from data. We first look at codification and then at abstraction.

3.4.1. *Codification and Fuzziness*

Codification makes it easier to distinguish between the categories—both personal and socially agreed—to which phenomena are subsequently assigned, through which they can be compared and contrasted, and through which relationships between phenomena are gradually articulated. Fuzzy sets, a generalization of set theory that covers collections of entities whose boundaries are not sharply defined (Zadeh 1965), can help us grasp the process of codification (McCloskey and Glucksberg 1978). Fuzzy sets extend the concept of a set, whose membership function takes on only two values {0,1}, to situations where the membership function can take on any value in the interval between 0 (complete exclusion) and 1 (complete inclusion). As a consequence of operating in the interval between 0 and 1, fuzzy sets do not satisfy the laws of contradiction and the excluded middle—respectively, $A \cap A' = 0$ and $A \cup A' = X$. The greatest deviation occurs for the membership value of $1/2$ over X. At this value, a set is at its fuzziest, making it impossible to achieve coherence using traditional two-valued logic since one cannot satisfy the constraints imposed by set membership to any degree at all (Lakoff 1987). Coherence will then require a multivalued fuzzy logic, and this will incur a higher computational cost than a classic two-valued logic.

Sets, then, can be either *crisp* or *fuzzy* and the extent to which codification is then possible will be a function both of the degree of crispness of candidate categories and of the degree of independence between them. If crispness establishes the clarity of category boundaries, independence establishes whether categories can be meaningfully related to each other. The concepts of crispness and fuzziness apply to the *boundaries* between entities to be classified, to the categories to which these are assigned, and to the *relationships* between entities or categories.

Codification aims to economize on computational costs by extracting relevant information from data—that is, by exploiting and retaining whatever regularities are perceived to be present in the latter that would help to distinguish relevant phenomena from each other and shedding extraneous random data as noise. It is a data-processing activity that is subject to error since information-bearing data might get discarded by mistake and noise, in turn, might be mistaken for information. One must then ask: how much data processing does one need to carry out in order to perform a valid discrimination between, say, sets A and B? Note that the problem is similar to the one of trading off type I versus type II error in statistics. So how should we measure codification? Since fuzziness increases the data-processing load, it works to undermine the computational economies that codification aims for. *Clearly, fuzziness and codification are inversely related.* Both might therefore be captured by some single data-processing measure.

De Luca and Termini (1972), among others, have developed entropy measures of fuzziness that reflect the extent to which two sets are distinguishable from each other. Entropy measures of fuzziness will be affected both by the fuzziness of sets themselves *and* by the distance between them. Sets that are fuzzy but do not overlap, for example, will have a lower entropy than sets that are fuzzy and do overlap. The former are easier to distinguish from each other in spite of their fuzziness and hence easier to codify. If we take fuzziness and codification to be inversely related, we could use an entropy measure of fuzziness to gauge the degree of codification of entities or categories. Such a measure would be quite different from Shannon's *H*, an entropy measure of information based on the probabilistic distribution of entities such as letters of the alphabet across preset categories in which the more equiprobable the entities, the higher the value of *H* (Shannon and Weaver 1949). Shannon assumed that such entities were initially given and were crisp—that is, well codified—and the uncertainty that he addressed with *H* concerned only their frequency of appearance. One entity might be mistaken for another, but not on account of any ambiguity or fuzziness of their respective forms. Fuzziness and probability, then, are orthogonal concepts (Pedrycz and Gomide 1998), and as we shall see below, the probabilistic distribution of events across the dimensions and categories of experience will lead us to the concept of abstraction.

The foregoing brings out the distinction between data and information that we drew in Section 3.1. According to Landauer (1999), information is inevitably tied to physical representations; it can only be extracted from discernable differences between states that are ultimately physical in nature. As Bateson (1972) puts it, 'information is the difference that makes a difference'. Where such differences are not easily discernable— that is, where they are characterized by fuzziness—then some of the data has to be classified as noise and needs to be discarded. Yet, according to Landauer (1999), data-processing operations that discard data, whether information-bearing or not, unavoidably incurs some minimal dissipation of energy. Landauer's arguments suggest that we should associate issues of data distinguishability—codification—with *thermodynamic entropy* and that we should associate the process of extracting useful information from data—abstraction—with *Shannon entropy.*

To illustrate the difference between the two, imagine that you come across what at first sight looks like the carving of symbols on a rock. The rock is well worn and your first problem is to decide whether these marks are just accidental features of the rock's shape or whether they are indeed something more intentional, like carvings that have been eroded by the passage of time—that is, that have been subjected to thermodynamic entropy. If the latter, you next have to decide whether the carvings are drawn from a given set of symbols, and if so, from what set? A Roman alphabet? Chinese ideograms? Deciding whether the different markings all belong to a given data-set—their codification—is one thing and extracting the information relevant to that decision is likely to be affected by the level of thermodynamic entropy. Establishing the frequency with which specific members of the set will then appear— their Shannon entropy—and in what order, is something else. You may, after all, conclude that you are dealing with a Roman alphabet even if the symbols are in a random sequence rather than specifically ordered to deliver a message in French or English. Clearly, though, if you cannot make the first decision, then you are unlikely to be able to make the second.

Having established what we mean by codification we next turn to abstraction.

3.4.2. Abstraction and Coding

The phenomena that make up the world of living systems first have to be distinguished from each other and then integrated into larger schemas if such systems are to achieve a coherent construction of objects and of relationships between objects. Depending on the system being studied, the number of potential relationships between objects or categories may actually grow at a faster pace than that at which the number of objects or categories themselves grows: for any system of n objects or categories, for example, there are $(n^2 - n)/2$ candidate relationships to choose from. Clearly, concrete phenomena, being closer to the world of direct embodied experience than abstract ones, will be characterized by a higher dimensionality than these—that is, by a larger number of candidate categories and relationships between them—and for that reason could potentially be categorized in a much larger number of ways. Yet the greater the number of categories available to classify phenomena within a given field, the lower the mean probability of anyone category being drawn upon and hence the greater will be the Shannon entropy, H, of the field. Concrete phenomena will thus typically tend to display a higher level of Shannon entropy than abstract ones.

Indeed, when faced with a concrete and complex experience, a concern with parsimony could well lead an agent to abandon any attempt at classification altogether, thus keeping such an experiences embodied (Clark 1997; Thelen and Smith 1994). This might happen, for example, if viable categories were not readily available and if the setup cost of creating them from scratch were too high. Alternatively, the agent might attempt to reduce the number of categories required to achieve a viable representation of the experience, and hence the entropy associated with them. The pursuit of parsimonious forms of representations, therefore, if it is undertaken at all, has the effect of moving us away from embodied and concrete experiences and toward more abstract disembodied forms of representation. How, specifically, is this done?

Abstraction treats things that are different as if they were the same (Dretske 1981). In effect, abstraction, while preserving relevant information, erases the differences that make *no* difference! Shannon's theory of efficient coding, by allowing one symbol to stand for another when the two are correlated, turns out to describe a process equivalent to that of abstraction (Shannon and Weaver 1949). Both efficient coding and abstraction involve mappings based on statistical correlations—between symbols in a repertoire in the case of efficient coding; between the categories that empirical phenomena are assigned to in the case of abstraction. And just as efficient coding economizes on data processing and transmission costs by exploiting the underlying statistical structure of the symbols appearing in a message to achieve compact representations, so does abstraction with categories.

Abstractions that are established through analytically derived functional relationships between objects or between categories will be crisp and hence strong and well codified. Those that are derived empirically will be less so—at least to start with: they will exhibit variance and hence fuzziness. The difference between, say, cladistics and phenetics as approaches to classification illustrate the point. The first is theory-driven and analytical; the second is not. *Fuzzy relations* generalize the generic concept of relation by admitting the notion of partial membership (association) between the elements in a universe of discourse. In science, for example, we attempt to move from fuzzy to well codified relationships through statistical analysis (Kachigan 1986). This process of formalization of our knowledge can never be complete: our cognitive processes (Popper 1972) and logic itself (Gödel 1931) make it impossible. Nevertheless, scientific progress requires crispness and by implication, codification, and abstraction. Science also requires a measure of alignment between the concepts and categories deployed by different individuals and groups. This is achieved by conventions that establish common codification and abstraction strategies among the different players. Yet to the extent that our formalizations remain incomplete, so do our conventions. In our everyday dealings with the real world, where the returns to formalization for the bulk of our situated experiences remains low, we are more often than not happy to live with the resulting fuzziness.

Abstraction, then, achieves a compact representation of phenomena using the same procedures as Shannon's theory of efficient coding. The value of doing this is clear. Shannon was concerned with achieving data processing and transmission economies by exploiting the statistical structure of messages in order to reduce their length. Insofar as abstraction and efficient coding use the same procedures in order to achieve compact representations, we can plausibly argue that abstraction also achieves data processing and transmission economies. But might codification and abstraction also be sources of epistemic heterogeneity?

3.4.3. *Codification, Abstraction, and Heterogeneity*

Codification and abstraction, by reducing transmission costs between agents, facilitate sharing. But what gets shared turns out to be data rather than information and knowledge (Boisot and Canals 2004). Whether sharing data subsequently gives rise to similar information extraction strategies and then to similar interpretative schemata is a more difficult question. The requirement here is for extensively shared *prior* data, information, and experiences rather than for either shared information or for shared experiences *tout court*. Whether it be at the level of a group, an organization, an industry, or a nation-state, this prior sharing secures an important role for culture in the development of collective sense-making and in the generation of collective forms of representation (Durkheim and Mauss 1963). A shared culture at the level of a group, for example, will be a source of *persistence* in these forms of representation (Weeks and Galunic 2003). Indeed, a shared culture, the product of a common socialization process that gradually aligns and attunes the different members of a group, underpins the emergence of a dominant logic.

Culture promotes shared codifications and abstraction strategies across groups of varying sizes. These give rise to conventions that in turn facilitate an alignment and common interpretation of experiences. Yet as we have seen, not only are conventions unable to completely capture the meanings around which social alignment is sought, but cultures, in turn, vary in how much alignment they actually require from their members. Cultures that Durkheim (1933) characterized as having organic solidarity, for example, will typically require alignment over a narrower range of phenomena than those he characterized as having mechanical solidarity. Furthermore, the homogenizing influence of cultural conventions and pressures notwithstanding, agents only ever work together with partially overlapping knowledge sets (Kelly 1963). We can thus either focus on the overlap between sets (common understanding) or on the differences between them (mutual understanding).

What might generate the differences? Assume that agents share the same physiology and hence, in the language of Figure 3.1, the same tunable filters. In identical situations, therefore, they will be called upon to react to the same range of external data—an important source of alignment. Yet while agents may confront the same data, being driven by situated and path-dependent memories as well as by idiosyncratic cognitive dispositions, they will each apply their filters—as reflected in their individual codification and abstraction strategies—so as to extract somewhat different information from this data. Furthermore, even if they were to extract identical information from the data, differences in individual memory and cognitive orientation would prevent them from embedding such information in the same context and of interpreting it in the same way. In other words, and as indicated by Figure 3.1, given an agent's prior knowledge base, even identical information items do not get internalized by different agents as identical knowledge items.

Codification and abstraction emerge from our analysis as double-edged; as sources both of heterogeneity and of homogeneity. Which of these sources will be emphasized will depend on circumstance. Under conditions of fuzziness, for example, different data-processing agents—individuals or organizations—may end up producing subtly different categories for themselves. They are then less likely to extract the same information from a given data-set than under conditions of crispness. What they subsequently internalize as knowledge is then even more likely to differ. Fuzziness thus provides an epistemic basis for both intra- and interagent heterogeneity. And even if a shared culture, through conventions, can constrain the variability of data and information processing strategies across agents—that is, can increase their crispness—differences in the interpretation of such information will remain, reflecting the diversity of prior contexts in which it gets embedded.

Another important source of epistemic heterogeneity resides in the complexity of knowledge that an agent is dealing with. Complex knowledge, in contrast to simple knowledge, allows for a much greater variety of alternative patterns to be wrought from the same data than simple knowledge—whatever their level of codification and abstraction (Wolfram 2002). Thus there is a much lower probability that any two agents will share similar interpretations when dealing with complex knowledge. Finally, what appears to be heterogeneous at one level may look homogeneous at another—neighboring villages, for example, may perceive each other as being radically different where to an outsider they may appear to be much the same. Whether different agents see similar or different things will therefore be partly a function of their respective distances from the phenomena being observed.

We conclude that differences in the situation of agents, differences in their respective interests and orientation, and differences in their cognitive styles will generate an irreducible level of epistemic heterogeneity that a shared culture can mitigate but never eliminate.

3.5. Implications for Firms

In this section, we move from a general discussion of epistemic heterogeneity in living systems to one focused more specifically on its instantiation in those human organizations called firms. We now address in turn the three questions that we posed earlier.

3.5.1. *Are Firms Epistemically Different?*

In Section 3.4 we identified three ways in which the codification and abstraction strategies of different agents might vary as a function of their respective circumstances: their location with respect to phenomena and their distance from them, their respective interests and orientations, and their respective cognitive styles. Taking each in turn:

(a) *The agent's circumstances.* No two agents can ever occupy the same spatiotemporal location. By definition, therefore, they cannot receive identical data with respect to an event. Even if it is almost imperceptible, they are differentially 'situated'. Culture acts to filter out agent awareness of minor variations in context and may in this way increase the agent's feeling that they share the same context. This will allow them to effectively coordinate their actions in most cases, but the question remains of how sensitive agents' cognitive processes might be to 'minor' variations in context. Gestalt psychology has taught us that such variations are nonlinear, and that small discontinuities in context can radically modify the patterns that we perceive (Kohler 1947). We thus take the agent's circumstances as constituting a first source of heterogeneity.

(b) *The agent's interests and orientation.* In any physical communicative process it is data that flows between intelligent agents, not information or knowledge (Boisot and Canals 2004). This data may or may not be information-bearing, and an agent may or may not gain access to it. But only if information is successfully extracted from data and subsequently internalized by an agent does it give rise to knowledge. As was earlier indicated in Figure 3.1, an agent extracts information from data as a function of its prior interests, and its prior expectations or knowledge. Two agents looking at the same data, for example, might be looking for, and thus attending to, quite different things. *Information, therefore, far from being a thing, expresses a relationship between external data and a knowing agent. And since the prior expectations or knowledge of such an agent will be strongly path dependent, it is highly improbable that the prior expectations or knowledge of any two agents—individual or organizational—will be identical.* We have here a second source of agent heterogeneity. As suggested earlier, agent heterogeneity may be constrained by prior conventions—as in the case of language—but it cannot be eliminated.

(c) *The agent's cognitive style.* Codification and abstraction are economizing strategies that agents use to extract information from data. The process of structuring data in this way, however, is subject to friction, both thermodynamic and informational. Codification and abstraction activities, therefore, generate data structures that have an irreducibly hypothetical character. They constitute acts of selection that are subject to refutation, revision, erasure, and reformulation. As Popper (1972) puts it, they are 'hypotheses that die in our stead'. The generation of hypotheses will reflect an agent's cognitive orientation. This might show up as a preference for clarity over fuzziness (codification), for an active rather than a reflective engagement with phenomena, or for concrete over abstract representations of phenomena (Kolb 1976). *The codification and abstraction strategies used by situated agents as they develop their hypotheses; therefore, will be partly idiosyncratic—reflecting not only differences in prior experience, but also differences in cognitive preferences and style.* We have here a third source of agent heterogeneity, and again, prior conventions with respect to what constitutes legitimate hypotheses may constrain such heterogeneity but cannot eliminate it.

The above considerations, taken together, vastly reduce the probability that any two agents will share exactly the same information and knowledge structures. Being players in a CAS, then, when two agents coordinate their actions, they do so on the basis of partially overlapping information and knowledge sets. Traditionally, the economic and organizational sciences have focused on the overlap between the information and knowledge sets held by different agents. In both disciplines, the growing interest in agent heterogeneity and in CASs is shifting the focus to the nonoverlapping parts of such sets (Shackle 1972; Weick 1995).

Although Coase (1937) and Williamson (1975) argued for a symmetrical treatment of firms and markets, the new institutional economics perspective on transaction costs—that is, friction—has accounted for the existence of firms through the phenomenon of market failure. The earlier neoclassical presumption in favor of markets, however, turns out to be a presumption in favor of the frictionless flow of data, information, and knowledge within a population of economic agents—that is, a presumption in favor of information and knowledge symmetries. Yet, *given that information extraction and its internalization as knowledge by agents is idiosyncratic and path-dependent, information and knowledge asymmetries constitute the default assumption. It is therefore information and knowledge symmetries that need to be explained, not information and knowledge asymmetries. It is also, by implication, firm similarities and not firm dissimilarities that need accounting for.*

The neoclassical economic presumption in favor of information and knowledge symmetry between agents implies that the existence of firms—reflecting, as it does, the absence of such symmetry—is a *deficiency*. Our analysis of the processes of codification and abstraction, however, highlights the point that even if we could get friction-free flows of data, we would still be left with the fact that, guided by their situated and path-dependent knowledge bases, agents extract information from data idiosyncratically. Seen in this way, *symmetric information and knowledge across agents is not just difficult to achieve, it is impossible.* Data-sets may well overlap where agents share the same experience—of sunsets, stock prices, etc.—yet given the application by each agent of its own tunable filters, the information sets constructed from these, and the knowledge sets that incorporate such information will do so to a much lesser extent.

The key issue, however, is how much cognitive overlap will actually be needed, both within and between organizations. Cultures focused on task efficiency, for example are likely to aim for a higher degree of overlap in the knowledge sets of their members than cultures focused on innovation. A concern with efficient coordination calls for alignment whereas a concern with innovation calls for diversity. Yet as Weick and Roberts (1993) point out, the high reliability of organizational processes does not come from the epistemic homogeneity required for alignment alone, but also from having just the right amount of overlap between heterogeneous mindsets (see also Tsoukas 1996). These, to be sure, will then be a source of noise in the system, but one can often get new order emerging from noise (Von Foerster 1960). Epistemic heterogeneity then becomes a source of novel order for firms. The question is whether such order can be made to persist.

3.5.2. *What Sustains Such Epistemic Differences?*

We submit that sustainable performance differences between firms can be secured by managers or other organizational players *reframing* faster than others to achieve a better fit between changing situations and their construal. Reframing is a form of adaptation to threats and opportunities that requires organizational agents to keep their tunable filters well tuned. By implication the cognitive activities of codification and abstraction must be kept plastic and flexible. A manager, for example, if she is a Schumpeterian entrepreneur, should be able to sense when the situation is familiar enough to justify using established codification strategies and when its novelty requires a more fuzzy approach; when to treat a given situation with all its concrete particulars as *sui generis* and when to seek out more general and abstract principles. Epistemic heterogeneity within the firm facilitates such reframing. Here, dominant logic works in two ways. It introduces cognitive friction and makes it more difficult to switch. But if the switch can be brought about, it then helps it to persist. This argument also applies to a firm's competitors. *Cognitive switching costs* allow differences in framing habits between organizations to persist. Knott (2003) has shown that such heterogeneity can emerge and persist without the help of isolating mechanisms—evidence, perhaps, of dominant logic at work. Dominant logic reflects the path-dependent, sunk costs of codification and abstraction incurred by dominant groups within a firm in pursuit of efficiency. Its very existence favors managerial rather than economic explanations of firm behavior (Prahalad and Bettis 1995). Dominant logic introduces friction and hence cognitive inertia into the system. But whereas Barney (2001), in line with neoclassical economic thinking, sees such persistence as ultimately leading to equilibrium conditions, its emergent qualities initially make it a far-from-equilibrium phenomenon.

Cognitive switching costs have two components: one associated with a changing context; another associated with mastering new codifications and abstractions. These costs are mutually reinforcing. The more tightly the codes are derived from and interpretatively embedded in a given context, for example, the more difficult it will be for those who do not share the context either to acquire and master the codes or to embed these in a different context. This will make it difficult for outsiders to reframe. But the tight coupling between codes and context also makes it difficult for insiders to reframe. Cognitive plasticity is therefore needed for intra-firm as well as for interfirm processes.

Heterogeneity is the product of both random and path-dependent processes. We have argued here that heterogeneity as such requires no explanation; it is our default assumption. What does require explanation is the sustainability of a difference in the performance of firms that such heterogeneity gives rise to, not the difference itself. In line with Ashby's law, epistemic heterogeneity must in some way reflect onto-logical heterogeneity—that which actually resides in environments and resources rather than in how these are construed—and it must do so in a timely fashion. The sustainability of firm performance differences is only valuable if it arises from a good fit between a given situation—and the opportunities and threats that it gives rise to—and a manager's framing or construal of that situation. But as situations change, so must their construal, failing which persistence becomes a liability—a competence trap (Leonard-Barton 1995). The challenge will then be to strike the right balance between a cognitive plasticity that facilitates adaptation and change on the one hand, and the cognitive commitments that give rise to persistent advantages on the other. In this sense a firm's dominant logic can have positive or negative outcomes.

As the foregoing implies, if interfirm heterogeneity is a natural con-dition, then, *pace* the arguments of transaction-costs economics, so is *intra-firm* heterogeneity. The assumption of easily shared information and knowledge inside the firm is thus equally problematic (Weeks and Galunic 2003) and a challenge both to organizational scholars and practitioners of knowledge management and to those who continue to view the firm as a unitary actor on the economic scene. Firm-specific conventions such as rules and routines (Nelson and Winter 1982) are designed to constrain intra-firm heterogeneity as much as they are to overcome agency prob-lems. And, as with interfirm homogeneity, the intra-firm homogeneity made possible by such conventions should therefore be regarded as an *achievement* rather than the unproblematic implementation of managerial will. The codification and abstraction of organizational routines into firm-specific rules will help, but only up to a point. Managerial coordination will often be more efficient than market coordination, but the very fact that it is needed at all and that firms are willing to incur substantial overhead costs to secure it speaks in favor of intra-firm heterogeneity. And, clearly, the greater the level of *intra-firm* heterogeneity, the more difficult it becomes to achieve *interfirm* homogeneity.

3.5.3. *Can Sustainable Epistemic Differences Be a Source of Competitive Advantage?*

The RBV's interest is in sustainable differences in performance between firms. Interfirm performance differences are attributed to competitive advantages that some firms possess and that others do not. This cuts two ways. Performance differences can themselves become a source of competitive advantage. In both cases competitive advantage has been explained by sustainable difference in resources between firms—and in knowledge-based theories of the firm, more specifically, by the difference in epistemic resources between firms. Yet, if as we have argued, such heterogeneity is pervasive—that is, the default assumption—it might be a necessary, but hardly a sufficient condition for competitive advantage to obtain, even if it proves to be sustainable. Competitive advantage, as the RBV well understood, comes from the *scarcity* of resources, and not just from their heterogeneity. What, then, is the relationship between scarcity and heterogeneity? The question leads us back to the concept of information.

As we saw, Bateson (1972) defined information as 'the difference that makes a difference'. If heterogeneity focuses on differences per se, we can think of *strategic heterogeneity* as that subset of the organizational differences that makes a difference. In this sense, strategic heterogeneity is information-bearing to managers and hence a source of opportunities and possible competitive advantage. It also introduces a legitimate role for managerial choice (Child 1972). Both codification and abstraction involve selecting from alternatives—from noisy data-sets in the case of codification; from competing categories in the case of abstraction. Where managers constitute an organization's dominant coalition, their codification and abstraction choices will shape its epistemic practices, its goals, its rules, its routines, and through all these, its dominant logic. Managerial choices will thus heavily influence what counts as an opportunity and what counts as a threat, and Porter (1991), for one, has explicitly linked the choices made by a firm's managers to the emergence of competitive advantage.

Consider, for example, Hamel and Prahalad's concept (1994) of stretch goals and of strategic intent. Two firms may have identical physical resources, but managers in the one may construe them in such a way as to deliver outstanding performance compared to those in the other. Here it is clearly not physical resources per se that are scarce. Rather it is the managerial ability to relate them in a feasible way to stretch goals that is scarce. And it is this cognitive skill that constitutes a source of competitive advantage. Stretch goals, where successfully implemented, are generators of superior performance and since by definition such performance is scarce, it constitutes a source of competitive advantage. Thus successful construal of goals and resources leads to superior outcomes that in turn lead to more ambitious construals, a virtuous circle that imparts a distinctly dynamic quality to the concept of persistence. It is a variant on this line of thinking that led Barney (2001) to suggest that the RBV needs to be augmented by theories of the creative and entrepreneurial process—epistemic theories of resources, by any other name.

We conclude that sustainable epistemic heterogeneity will be a source of competitive advantage, but only where epistemic content is constantly changing. Under such circumstances, *fast learning*, as noted by Arie de Geus (1997), becomes the only durable source of competitive advantage, and, by implication, so must be the speed and the flexibility with which an organization deploys its codification and abstraction skills.

Given their contribution to the epistemic heterogeneity of agents, how might a more focused knowledge-based theory of the firm incorporate the constructions of codification and abstraction? Knowledge is that subset of an agent's beliefs that it is willing to act upon. The concept of knowledge creation—the production of actionable beliefs—is applicable to living systems in general and is therefore scalable. In this chapter, we have so far taken abstract agents to be our data processors. But in their respective contexts, firms, organizations, and institutions all qualify as data-processing agents (Prietula, Carley, and Gasser 1998). There may be differences in the physical implementation of their different computational capacities but not in the logic of the process. Each type of implementation will involve acts of discrimination and association between states—that is, of codification and abstraction. The epistemic heterogeneity that characterizes agents in general, when viewed from the perspective of evolutionary epistemology, is a source of intelligence and of strategic opportunity. Applying this point at the level of the knowledge-based firm has the

effect of shifting the emphasis from a concern with *knowledge sharing*—
an activity that facilitates decentralization based on the commonality of
knowledge—to one focused on *distributed processing*—an activity that facilitates self-organization based on knowledge differences (Tsoukas 1996). As
Hayek had foreseen, epistemic heterogeneity is intrinsic to the concept of
distributed processing (Hayek 1945).

To summarize, the articulation of path dependent and situated experience through acts of codification and abstraction is a source of perceived
differences between firms—that is, of epistemic heterogeneity—as well as
of perceived similarities between them. A firm's dominant logic has the
effect of maintaining such differences. It is a source of inertia—and hence
of persistence—that simultaneously abets and constrains heterogeneity,
facilitating it between groups and constraining it within them. Culture
is a product of inter- and intra-group interactions, that is, of communication. It refers to the sharing of meanings and values among groups of
different sizes—at the level of departments within firms, at the level of
firms themselves, at the level of industries (Boisot 1995). Organizational
meanings and values are path-dependent sedimentations of the prior
codification and abstraction of experiences—organization-specific forms
of knowledge—that condition future ones. Differences in organizational
culture and history are not alternative sources of firm differences to those
brought about by the codification and abstraction of experience, but
rather different manifestations of this articulation process at work.

3.6. Conclusions

This chapter has argued that: (*a*) the cognitive activities of codification
and abstraction are important sources of epistemic heterogeneity; (*b*) epistemic heterogeneity is pervasive; (*c*) epistemic heterogeneity is sustainable; and (*d*) sustainable epistemic heterogeneity is a source of competitive
advantage. By making epistemic heterogeneity the default assumption, we
unshackle the knowledge-based theory of the firm from the burdensome
and unrealistic neoclassical assumptions of similarity. We also shift from
a perspective inspired by nineteenth-century physics (Mirowski 1989)
to one firmly rooted in twentieth-century biology and, more generally,
associated with the CASs perspective. Such a bioeconomic approach poses
new research challenges for organization scholars.

Heterogeneity and similarity are conceptual lenses through which we
look at the world. Different lenses are appropriate at different distances

and levels of resolution. Seen from outside, the action of firms appears to be shaped by their environment. Seen from within, however, firm players perceive degrees of freedom that may be invisible to outsiders but that they nevertheless can exploit to their advantage. The research challenge will be to identify how the epistemic homogeneity and heterogeneity of organizational agents interact and mutually constrain each other to create what Hayek described as 'spontaneous order' (Hayek 1945)—that is, *emergence*, by any other name (Holland 1998). In this scheme, the RBV becomes the story of how managers create and maintain focus, order, and some measure of homogeneity—perhaps through a shared culture—while responding adaptively to the diversity-generating competition around them.

The focus on emergent processes has implications for how one investigates the knowledge-based firm. Whether viewed as a resource or as a capability, knowledge is nonlinear in its effects. Small changes in the data being processed can produce disproportionately large changes in an agent's knowledge base. The magnitude of such changes is often concealed by a focus on population means, and investigating heterogeneity requires a shift of focus from population means to population variances. Yet the essential nonlinearity of knowledge makes it more complex to deal with than what is assumed by traditional forms of analysis—both idiographic and nomothetic—and knowledge management tools drawing on the new sciences of complexity, such as agent-based simulation modeling (McKelvey 2004; Prietula, Carley, and Gasser 1998; Tsoukas 1996; Wolfram 2002), will be needed to address the theoretical and empirical challenges posed by the knowledge-based organization.

References

Aldrich, H. (1999). *Organizations Evolving*. London: Sage.

Arrow, K. (1984). 'Information and Economic Behaviour', in the Economics of Information: Collected Papers of Kenneth J. Arrow. Cambridge, MA: Belknap Press of Harvard University, pp. 136–52.

Ashby, R. W. (1956). *An Introduction to Cybernetics*. London: Methuen.

Bain, J. (1959). *Industrial Organization*. New York: John Wiley & Sons.

Barney, J. (1986a). 'Strategic Factor Markets: Expectations, Luck and Business Strategy', *Management Science*, 32: 1231–41.

Barney, J. (1986b). 'Organization Culture: Can It Be a Source of Sustained Competitive Advantage?', *Academy of Management Review*, 11: 656–65.

—— (1991). 'Firm Resources and Sustained Competitive Advantage,' *Journal of Management*', 17(1): 99–100.

—— (2001). 'Is the Resource-Based "View" a Useful Perspective for Strategic Management Research?', Yes, *The Academy of Management Review*, 26(1): 41–56.

Barrow, J. and Tipler, F. (1986). *The Anthropic Cosmological Principle*. Oxford: Oxford University Press.

Bateson, G. (1972). *Steps Towards an Ecology of Mind: Collected Essays in Anthropology, Psychiatry, Evolution and Epistemology*. St. Albans, Herts: Paladin.

Bennett, C. (1999). 'Quantum Information Theory', in A. Hey (ed.), *Feynman and Computation: Exploring the Limits of Computers*. Reading, MA: Perseus Books, pp. 177–90.

Boisot, M. (1995). *Information Space: A Framework for Learning in Organizations, Institutions and Culture*. London: Routledge.

—— (1998). *Knowledge Assets: Securing Competitive Advantage in the Information Economy*. Oxford: Oxford University Press.

—— and Canals, A. (2004). 'Data, Information, and Knowledge: Have We Got It Right?', *The Journal of Evolutionary Economics*, 14: 43–67.

Bromiley, P. and Fleming, L. (2002). 'The Resource-Based View of Strategy: A Behavioral Critique', in M. Augier and D. M. James (eds.), *Change, Choice and Organization: Essays in Memory of Richard M. Cyert*. Cheltenham, UK: Edward Elgar, pp. 319–36.

Caves, R. (1982). *Multinational Enterprise and Economic Analysis*. Cambridge: Cambridge University Press.

Child, J. (1972). 'Organizational Structure, Environment and Performance: The Role of Strategic Choice,' *Sociology*, 6: 1–22.

Clark, A. (1997). *Being There: Putting Brain, Body, and World Together Again*. Cambridge, MA: MIT Press.

Coase, R. (1937). 'The Nature of the Firm,' *Economica, N.S.*, 4: 386–405.

Conner, K. and Prahalad, C. K. (1996). 'A Resource-Based Theory of the Firm: Knowledge versus Opportunism', *Organization Science*, 7(5): 477–501.

Cotterill, R. (1998). *Enchanted Looms: Conscious Networks in Brains and Computers*. Cambridge: Cambridge University Press.

Cyert, R. M. and March, J. G. (1963). *A Behavioral Theory of the Firm*. New Jersey, NJ: Prentice-Hall.

David, J. S., Yuhchang, H., Pei, B. K. W., and Reneau, J. H. (2002). 'The Performance Effects of Congruence between Product Competitive Strategies and Purchasing Management Designs', *Management Science*, 48(7): 866–85.

De Geus, A. (1997). 'The Living Company', *Harvard Business Review*, 75(2): 51–9.

De Luca, A. and Termini, S. (1972). 'A Definition of Non-Probability Entropy in the Setting of Fuzzy Sets', *Information and Control*, 20: 301–12.

Dierickx, I. and Cool, K. (1989). 'Asset Stock Accumulation and Sustainability of Competitive Advantage', *Management Science*, 35(12): 1504–14.

Dretske, F. (1981). *Knowledge and the Flow of Information*. Cambridge, MA: MIT Press.

Durkheim, E. (1933). *The Division of Labor in Society*. New York: Free Press.

—— and Mauss, M. (1963). *Primitive Classification*. London: Cohen & West.

Feynman, R. (1996). *Feynman Lectures on Computation*. Reading, MA: Addison-Wesley.

Foss, N., Knudsen, C., and Montgomery, C. (1995). 'An Exploration of Common Ground: Integrating Evolutionary and Strategic Theories of the Firm', in C. Montgomery (ed.), *Resource-Based and Evolutionary Theories of the Firm: Towards a Synthesis*. Boston, MA: Kluwer Academic, pp. 1–17.

Frawley, W. (1997). *Vygotsky and Cognitive Science: Language and the Unification of the Social and the Computational Mind*. Cambridge, MA: Harvard University Press.

Gödel, K. (1931). 'Uber formal unentscheidbare Siitze der Principia Mathematica und verwandter Systeme, 1', *Monatshefte fur Mathematik und Physik*, 38: 173–98.

Grant, R. (1996). 'Toward a Knowledge-Based Theory of the Firm', *Strategic Management Journal*, Winter Special Issue 17: 109–22.

Green, H. (2000). *Information Theory and Quantum Physics: Physical Foundations of Understanding the Conscious Process*. Berlin: Springer.

Hahn, U. and Chater, N. (1998). 'Similarity and Rules: Distinct? Exhaustive? Empirically Distinguishable?', in S. Sloman and L. Rips (eds.), *Similarity and Symbols in Human Thinking*. Cambridge, MA: MIT Press, pp. 111–44.

Hamel, G. and Prahalad, C. K. (1994). *Competing for the Future*. Boston, MA: Harvard University Press.

Hannan, M. and Freeman, J. (1989). *Organizational Ecology*. Cambridge, MA: Harvard University Press.

Haugeland, J. (1987). 'An Overview of the Frame Problem', in Z. Pylyshyn (ed.), *The Robot's Dilemma*. Norwood, NJ: Ablex, pp. 77–93.

Hayek, F. (1945). 'The Use of Knowledge in Society', *American Economic Review*, September: 519–30.

Hilderbrandt, S. and Tromba, A. (1996). *The Parsimonious Universe: Shape and Form in the Natural World*. New York: Springer-Verlag.

Hodgson, G. (1993). *Economics and Evolution: Bringing Life Back Into Economics*. Cambridge: Polity Press.

Holland, J. (1998). *Emergence: From Chaos to Order*. Reading, MA: Addison-Wesley.

Hoopes, D. G., Madsen, T., and Walker, G. (2003). 'Why Is There a Resource-Based View? Towards a Theory of Competitive Heterogeneity', *Strategic Management Journal*, 24: 889–902.

James, W. (1890). *Principles of Psychology*, vol. II. New York: Henry.

Johnson, D. R. and Hoopes, D. (2003). 'Managerial Cognition, Sunk Costs, and the Evolution of Industry Structure', *Strategic Management Journal*, Special Issue 24(10): 1057–68.

Kachigan, S. K. (1986). *Statistical Analysis: An Interdisciplinary Introduction to Univariate and Multivariate Methods*. New York: Radius Press.

Kelly, G. (1963). *A Theory of Personality: The Psychology of Personal Constructs*. New York: W.W. Norton.

Kirzner, I. (1979). *Perception, Opportunity and Profit: Studies in the Theory of Entrepreneurship*. Chicago, IL: University of Chicago Press.

Knott, A. (2003). 'Persistent Heterogeneity and Sustainable Innovation', *Strategic Management Journal*, 24(8): 687–706.

Kogut, B. and Zander, U. (1992). 'Knowledge of the Firm: Combinative Capabilities and the Replication of Technology', *Organization Science*, 3(3): 383–97.

Kohler, W. (1947). *Gestalt Psychology: An Introduction to New Concepts in Modern Psychology*. New York: Liveright.

Kolb, D. (1976). *The Learning Style Inventory: Technical Manual*. Boston, MA: McBer.

Lakoff, G. (1987). *Women, Fire, and Dangerous Things*. Chicago, IL: University of Chicago Press.

Landa, J. T. (1981). 'A Theory of the Ethnically Homogeneous Middleman Group: An Institutional Alternative to Contract Law', *The Journal of Legal Studies*, X(2): 349–62.

—— (1982). 'Uncertainty Principle and Minimal Energy Dissipation in the Computer', *International Journal of Theoretical Physics*, 21: 283–97.

—— (1999). 'Information Is Inevitably Physical', in A. Hey (ed.), *Feynman and Computation: Exploring the Limits of Computers*. Reading, MA: Perseus Books, pp. 77–92.

Lawrence, P. and Lorsch, J. (1967). *Organization and Environment: Managing Differentiation and Integration*. Illinois, IL: Richard Irwin.

Leibenstein, H. (1987). *Inside the Firm: The Inefficiencies of Hierarchy*. Cambridge, MA: Harvard University Press.

Leonard-Barton, D. (1995). *Wellsprings of Knowledge: Building and Sustaining the Sources of Innovation*. Boston, MA: Havard Business School Press.

Lippman, S. A. and Rumelt, R. (1982). 'Uncertain Imitability: An Analysis of Inter-Firm Differences in Efficiency under Competition', *Bell Journal of Economics*, 13: 418–38.

—— —— (2003). 'The Payments Perspective: Micro-Foundations of Resource Analysis', *Strategic Management Journal*, 24: 903–27.

McCarthy, I., Leseure, M., Ridgeway, K., and Fieller, N. (2000). 'Organizational Diversity, Evolution and Cladistic Classifications', *The International Journal of Management Science—OMEGA*, 28: 77–95.

McCloskey, M. and Glucksberg, S. (1978). 'Natural Categories: Well-Defined or Fuzzy Sets?', *Memory and Cognition*, 6: 462–72.

McKelvey, W. (1978). 'Organizational Systematics: Taxonomic Lessons from Biology', *Management Science*, 24: 1428–40.

105

McKelvey, W. (2004). 'Toward a 0th Law of Thermodynamics: Order-Creation Complexity Dynamics from Physics and Biology to Bioeconomics', *Journal of Bioeconomics* 6(1): 65–96.

Mainzer, K. (1994). *Thinking in Complexity: The Computational Dynamics of Matter, Mind, and Mankind.* Berlin: Springer.

Marshall, A. (1920). *Principles of Economics.* London: MacMillan.

Michod, R. (1999). *Darwinian Dynamics: Evolutionary Transitions in Fitness and Individuality.* Princeton, NJ: Princeton University Press.

Miller, J. (1995). *Living Systems.* Niwot, CO: University Press of Colorado.

Mirowski, P. (1989). *More Heat Than Light: Economics as Social Physics, Physics as Nature's Economics.* Cambridge: Cambridge University Press.

Mirowski, P. (2002). *Machine Dreams: How Economics Became a Cyborg Science.* Cambridge: Cambridge University Press.

Nelson, R. (1991). 'Why Do Firms Differ, and How Does It Matter?', *Strategic Management Journal*, 14: 61–74.

—— and Winter, S. (1982). *An Evolutionary Theory of Economic Change.* Cambridge, MA: Belknap Press of Harvard University Press.

Nielsen, M. and Chuang, I. (2000). *Quantum Computation and Quantum Information.* Cambridge: Cambridge University Press.

Norman, D. (1976). *Memory and Attention.* New York: John Wiley & Sons.

Pedrycz, W. and Gomide, F. (1998). *An Introduction to Fuzzy Sets: Analysis and Design.* Cambridge, MA: MIT Press.

Penrose, E. (1959). *The Theory of the Growth of the Firm.* Oxford: Oxford University Press.

Pesic, P. (2002). *Seeing Double: Shared Identities in Physics, Philosophy, and Literature.* Cambridge, MA: MIT Press.

Peteraf, M. A. (1993). 'The Cornerstones of Competitive Advantage: A Resource Based View', *Strategic Management Journal*, 14(3): 179–91.

Popper, K. R. (1972). *Objective Knowledge: An Evolutionary Approach.* Oxford: Clarendon Press.

Porter, M. (1980). *Competitive Strategy: Techniques for Analysing Industries and Competitors.* New York: Free Press.

—— (1991). 'Towards a Dynamic Theory of Strategy', *Strategic Management Journal*, 12: 95–117.

Prahalad, C. K. and Bettis, R. A. (1986). 'The Dominant Logic: A New Linkage between Diversity and Performance', *Strategic Management Journal*, 7: 485–501.

—— —— (1995). 'The Dominant Logic: Retrospective and Extension', *Strategic Management Journal*, 16: 5–14.

Priem, R. L. and Butler, J. E. (2001). 'Is the Resource-Based 'View' a Useful Perspective for Strategic Management Research?', *Academy of Management Review*, 26: 22–44.

Prietula, M., Carley, K., and Gasser, L. G. (eds.) (1998). *Simulating Organizations: Computational Models of Institutions and Groups.* Cambridge, MA: MIT Press.

Prigogine, I. (1980). *From Being to Becoming: Time and Complexity in the Physical Sciences.* New York: W.H. Freeman.

Rosch, E. (1975). 'Cognitive Representations of Semantic Categories', *Journal of Experimental Psychology*, General 104: 192–232.

Rumelt, R. (1984). 'Towards a Strategic Theory of a Firm', in R. B. Lamb (ed.), *Competitive Strategic management.* Englewood Cliffs, NJ: Prentice-Hall.

Schoemaker, P. (1990). 'Strategy, Complexity, and Economic Rent', *Management Science*, 36: 1178–92.

Schumpeter, J. (1961). *The Theory of Economic Development.* Oxford: Oxford University Press.

Shackle, G. (1972). *Epistemics and Economics: A Critique of Economic Doctrines.* Cambridge: Cambridge University Press.

Shannon, C. E. and Weaver, W. (1949). *The Mathematical Theory of Communication.* Urbana, IL: University of Illinois Press.

Spender, J. C. (2002). 'Knowledge, Uncertainty, and an Emergent Theory of the Firm', in C. W. Choo and N. Bontis (eds.), *The Strategic Management of Intellectual Capital and Organizational Knowledge.* Oxford: Oxford University Press, pp. 149–62.

Suchman, L. A. (1987). *Plans and Situated Actions: The Problem of Human-Machine Communication.* Cambridge: Cambridge University Press.

Thelen, E. and Smith, L. (1994). *A Dynamic Systems Approach to the Development of Cognition and Action.* Cambridge, MA: MIT Press.

Tsoukas, H. (1996). 'The Firm As a Distributed Knowledge System: A Constructionist Approach', *Strategic Management Journal*, 17: 11–25.

Vermeij, G. J. (2004). *Nature: An Economic History.* Princeton, NJ: Princeton University Press.

Von Foerster, H. (1960). 'On Self-Organizing Systems and Their Environments', in M. Yovitz and H. Cameron (eds.), *Self-Organizing Systems.* London: Pergamon Press, pp. 31–50.

Vromen, J. (1995). *Economic Evolution: An Enquiry Into the Foundations of Institutional Economics.* London: Routledge.

Walras, L. (1874). Elements d'economie politique pure (Theorie de la richesse sociale). Premier Fascicule Lausanne.

Weeks, J. and Galunic, C. (2003). 'A Theory of the Cultural Evolution of the Firm: The Intra-Organizational Ecology of Memes', *Organization Studies*, 24(8): 1309–52.

Weick, K. (1995). *Sensemaking in Organizations.* Thousand Oaks, CA: Sage.

—— and Roberts, K. (1993). 'Collective Mind in Organizations: Heedful Interrelating on Flight Decks', *Administrative Science Quarterly*, 38(3): 357–81.

Wernerfelt, B. (1984). 'A Resource-Based View of the Firm', *Strategic Management Journal*, 5: 171–80.

Williamson, O. (1975). *Markets and Hierarchies: Analysis and Antitrust Implications*. Glencoe, Scotland: Free Press.

Wolfram, S. (2002). *A New Kind of Science*. Champagne, IL: Wolfram Media.

Yourgrau, W. and Mandelstam, S. (1968). *Variational Principles in Dynamics and Quantum Theory*. New York: Dover.

Zadeh, L. A. (1965). 'Fuzzy Sets', *Information and Control*, 8: 338–53.

4

Organizational versus Market Knowledge: From Concrete Embodiment to Abstract Representation

Max H. Boisot and Yan Li

4.1. Introduction

How far knowledge gets articulated determines how speedily and extensively it can be shared (Boisot 1995). Sharing knowledge is typically viewed as a benefit that affects how we view the options of transacting within or between organizations. Transactional options, first identified by Coase (1937) and then further articulated by Williamson and others (Cheung 1983; Williamson 1975, 1985), rest on a number of unstated assumptions concerning how agents process and share the data of experience. Coase was in effect suggesting that where things cannot be readily articulated—that is, where the cost of writing complete contracts and hence of using the price mechanism was too high—they should be internalized, thereby becoming the province of organizational theory. Where they could be so articulated—that is, be fully specified and priced— they should belong to market processes and be left to economists. The transaction cost perspective invites a more penetrating analysis of the information question than neoclassical economics has traditionally been willing to countenance. The latter has taken as its default assumption that 'in the beginning there were markets' (Williamson 1975: 20)—an assumption that favors the view that transactionally relevant information can be readily articulated and shared (Boisot 1986; Debreu 1959;

Hurwicz 1972). The transaction cost perspective, as formulated by Williamson, frames the choice between organizations and markets as essentially a symmetrical one.

Our analysis in this chapter challenges both the primacy-of-markets and the market-organization symmetry perspectives on information grounds. These perspectives are predicated on assumptions of agent homogeneity. In Boisot and Li (2005), we argued that the heterogeneity of organizations, not their homogeneity, had to be taken as a default assumption when analyzing organizational strategies. The heterogeneity of organizations expresses the situatedness and path-dependent complexities of their knowledge base. These impede articulation and sharing. Hence, new ICTs notwithstanding, transaction costs and benefits remain heavily stacked against the kind of articulation of knowledge that would be required to make the choice of markets either ubiquitous or even symmetric with that of organizations. By implication, we argue, a default assumption in favor of organizational heterogeneity entails another, namely, that 'in the beginning, there was organization'. By proposing to make organization rather than markets a new default assumption for economics, we implicitly invite the discipline to look more toward biology than toward physics for its models—as Marshall had originally suggested that it should (Boisot and Cohen 2000; Marshall 1920; Mirowski 1989). And biology provides a fair amount of support for the plausibility of our proposal. Culture, for example, the transmission of information by behavioral rather than genetic means—by means of imitation, of signs, and later of language—is a phenomenon that humans share with animals (Bonner 1980; Landa 1999). Hamilton's notion (1964) of inclusive fitness, the idea that fitness should include the reproduction and survival of kin, certainly provides a motivation for such information transmission. Such concepts orient us more readily toward the richness of organizational behavior than toward thin and impersonal market processes.

Theories of organization have oscillated between two quite different ways of thinking about knowledge. The first takes knowledge to be an object that can be explicitly described, manipulated, transmitted, and stored. The second takes it to be a condition for and a product of the activities—individual or collective—in which it is embedded (Spender 2002). The first is steeped in a positivistic tradition that discounts that which cannot be articulated or measured (Tsoukas 1996). This perspective views knowledge as abstract, decontextualized, objective and robust, and has tended to appeal to IT practitioners of a practical cast (Spender

2002). Such knowledge can be articulated and codified. On the second view—which draws on Ryle's distinction between 'knowing what' and 'knowing how' (Ryle 1949)—knowledge always involves 'more than one can say' (Polanyi 1958) and is hard to disentangle from the activities themselves. For that reason it often resists articulation. Polanyi distinguishes between tacit and explicit knowledge. The former is typically unconsciously held, does not readily lend itself to explicit forms of representation, and is thus inaccessible to the knower (Reber 1993). Following Polanyi, tacitness has been taken by knowledge management to refer to the incommunicability of certain types of knowledge.

Tacit knowledge, however, is not always intrinsically incommunicable. Knowledge can remain tacit, for example, when all present share a common context—that is, a tacit understanding—that could be articulated but under the circumstances does not have to be (Johnson 1987). Nonaka and Tacheuchi (1994), building on Polanyi's distinction between tacit and explicit knowledge, take the position that knowledge only ever really becomes useful to an organization if it can somehow be communicated, whether or not it can be articulated. Their approach challenges the neo-classical economic position which assumes complete foresight and complete contracting—that is, that all transactionally relevant information can be codified, captured in prices, and instantly communicated (Arrow 1984; Debreu 1959; Mirowski 2002).

All forms of knowing and of communicating knowledge by intelligent agents incur data-processing costs and moving between the tacit and the explicit in either direction will express their concern both to economize on such costs and to secure some benefit for having incurred them. Building on Boisot (1986, 1995), we frame these moves as data-processing strategies that judiciously combine the activities of *codification* and *abstraction*, activities which respectively distinguish between, and economize on the categories used to make sense of experience. This leads to two questions:

1. Under what circumstances will an agent find it worthwhile to engage in the codification, abstraction, and sharing of knowledge?
2. How do these three activities affect the emergence of economic organization?

The structure of the chapter is as follows: In Section 4.2, we distinguish between two types of knowledge, Zen knowledge and market knowledge, and briefly discuss the characteristics of each. The first is low in codification and abstraction, whereas the second is high in both. We show that moving from tacit to explicit means moving from the first type of knowledge to the second—that is, from a form of knowledge that is mainly embodied to one that is mainly representational. The move offers benefits, but also incurs costs. In Section 4.3, we explore the nature of the interactions between the codification and abstraction of knowledge. We show that with moves toward greater codification and abstraction, embodied knowledge first gives way to narrative knowledge and then finally to abstract symbolic knowledge. Next, following Boisot (1995), we introduce a third dimension into our framework to allow us to represent the diffusibility of knowledge within a population as a function of its degree of abstraction and codification. Finally, placing both Zen and market knowledge in our framework, we discuss the implications of our analysis for the emergence of economic organizations. A conclusion follows.

4.2. Embodied, Narrative, and Abstract Symbolic Knowledge

4.2.1. *Zen versus Market Knowledge*

Consider two different instances of knowledge and its transmission: (*a*) that held by a Zen master and his disciples and (*b*) that held by a bond analyst operating in the market. The Zen master and the bond analyst, of course, may well be one and the same person, holding two quite different kinds of knowledge and beliefs and applying these at different moments.

ZEN KNOWLEDGE

Zen Buddhism stresses the intuitive grasp of the reality of things acquired, not through analytical reasoning, but through meditation and physical exercises of various kinds (Suzuki 1956). Zen knowledge is typically nonrepresentational—literally 'mindless'—and often embodied in very concrete forms of behavior such as Zen archery, painting, swordsmanship, or the tea ceremony. A Zen master uses ambiguity, puzzles, and paradoxes (Zen Koans) to force his disciples to abandon analytical and critical thought and to rely on unmediated intuition. To free a disciple's mind, he will not allow it to 'stop' anywhere, arguing that the mind only 'stops' when thinking substitutes for knowing, and trying substitutes for letting-go (Brannigan 2002). The Zen master displays a deep distrust of analytical reasoning as a way of attaining valid knowledge of the ultimate reality as well as of verbal communication as a way of transmitting it. Therefore, he does not explain things much to his disciples but rather places them in situations in which they will have to figure things out for themselves (Suzuki 1967: 126). In their quest for enlightenment—*satori*—disciples can only watch and listen to the master's sparse and puzzling pronouncements, and think deeply. They may then 'get it' or they may not. Faced with the complexity of the master's 'message', imitation becomes a disciple's rational strategy for gaining access to his knowledge. Yet, as Dupuy points out, imitation is also the source of all illusion (Dupuy 2004). Devoting several years of one's life to the mastery of Zen is, therefore, to put it mildly, an uncertain and risky business.

Because a tolerance for ambiguity and paradox lies at the heart of what the Zen master imparts to his disciples, he necessarily stands in a relationship of trust with them. Such trust is built up slowly by both parties in numerous face-to-face encounters. Together, the Zen master and his disciples constitute a small group whose size is limited by the need for trust and for continued face-to-face interaction [the thirteenth-century Zen monk Dogen famously said that he only really wanted one disciple, but that he wanted him for life (Hori 1967)]. They live together as a tightly knit community, and over a number of years, they get to know each other intimately. Because of his own ineffable knowledge, the Zen master thus acquires a very personal and charismatic kind of authority over his disciples. In return these offer their master loyalty and obedience.

MARKET KNOWLEDGE

To grasp the difference between Zen and market knowledge, picture now a bond analyst in a crowded trading room. She sits in front of a bank of monitors, for the most part ignoring the bustle around her, and working largely on her own. Through 'buy' and 'sell' instructions, she communicates with people working in other organizations, many of whom she has likely never met face-to-face. In contrast to the Zen master, she can communicate with them instantaneously and unambiguously wherever they may be located around the world by simply pressing down one or two keys on her computer. Her message will be transmitted at electronic speed.

The transactions our bond analyst engages in typically involve millions or even hundreds of millions of dollars. Any opportunistic behavior on her part or that of other transacting parties she deals with could bankrupt firms and ruin the lives of thousands of people. Yet, in spite of this, comparatively little interpersonal trust is involved. In contrast to the Zen master and his disciples, the parties do not really have to trust each other much. They do, however, have to trust the institutional, organizational, and technological setting in which their transactions take place. They have to believe that the information on the transactions that they commit to will be faithfully transmitted, the transaction itself will be reliably executed, and if it were not, the contractual arrangements that describe and regulate it are legally enforceable.

Given the stakes involved in any given transaction, our bond analyst deeply distrusts vagueness, ambiguity, and paradox in the information that she has to deal with—the very qualities that the Zen master prizes so highly. Rather, she looks for the kind of clarity, simplicity, and conciseness that will make it easier for her to analyze the relevant figures, contractual provisions, etc., speedily and accurately. She seeks transactional efficiency rather than Zen-like enlightenment, and to this end, spends a large part of her time analyzing abstract figures and text. She knows that she will incur a heavy opportunity cost in terms of lost time should these prove to be opaque.

Perhaps the many differences between the Zen master and the bond analyst are best summarized by observing that whereas the former achieves his aims by dissolving the boundary between self and nonself— or more generally, between subject and object (Kishimoto in Moore 1967: 118)—the latter's success, by contrast, depends on rigorously maintaining and articulating it. In effect, the bond analyst's transactionally relevant knowledge consists for the most part of Ryle's 'knowledge about', which resides largely (although not completely) outside the self (Ryle 1949). Zen knowledge and market knowledge are respectively instantiations of *embodied* and *abstract symbolic* knowledge. The first is primarily experiential, concrete, and tangibly expressed in 'situated' physical behavior (Johnson 1987), whereas the second primarily representational, mental, and can typically be disconnected from behavior—that is, it can be non-situational. In any intelligent being, these necessarily coexist and interact, reflecting some kind of a division of labor between the body and the brain as shown in Figure 4.1 (Clark 1997; Hacking 1983; Thelen and Smith 1994). As one moves from right to left in the diagram, the proportion of one's experience that can be captured by abstract symbolic knowledge increases, and by implication, so does the proportion of one's experience that one can communicate to others. Thus a third kind of knowledge, *Narrative* knowledge, can be located somewhere in between

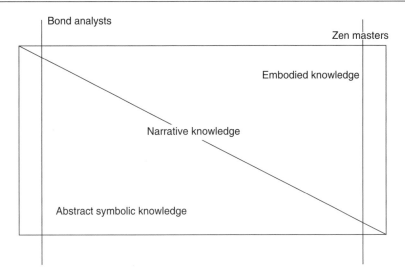

Figure 4.1. Different Knowledge Mixes for Zen Masters and Bond Analysts

fully embodied and fully abstract symbolic knowledge, to mediate the relationship between them (Lackoff and Johnson 1999; Mac Cormac 1985). It partakes both of the expressiveness of the first and the symbolic reach of the second.

Toward the right in Figure 4.1, knowledge is to be found mostly in an embodied form, locked into patterns of behavior and in concrete experiences that are hard to articulate and transmit to others. To some extent, it can be shared through co-presence with those who participate in either the behavior or the experience. But it can only be partially expressed rather than fully articulated, and for this reason it can never be reliably replicated (Thelen and Smith 1994). This is the only kind of knowledge that the Zen master considers valid for gaining access to the ultimate reality. On the left in the figure, by contrast, knowledge takes mostly a disembodied form. It exhibits recurrent regularities that can be mapped on to codes or other conventional structures that free it from the substrates whence it originates. Such knowledge can be communicated to others and forms the basis of intersubjective objectivity (Popper 1972). Such knowledge can be justified (Kornblith 1994); it is the only kind that the bond analyst, as an instance of what McQuade and Butos call an *adaptive classifying system*, is legally entitled to rely on. Such a system needs to remain distinct from its environment in order to generate 'knowledge' of that environment (McQuade and Butos 2005).

4.2.2. *From Zen to Market Knowledge*

When meditating, the Zen master distrusts representational knowledge and wants to dwell on the right in the diagram. But given the difficulties associated with the transmission of embodied knowledge, he prefers to stay silent. The bond analyst, by contrast, distrusts Zen knowledge as a way of assessing a bond and wants to get to the left in the diagram. She wants a clear articulation and an objective representation of the knowledge that is involved in a transaction. Any attempt to communicate one's knowledge to others—even when these are co-present—entails a move from the right toward left in the diagram that reduces the embodied component of such knowledge and increases both narrative and its representational component. The cost of a leftward move is measured in the amount of data-processing work involved. It is a cost that is shared by sender and receiver. How much work is involved depends on: (*a*) the *complexity* of the sender's message, (*b*) how much of the sender's prior *experience* is already shared by the receiver, and (*c*) how many of the sender's codes and concepts are already shared by the receiver.

These considerations will determine how far to the left one needs to move in the diagram and hence what data-processing costs one will incur in doing so. The leftward move has the effect of converting tacit into explicit knowledge (Nonaka and Takeuchi 1994). Nonaka and Takeuchi discuss this move in organizational terms. In this chapter, we argue that such knowledge articulation also needs to be framed in data-processing terms. Extracting information from data and converting it into knowledge—whether of the Zen or market variety—are data-processing activities that consume time, space, and energy (Boisot and Canals 2004), and intelligent agents will be concerned to minimize their consumption of such resources. Indeed, intelligent behavior is far more frugal in its use of such resources than unintelligent behavior. In Boisot and Li (2005), we argued that:

- All living things are concerned to minimize their rate of entropy production in order to make efficient use of the scarce physical resources—space, time, and energy—available to them.

- All living things minimize their production of entropy by substituting the data of experience that they accumulate over time for physical resources—data here, being taken as a low-energy phenomenon. Those that succeed, through a mixture of inheritance and learning, gradually evolve into intelligent agent's. The scope of the substitution process, however, is limited by an intelligent agent's data-processing and transmission's capacities. Clearly, the larger an agent's memory and intelligence, the greater the scope for substitution will be.

- Given their cognitive limitations, intelligent agents will also be concerned to minimize their consumption of scarce data-processing and transmission resources. They do this by selectively extracting information from data through processes of *codification* and *abstraction*. Codification reduces the production of thermodynamic entropy—associated with the consumption of the data's energy substrate—abstraction reduces the production of Shannon entropy—associated with the consumption of information.

- Information then becomes that subset of the data of experience that has relevance for an intelligent agent. Knowledge is the set of beliefs held by an intelligent agent that can be modified by the reception of new information and on which the agent is disposed to act.

Under what circumstances will the need to economize on scarce data-processing resources lead one up toward greater codification and abstraction and hence move us away from embodied and toward representational knowledge—the kind of knowledge that makes up an adaptive classifying system (McQuade and Butos 2005)? And, in moving toward representation, do codification and abstraction work independently of each other or do they work together in synergistic ways? We turn to these questions next.

4.3. Codification and Abstraction: The Epistemological Space or E-Space

4.3.1. *Economizing on Data Processing*

Codification and abstraction achieve data-processing economies for intelligent agents by first differentiating and then integrating the data of experience in order to secure compact representations of the phenomena that need attending to. Differentiation and integration—corresponding respectively to codification and abstraction—appear to be two phases of a single data structuring process. How are they related to each other?

Codification creates categories in order to make clear and reliable distinctions between relevant states of the world that one can act upon—between black and white, between heavy and light, between right and wrong, between cases that will be reimbursed by one's medical insurance and those that will not, and so on. In creating and clarifying categories, codification aims to take the fuzziness out of phenomena; it is analogous to de-fuzzifying a fuzzy set (Pedricz and Gomide 1998). Codification entails time-consuming data-processing efforts, and the larger and more complex the number of categories that one has to deal with, the greater the data-processing effort involved. Where codification is effective, it allows one to subsequently assign phenomena unproblematically to a given set of categories—the specific activity of assigning phenomena to well-formed pre-extant categories we call *coding*. If codification corresponds to what Ghiselin and Landa refer to as *classification*, coding corresponds to what they refer to as *identification* (Ghiselin and Landa 2005). Our general information-theoretic categories thus map nicely onto their more specific bioeconomic ones. Effective codification, like classification, acts to reduce the cost of processing the data of experience.

Abstraction reduces the number of categories that one needs to draw upon when classifying phenomena. How far one can abstract will depend on the purpose of the classification. By treating things that are different as if they were the same (Dretske 1981)—a *ceteris paribus* assumption—abstraction allows one to focus on what is essential. What is essential, of course, will vary according to purpose. A painter and a geologist, for example, would abstract very different features when contemplating a landscape. Abstraction is built out either out of empirical correlations—those similarities that prove to be robust across differences between phenomena—or out of logical inferences that relate phenomena to each other. A mix of correlations and inferences will allow one thing to stand for another. Just as an efficient coding process allows one letter to stand for another (Shannon 1948), abstraction, by economizing on the number of categories that we need to deal with in apprehending a given phenomenon, allows us to reduce our data-processing costs.

There are, in fact, two quite different payoffs to well-performed codifications and abstractions. The first is that by assigning phenomena to pre-extant classes, we can draw useful inferences from our prior knowledge of the classes to which they have been assigned to increase our understanding of the phenomena in question. Thus, for example, prior knowledge allows us to classify a light point in the night sky as a star, as a planet, or as an aircraft coming into land. Each of these alternative classifications, combined with our prior knowledge, will lead us to expect the light point to move in a different way and at a different speed. The second payoff is a more compact and economic representations of the phenomena we are called upon to deal with. The first payoff allows us to respond to phenomena in more discriminating and adaptive ways; the second payoff allows us to respond to them faster.

Yet if codification and abstraction activities offer benefits, these activities also incur setup and operating costs, that is:

- Technical costs—those incurred in the capturing, processing, and transmission of the relevant data. Such costs may be measured either in terms of the physiological effort involved, or in terms of developing artifactual substitutes that can take over from physiology where required—that is, measuring instruments, etc.

- Negotiation and decision costs—getting agreement from the relevant stakeholders on the categories to be created by codification or those to be eliminated by abstraction. Since different ways of codifying and abstracting often creates winners and losers, such negotiation costs will not necessarily be trivial.

- Psychological costs—the emotional and cognitive costs associated with categories forgone when new codifications and abstractions come into play. We can associate such costs with losses of 'meaning'.

- Learning costs—the time and effort required to internalize new categories. Having created new narratives or abstract representations, one must learn how and under what circumstances to use them.

These costs can be large or small depending on the degree of refinement one is after. Working to a tolerance of 1 mm, for example, will be less costly in information processing terms than working to a tolerance of 0.001 mm. If the first proves acceptable when, say, plastering a wall, it will not do when it comes to manufacturing microprocessors—nor, indeed, will a tolerance of 0.001 mm. The refinement needed is task dependent, and sometimes it can be pursued to the point of diminishing returns. The marginal costs of either creating a new category, or as in the case of tolerances, a new subdivision within an existing category, will then exceed the marginal benefit of using it. Agents, however, vary in their capacity to codify and abstract and they often have recourse to artifacts that can move them beyond what their senses on their own can achieve. Mechanical and electronic measuring instruments, for example, simultaneously reduce the costs of operating at higher levels of precision and help to eliminate interagent variations in data-processing skills by creating measurement conventions that amplify those skills (Wise 1995*a*, 1995*b*).

If what can be codified as categories establishes what can meaningfully be abstracted, the products of abstraction, in turn, act to orient subsequent efforts at codification. Recast in the language of the philosophy of science, if theorizing is constrained by what can be observed, then observing is in turn informed by theory (Hanson 1965). Prior knowledge sets expectations, teaching one to look for manifestations of specific phenomena at a given level of codification. An effective allocation of scarce data-processing and transmission resources respectively to codification and abstraction activities must take into account the existence of such prior knowledge. But how is such an allocation achieved?

4.3.2. *The Cognitive Production Function*

Codification and abstraction are productive activities that are subject to economizing. What resources are required to perform the articulating activities of codification and abstraction? Three physical resources that are needed are time, space, and energy (Boisot and Canals 2004). Articulation, like the computational activities that it often gives rise to, involves moving data from one spatially located register to another over time, and in doing so, it consumes all three types of physical resource (Bennett 1999; Landauer 1999). Articulation will be efficient in its use of resources to the extent that the categories that it draws upon to capture some phenomenon are distinct from each other (i.e. well-codified) and few in number (i.e. abstract). If we think of codification and abstraction as each minimizing the quantity of data inputs that are required in different mixes to produce a given level of embodied, narrative, or abstract symbolic output, then we can view the curves of Figure 4.2 as constituting an intelligent agent's *cognitive production function*, with one of the data factors associated with the cognitive activity of *discrimination* (codification) and the other associated with the cognitive activity of *association* (abstraction) (Hahn and Chater 1998). Although both axes in the diagram are measured in data, for the purposes of illustration we shall take the physical resources consumed in the act of computation to be proportional to the quantity of data to be processed. An intelligent agent makes best use of her limited data-processing resources and capacities by operating on the efficiency frontier of her production function.[1] That is to say, for any desired level of computational output, O_i, an agent minimizes her data-processing costs

[1] Where the data describes complex states giving rise to aesthetic experiences, one aims at effectiveness rather than efficiency and does not necessarily attempt to locate oneself on the efficiency frontier.

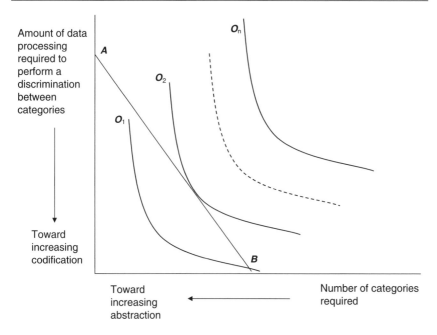

Figure 4.2. The Cognitive Production

by moving as far as possible toward origin of Figure 4.2. In doing so, the agent will minimize the total entropy costs, H_i, associated with achieving that output with different mixes of codification and abstraction. This idea is further elaborated in the Appendix.

The line AB represents a given agent's data-processing budget. The slope of the line gives the relative cost to the agent of engaging in codification relative to engaging in abstraction. In the case of a human agent, the slope of the line is partly determined by her biological makeup, and partly by the artifacts available to assist her in processing data.

A good example of how the number of categories used in the process of abstraction can be optimized is given in Landa's study of Chinese middlemen in the trading networks of Southeast Asia (Ghiselin and Landa 2005; Landa 1981). What Landa terms an ethnically homogeneous middleman group (EHMG), a low-cost club-like institutional arrangement that operates personalized exchange relations and simultaneously facilitates exchanges between Chinese middlemen and constrains breaches of contract. Members of this group typically classify the traders they interact with into a hierarchical system that grades these into seven categories of trustworthiness. In declining order these are: (*a*) kinsmen belonging to the same nuclear family, (b) distant kinsmen from the same extended family and lineage, (c) fellow clansmen, (d) fellow villagers, (e) people speaking the same dialect and coming from the same province in China, (f) Chinese speaking a different dialect, and (g) non-Chinese. Such a categorization strategy is informationally efficient for two reasons. First, candidate traders can be readily identified as falling into one of these categories—that is, the codification into categories facilitates efficient coding. Secondly, the codification operates at an appropriate level of abstraction by creating the optimal number of categories that can be speedily processed in one's head—Miller's famous number 7, ± 2 (Miller 1956)—and thus helps to minimize the costs of transacting with traders who might behave opportunistically.

The cognitive production function depicted in Figure 4.2 can now be inverted to create a two-dimensional space that we shall label an Epistemological Space or *E-Space* (Boisot 1995). Along the vertical axis, one measures the degree of codification required to distinguish between the categories that capture a given phenomenon. The degree of codification is inversely related to the degree of fuzziness, and hence to the amount of data-processing required to distinguish between any two of the categories to which the phenomenon is to be assigned—that is, low degrees of codification are associated with high data-processing requirements and vice versa (we are using here Chaitin's Algorithmic Information Content [AIC] approach to measuring complexity. See Chaitin [1974]).

Along the horizontal axis, one measures the degree of abstraction required to deal with the phenomenon in question—one abstracts for a particular purpose, selecting among available categories those that will serve that purpose. Abstraction is inversely related to the number of categories required to properly capture a phenomenon for a given purpose. The larger the number of categories required, the more concrete one's apprehension of the phenomenon will be and, consequently, the lower will be the level of abstraction achieved. Conversely, the fewer the numbers of categories required, the higher will be the level of abstraction achieved and, by implication, the lower the data-processing load.

The line AB in Figure 4.3 marks out the region E within the space below which an agent cannot profitably articulate her experiences. The amount of data processing required to distinguish categories either from the surrounding noise or from each other becomes so large that for most practical purposes it puts any attempt at establishing meaningful correlations between them beyond reach. Below point A on the codification dimension, therefore, an agent cannot extract information from

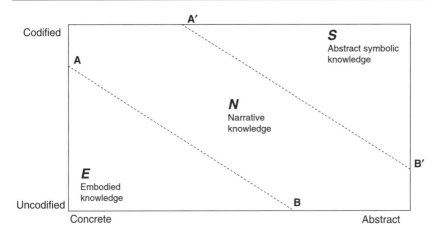

Figure 4.3. The E-Space

data without incurring data-processing costs that are judged unacceptable relative to the benefits on offer for doing so. The further one moves toward the origin, the higher become those costs. Likewise, if an agent faces limits to what she can codify, she also faces limits on her capacity to abstract. To the left of point B on the abstraction dimension—that is, above a certain density of categories available to abstract from—an agent gets overwhelmed by the number of possible categorial choices and is no longer able to identify suitable candidates for profitable attempts at abstraction without incurring unacceptably high data-processing costs. In short, the agent finds it difficult to *objectify* anything—that is, to constitute independent objects of experience (Smith 1996). Here again, the further one moves to the left along the abstraction dimension the higher the data-processing costs rise.

Does that mean that below line AB no form of knowledge is actually achievable? No. The point identifies the region, E, in which knowledge is for the most part likely to remain *embodied* (Clark 1997; Johnson 1987; Thelen and Smith 1994) and so deeply embedded in physical experiences and behaviors and that can only be profitably articulated—and hence give rise to representations—under exceptional circumstances if at all. In this area, data continues to get *processed* even if it does not always get *structured*. It gives rise to experiences that can be shared but not articulated and hence transmitted (Johnson 1987). Such personal knowledge can resonate with that of others but cannot count as public, objectively verifiable knowledge (Dupuy 1992; Maturana and Varela 1980; Ziman 1968). And yet, for the Zen master, this is the only kind of knowledge that gives access to reality.

The area AA'B'B marks out a region, N, in which we encounter knowledge operating at medium levels of codification and abstraction—we earlier referred to this type of knowledge as narrative knowledge. It is a world of texts and images, of metaphors and icons, all of which derive their coherence and plausibility from their links with the embodied experiential knowledge from which they spring (Deacon 1997; Lackoff and Johnson 1999; Mac Cormac 1985). A further move northeast of line A'B' takes us into the region, S, of abstract symbolic knowledge, a late arrival on the scene on an evolutionary timescale (Barkow, Cosmides and Tooby 1992; Deacon 1997; Pinker 1997). This kind of knowledge, dealing with highly compressed representations of classes and of relationships between classes, is now untethered from the world of embodied knowledge, even if it originated there. In the region of abstract codifications, symbols acquire a life of their own and can move frictionlessly from agent to agent and from context to context.

The costs of articulating knowledge vary as a function of location in the E-Space. They will be at a maximum for an agent in region E of the space—that is, where knowledge is at its most embodied. They will be at a minimum in region S of the space, a region in which the levels of codification and abstraction achievable allow the data to be structured into abstract symbolic representations. Whether the costs of articulating knowledge are worth incurring at all will depend on what benefits they offer and these, in turn, will be related to the nature of the tasks undertaken or the experiences sought. Such costs have two components:

- *Fixed costs* are incurred by the *creation* of new information and knowledge structures in the E-Space—these may reside inside the heads of intelligent agents, or outside their heads in the form of artifacts (Stewart and Cohen [1997] label these *extelligence*. Clark [1997] labels them *external scaffolding*). They may also be embodied in their behaviors in the form of learned routines (Nelson and Winter 1982). These costs do not vary with the extent to which the information and knowledge structures so created are subsequently used.

- *Variable costs* are incurred in *using* such structures to support either data-processing activities in one location in the E-Space or moves from one location in the space to another. These costs vary directly with the extent to which these structures are used.

The slope of the budget line of Figure 4.2 reflects prior expenditures in both fixed and variable costs and also conditions future expenditures. The variable costs of moving from one isoquant to another in the E-Space, for example, will partly depend on whether structural resources for data processing and transmission already exist to support such a move or whether they will have to be created afresh.

The benefits of investing in the codification and abstraction of information and knowledge are at their highest when these are subjected to repeated use. Whereas the creation of new information and knowledge incurs high-fixed costs, their actual reproduction and subsequent use incur low-marginal costs. Yet, although increasing bandwidth is changing the picture, low-marginal costs are typically only achieved under conditions of high codification and abstraction.

4.3.3. *Of Zen and Markets*

The foregoing now better allows us to understand where the Zen master and the bond analyst are coming from. Region E of the E-Space is the natural home of embodied knowledge. Region S, by contrast, is the natural home of abstract symbolic knowledge. When meditating, the Zen master distrusts any move that would move him away from region E and toward region S. He judges the sacrifice of embodied, experiential data to be too great. Since the Zen master discerns order in fuzziness, in paradox, and in noise, eliminating these incurs an opportunity cost. The analytically derived 'disembodied' knowledge that results is too impoverished for his purpose, *and this purpose resides in the quality of the experience itself.* For the Zen master, experiential knowledge is an end in itself, to be pursued for its own sake. The price he pays for the quality of the experience that he achieves, however, is its incommunicability. Others may acquire similar experiences, but not through the articulate transmission of his own. They can only do so through a resonance set-up by the sharing of experiences.

In contrast to the Zen master, the knowledge sought by the bond analyst, resides in region S. Unlike embodied knowledge located in region E, this knowledge can be efficiently transmitted and shared. It is the stuff that arm's length contracts are made of. For the bond analyst, such knowledge is not intrinsically valuable but rather resides in the different uses to which it can be put. For the bond analyst, therefore, *knowledge has instrumental rather than experiential value.* The loss of experiential data that is incurred in the move from E to S is compensated for by what you can do with it once it has become codified and abstract. Far from imprisoning her in rich but incommunicable experiences, knowledge residing in S links the bond analyst to the world beyond the trading room. Its compass may be narrower than that of the Zen master, but the knowledge available to the bond analyst gives her reach (Evans and Wuster 1997).

Which kind of knowledge is it better to have? It depends on your purpose. If that purpose is purely aesthetic or experiential, then the embodied kind of knowledge that is on offer in region E in the E-Space and in its neighborhood will serve you better than the more pallid symbolic stuff available in region S. If, on the other hand, your purpose is to accomplish some specific goal out there in the world, if it requires coordination with others, if it requires mobilizing their commitment, then you will be better off trying to articulate it by heading for region S.

Interposing itself somewhere between regions E and S in the space is narrative knowledge in region N. It draws much of its expressiveness from the fact that in part it still remains embodied. But unlike purely embodied knowledge, narrative knowledge can also draw on the representational powers of abstract symbolic resources as well. Thus, in contrast to purely embodied knowledge, narrative knowledge can be transmitted, albeit under conditions of greater fuzziness and ambiguity than highly abstract and symbolic types of knowledge.

Embodied, narrative, and abstract symbolic knowledge in the E-Space are linked to each other as shown in Figure 4.4. The arrows that move from abstract symbolic knowledge, S, to narrative knowledge, N, and

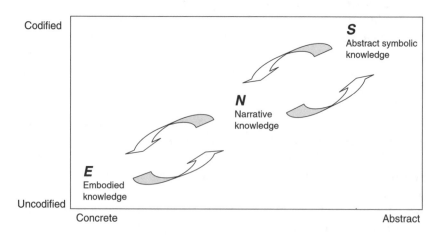

Figure 4.4. Moving through Different Knowledge Regimes in the E-Space

thence onto embodied knowledge, E, highlight the fact that the epistemic traffic does not flow in only one direction in the E-Space. Abstract symbolic knowledge gets stirred into narrative knowledge and can radically change its content—think of how much Newton's laws underpinned the narratives of the Enlightenment in eighteenth-century Europe. Narrative knowledge, in turn, helps shape embodied knowledge—a political discourse can trigger passionate reactions; a religious discourse can induce a state of meditation.

4.4. Diffusion: The Information-Space or I-Space

4.4.1. *Intelligent Interaction*

How do the above considerations affect the way that information diffuses within a population of agents? The key and well-established point is that articulating knowledge speeds up and facilitates its sharing by others (Boisot 1986, 1995). Investing in codification and abstraction, therefore, will make one's knowledge more readily accessible to other agents. Through what specific mechanism? Consider first a purely physical situation such as a perfume spreading throughout a room. Convection currents will play a role, but assuming that the room is in thermal equilibrium, the only way in which aromatic molecules can spread out on their own is through a mechanism of *diffusion*, a process that explicitly involves *time* and that is essential to photosynthesis, to respiration, to molecular transport in cells, to the absorption of digested food from the gut into the bloodstream, and to other biological activities (Haynie 2001). In a typical diffusion process, a given molecule will make an average of N collisions with other molecules per unit of time t. The process is linear. If we increase the length of the observation time to, say, $5t$, the molecules will make an average of $5N$ such collisions. The average time between collisions, τ, is just

$$\tau = t/N \qquad (4.1)$$

The odds that one molecule will collide with another molecule during a small unit of time, Δt, is just $\Delta t/\tau$. As $\Delta t \to \tau$, this ratio approaches unity at which point there is a 100 per cent chance of a collision taking place. Now, if instead of one molecule making N collisions, we have N molecules make as many collisions as they will in a short period of time Δt. The number of collisions becomes $N \times \Delta t / \tau$ (Haynie 2001).

In the case of a collision between molecules, we ignore the duration of the collision itself. Energy transfer between molecules is deemed to take place instantaneously. If, however, we wanted to model information diffusion processes between *communicating* agents, however, we would need to allow for the fact that any exchange of data between agents takes time and would affect the collision rate—that is, the rate of encounter—between them.

We would then obtain

$$E = \tau + i \qquad (4.2)$$

Where E is the rate at which agents encounter each other, and i is the time required for a data exchange between agents. The first term, τ, will be determined by spatial factors such as the density and spatial mobility of agents—as well as by the fact that one agent can now communicate simultaneously with several other agents—whereas the second term will be determined by the volume of data being transferred at each encounter. Information and communication technologies will affect the values of both τ and i. The collision rate, τ, between agents now ceases to be defined by purely physical fact-to-face encounters as they can now exchange data by e-mail, by mobile phone, by TV,[2] etc. The overall time, i, required by an exchange of data will be affected by the extent to which data-processing technologies are able to compress messages through acts of codification and abstraction in each of the communicative activities of message formulation, encoding, transmission, decoding, and interpretation (Shannon and Weaver 1949). Thus

$$i = f(V, C, A) \qquad (4.3)$$

Where V stands for the volume of data to be transmitted, C stands for codification and A stands for abstraction. We can minimize i by moving across the isoquants of Figure 4.2 toward the origin. As already discussed, however, there are costs, both fixed and variable, associated with these moves as well as costs to transacting in it from a given location. Whether either kind of cost is worth incurring depends on the payoff that one might expect. What is the nature of the payoff? We identify two broad categories of payoff:

---

[2] We can think of any broadcasting technology such as television as increasing the one-to-many collision rate.

1. Data-processing payoffs—we shall take these as occurring within the mind of a single agent, whether it be human, organizational, or other

2. Data transmission payoffs—we shall take these as occurring across the minds of different agents, whether these be human, organizational, or other.

One payoff to the faster transmission of data is more powerful data-processing capabilities—as evidenced by successive generations of ever-more compact microprocessors. Yet faster data processing itself leads to faster data transmission so that we could argue that the two kinds of payoff are mutually reinforcing. The coevolution of computing and communication technologies—the line that divides them is today becoming increasingly blurred (Sipser 1997)—is a source of *positive returns* (Arthur 1989) that has recently given rise to the idea that any form of social organization can be likened to a computer (Prietula Carley, and Gasser 1998).

4.4.2. *Economies of Transmission*

We can explore the communicative payoff to codification and abstraction by adding a third dimension to the E-Space that captures the transmissibility or diffusion of knowledge within a given population of agents. For our purposes, agents are any entities that can receive, process, and transmit data intelligently—that is, they can *act* on the basis of data. Agents might be individual human beings, but, at one extreme, they could also be as complex as firms, while at the other they could be as elementary as individual neurons. In the first case, our diffusion dimension would represent an industry; in the second, an individual brain—whether silicon- or carbon-based. Close to the origin, little or no diffusion takes place. At the end of the diffusion dimension, 100 per cent of a target population of data-processing agents can be reached with a given message.

The three-dimensional information space or *I-Space* that results is shown in Figure 4.5 (Boisot 1995, 1998). The curve AA′ shown in the figure indicates the number of agents within the target population that can be reached per unit of time with a given message at different levels of codification and abstraction. In effect, the curve tracks the communicative payoff to investments in knowledge articulation measured by the number of agents located along the diffusion curve that are reached

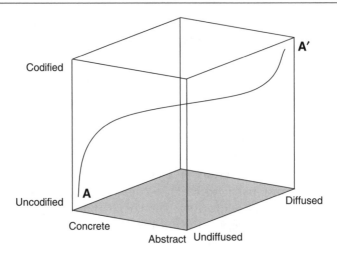

Figure 4.5. The I-Space

over time. The more codified and abstract one's message, the larger the number of agents within a given population that it can reach per unit of time. Note, however, that the curve, as such, says nothing concerning the internalization of such messages. For a message to be internalized at all, sender and receiver have to share codes as well as context at some minimum level. Furthermore, the process of internalization is often subject to all the subtleties of contextual interaction that Dupuy explored in his discussion of imitation (Dupuy 2004). We discuss the issue of context in greater detail in Section 4.5.

In addition to the factors that shaped the trajectories across the isoquants depicted in Figure 4.2, the specific form of the diffusion curve in the I-Space is also determined by a number of factors such as the nature of the communication technologies and data-structuring algorithms available, the spatial and structural characteristics of the diffusion population under study, and the nature of the messages being transmitted.

The diffusion curve of Figure 4.5 captures nothing more than the proportions of a given population, measured along the diffusion dimension, that can be reached given the different communication times $i_1, i_2, \ldots, i_n$ associated respectively with the entropy costs $H_1, H_2, \ldots, H_n$. Recall that these are incurred by different mixes of codification and abstraction. Clearly as one moves along the curve toward A' total communication time i between any one sender and anyone receiver goes *down*. And as the population of senders and receivers goes up, so the total savings in communication time achieved by moving across the isoquants toward H_n

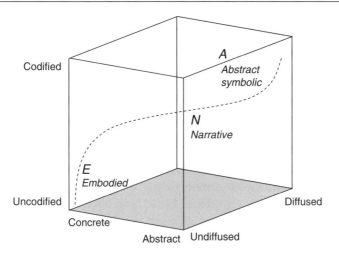

Figure 4.6. The Three Different Knowledge Regimes in the I-Space

go up. Thus we obtain the curve of Figure 4.5 and, as i tends to 0 in the expression $E = \tau + i$, the diffusion rate gets to approximate the collision rate between agents, now enhanced by ICTs.

The diffusion curve of Figure 4.5 makes it clear why embodied knowledge tends to stay local and does not travel well, why narrative knowledge travels somewhat better, and why well-compacted abstract symbolic knowledge is the most mobile and fluid of all (see Figure 4.6). Yet this gain in mobility as one moves from embodied to narrative and thence to abstract symbolic knowledge is paid for in data losses. Acts of codification and abstraction involve selection from a repertoire—of symbols and categories—and all selection implies foregoing contending alternatives. Only what is actually selected gets transmitted to the receiver, the remainder of the repertoire from which the selection was made staying behind with the message source. Is selected data information-bearing? Much depends on the ability of codes and abstractions to capture the communicative intention of the message source. As Boisot and Li (2005) observe, the moves toward greater codification and abstraction have an irreducibly hypothetical nature and can never be complete. Indeed, the limits to any attempt at formalization—what all codification and abstraction aspires to—were identified by Godel's famous incompleteness theorems (Godel 1962). The value of such moves, however, as Popper observed, is that they constitute hypotheses 'that die in our stead' (Popper 1972).

4.5. Implications

4.5.1. *General Implications*

How does the I-Space help us to understand the information perspectives of the Zen master and the bond analyst? For the Zen master only embodied knowledge gives access to real knowledge—to reality; for the bond analyst only abstract symbolic knowledge is valid. Yet as indicated by Figure 4.3, both in different degrees draw on narrative knowledge. Although there is a natural complementarity between the three kinds of knowledge, none on its own can give the whole picture. The Zen master's knowledge is rich but incommunicable. It must perforce remain subjective and its main value is experiential. The bond analyst trades-in the richness of knowledge for its easy communicability and the possibility of achieving intersubjective objectivity. Such knowledge—in contrast to the Zen master's—can be leveraged and used instrumentally.

The Zen master reckons that, for the kind of experiences that he seeks, the costs of codification and abstraction outweigh the benefits. The Zen master has an intuitive grasp of Godel's incompleteness theorems and of the limits of formalization (Casti and DePauli 2000) and thinks that too much of value is lost in the translation. Such is the case, for example, with aesthetic knowledge, an important component of Zen knowledge, which, as Moles has shown, one cannot codify (Moles 1968). For the bond analyst, by contrast, the benefits of formalization outweigh the costs. Note, however, that the bond analyst already has a large data-processing and transmission infrastructure available to her—computers, software, internet protocols, etc. Her fixed costs are already covered. She codifies and abstracts at the margin. Also, given the utilitarian nature of the knowledge being transacted—a bond analyst, when actually trading, is rarely concerned with the aesthetic dimension of the knowledge being used—the risks of information loss are judged to be small. In statistical parlance, we might say that whereas the Zen master seeks information in the variance of a distribution—that is, in a *situated context*—the bond analyst looks for it in the mean—that is, in *stable structures*—treating the variance as so much noise.

Both abstract symbolic knowledge and narrative knowledge have their origins in embodied knowledge (Deacon 1997). But cognitive neuroscience teaches us that by far the greater part of our knowledge remains embodied and therefore tacit (Thelen and Smith 1994; Clark 1997).

Articulating such knowledge will often be experienced as problematic.[3] It will therefore be implicitly subjected to a cost–benefit calculation in which the costs will be measured in data-processing efforts and the benefits will be measured in terms either of its enhanced instrumental utility or of its increased diffusibility. Moving up the diffusion curve of Figure 4.5 may then only be worthwhile for certain kinds of instrumental knowledge under certain task conditions. The specific contents of the knowledge in question will often act as a guide to what is worth formalizing; their location in the I-Space then indicates what the costs and benefits of doing so might be. But what goes round comes around. As indicated in Figure 4.3, once articulated, our abstract symbolic and our narrative knowledge feeds back into our embodied experiences and helps to shape them. In this way, the abstract representations that we construct of the world subsequently get to affect our bodily states.

The general implications of the above remarks can be summarized in three points:

(1) Godel's incompleteness theorems apply to the conversion of data into information, and, by implication to the conversion of information into knowledge. What Godel's incompleteness theorems suggest, is firstly that no single formal codification or abstraction scheme can ever capture in a narrative form the whole of our embodied knowledge, and secondly that no single formal codification and abstraction scheme can ever capture in an abstract symbolic form the whole of our narrative knowledge. To the extent that we then resort to using different codification and abstraction schemes together, much will fall between the cracks.

(2) Data that has not been codified and abstracted remains available to serve as contextual background for the subsequent interpretation of information. In this sense, codes and context mutually constitute each other (Dupuy 1992). We can thus think of any process of interpretation as a return movement from well-codified and abstract representational knowledge back to more narrative and embodied forms of knowledge. These latter forms are then partly shaped by the codified abstractions that are brought to bear on them. It is in this sense that all experiential knowledge is shot through with theoretical knowledge (Hanson 1965).

---

[3] On many occasions, the returns to articulating tacit knowledge will be low because such knowledge is already widely shared in the relevant groups.

(3) Since contextual data that has not been codified and abstracted does not readily diffuse, either the recipient has prior access to the contextual background within which the message originated or the recipient will not construe the message in the way intended by the receiver. Quine refers to this problem as the indeterminacy of translation and Fuller refers to it as the inscrutability of silence (Fuller 2002; Quine 1969). To the extent that the contextual background to a communication is shared between sender and receiver, the message is more likely to lead to the behavior desired by the sender (Shannon and Weaver 1949). To the extent that it is not, then the communicating parties face both data losses in transmission and divergent interpretations of what has been transmitted.

4.5.2. Implications for Economics

Economics is slowly coming to grips with the phenomenon of information in general and asymmetric information in particular. But except for a few (Nelson and Winter 1982; Teece 1986), it has not seriously addressed the nature of tacit knowledge or the way that it differs from explicit knowledge. The upshot is that economists are typically more comfortable dealing with the codified and abstract information environment of bond analysts than with that of Zen masters. Yet applying Godel's incompleteness theorems to the domain of information, one cannot have complete codification, complete abstraction, and complete diffusion. Some features of an economic good will never be captured within the formal code of the price. Incomplete contracting (Hart 1989; Williamson 1985) is thus a pervasive phenomenon.

Prices are formed through processes of codification and abstraction that have a hypothetical character. To the extent that codification and abstraction are always incomplete in their effects—the Godelian theorems—so pricing can never fully capture all the value-adding attributes of an economic good.[4] The I-Space teaches us that the assumption of a frictionless diffusibility of price information is at odds with the way that prices are formed through gradual and tentative moves up the I-Space. The diffusion of price information does eventually speed up, but only at the end of the pricing process. In efficient neoclassical markets, the existence of friction and information losses is either assumed away or is deemed it

---

[4] This point is implied by the economist's concept of the consumer surplus. The spot market price may be identical for all consumers, but the value that such a price attaches to will vary from consumer to consumer.

to be an undesirable impediment to the attainment of market equilibrium. Yet in a friction-free and reversible world, economic agents will experience little need to economize on data-processing and transmission resources, for their physical finitude is illusory. In such a world, nothing ever needs to *move* toward point A' in the I-Space—where information is well-codified, abstract, and diffused—since, by assumption, all the data that an agent will ever needs to process or transmit is *already* located there.

Our own analysis, however, suggests that the time and costs incurred by the processing and communicating of data will vary inversely with the extent of its codification and abstraction and hence will be a function of its location in the I-Space. Thus, other things being equal, the time and costs incurred in region A in the I-Space (Figure 4.5) will be maximal while those incurred in region A' will be minimal. It follows that data coming out of region A' will be more readily processed and will also reach more agents and in less time than data coming out of region A. Efficient market processes are then much more likely to occur in an information environment such as that offered by region A' than one such as that offered by region A.

For firms and similar types of organization, by contrast, the opposite will be true: they are much more likely to emerge in an information environment such as that which characterizes region A, even if their subsequent evolution leads them to gradually spread out beyond that region. And if they do spread out, they are initially likely to adopt trust-based strategies consistent with a region A information environment, strategies of the kind outlined by Landa in her studies of Chinese middlemen in Southeast Asia (Landa 1999). We have here an information-based interpretation of Coase's analysis (1937) of the emergence of firms and markets as institutions (Coase 1937). By establishing the economic basis on which an intelligent agent would move through the I-Space from region A to region A', we add to the Coasian perspective a dynamic element which challenges the default assumption made by neoclassical economists that 'in the beginning there were markets' (Williamson 1975: 21).[5] Moving in the I-Space is precisely what neoclassical economics cannot convincingly deliver. Stuck as it is in region A' of the space, it finds it hard to deal with any concept of change or becoming that goes beyond comparative statics.

---

[5] Williamson points out that he makes this assumption as an expositional convenience. Such 'conveniences', however, usually provide a reliable guide to the kinds of default assumptions that one is working with.

Our analysis gives us good reason to believe that *in the beginning there was organizing*. As we have already seen, a crucial issue concerns the sharing of context between transacting parties. A shared context between sender and receiver lowers both data-processing and transmission costs in the I-Space, whatever the level of codification and abstraction involved (Hall 1976). But, below a certain codification and abstraction threshold, a shared context becomes a presumption in favor of internalization, and of information asymmetries that lead to hierarchies rather than markets.[6] Indeed, the weight that we give in this chapter to the role played by embodied knowledge is also a presumption in favor of internalization, of favoring an in-group at the expense of an out-group, as exemplified by Landa's Chinese middlemen (Landa 1999). *Pace* Williamson, externalization into markets must then be considered an *achievement* and not something that we can take as a starting assumption. It involves costly and uncertain moves up the diffusion curve in the I-Space, from embodied to narrative knowledge, and thence to abstract symbolic knowledge in the form of prices and quantities. This places the concept of market failure in a new light since the burden of explanation now shifts: *what needs accounting for is the efficiency of markets not their failures.*

Efficient markets are made up of 'atomistic' agents whose behavior is driven by the impersonal 'forces' of rationality. For a long time, this way of framing things allowed economics to ignore issues of internal organization and strategic choice in favor of a model that looked to nineteenth-century physics for its inspiration (Mirowski 1989). The primacy that we accord to organization in this chapter requires a more holistic approach, one with a greater affinity for biological concepts than for purely physical ones (Boisot and Cohen 2000). Alfred Marshall had advocated that biology should become the economist's mecca. Our arguments militate in favor of such a reorientation.

4.5.3. *Implications for Organizations*

For most of the twentieth century, organization theory followed economists up the I-Space—from community into organization (Tönnies 1955) and from an enchanted into a rational–legal order (Boisot and Child 1988, 1996; Weber 1978). For both disciplines, codification and abstraction

---

[6] Huang (2003) has argued that a shared cultural context would have the effect of facilitating arm's length transactions. We do not disagree. What we are dealing with here are transactions whose complexity and uncertainty requires more than a shared set of cultural assumptions. Huang is dealing with comparatively simple transactions.

were the desiderata. The only question that divided them was where to locate decisions along the diffusion scale—the decentralization issue. Yet, if the Lange–Lerner debates of the 1920s attempted to establish the equivalence between efficient markets and efficient hierarchies (Lange 1937; Lerner 1936), the Aston studies of the 1960s and 1970s implied that formalization—codification and abstraction—had something to contribute to the decentralization debate (Pugh et al. 1969) and that to the extent that decentralization was desirable, then, by implication, so was formalization.

Yet by moving so hastily up the I-Space, organization theorists, like economists before them, assumed away almost all of the interesting problems relating to the nature of knowledge. Why have they felt obliged to favor the bond analyst at the expense of the Zen master? If, as current research suggests, most human knowledge is of the embodied kind, then it is either tacit because it is embodied and probably cannot be articulated or it turns out to be articulable but the cost and benefits are stacked up against the effort required. When used recurrently, such knowledge can give rise to *routines*, only some of which, over time, will be codified into rules (Boisot and Sanchez 2004).

What we need to understand is that any transaction will consist of a *configuration* of knowledge elements in the I-Space, with some being embedded in external scaffolding—that is, objects—and others being embodied in the minds and behaviors of agents. The urge to economize on data processing and transmission *may* lead you toward codified and abstract conceptual knowledge in region A', but the process is inherently highly *selective*. We have seen that movement in the E-Space is not all toward greater codification and abstraction. Abstract symbolic knowledge, for example, gets internalized and subsequently shapes both narrative and embodied knowledge. In this way an agent's corpus of tacit and embodied knowledge is constantly getting renewed. This dynamic underpins Williamson's fundamental transformation (Williamson 1985), wherein large-numbers bargaining gives way to small-numbers bargaining as a result of 'information impactedness'. It also echoes Nonaka and Takeuchi's scheme for moving from explicit to tacit (Nonaka and Takeuchi 1994). Nonaka and Tacheuchi derive their scheme from empirically observing the behavior of people in organizations, whereas we derive ours from theorizing on the nature of knowledge flows. Thus we all illuminate the same phenomenon but from two quite different perspectives.

A growing body of evidence suggests that most of our knowledge is of the tacit, embodied kind (Johnson 1987; Thelen and Smith 1994). It will never be made explicit. This kind of knowledge is constantly being recreated and abstract representational knowledge is but a precipitate of it. Williamson's quip that 'in the beginning there were markets' is a presumption in favor of the ubiquity and ready availability of well-codified and abstract knowledge—that is, prices. We have argued that such knowledge should really be viewed as a point of arrival rather than as a point of departure and that it must be considered a contingent achievement rather than an axiom. It follows that organizations are best thought of not as the product of market failure but as the natural response to the inherently local and situated nature of most of our knowledge. Interactions between agents start out as highly local and our transactional options reflect the ontological primacy of the local over the nonlocal, of the embodied over the abstract and the symbolic. Furthermore, because we are situated, the local constantly gets recreated. Efficient market phenomenon occupies but a small region around point A' in the I-Space. More general organizational phenomena occupy the rest of the space. If our analysis is correct, *organizational phenomena subsume the market rather than the opposite.* Markets will only appear under certain conditions so that internal organization, not external markets, has to be our default hypothesis. What needs to be explained, therefore, is the market phenomenon itself, not impediments to the market phenomenon.

4.6. Conclusions

Economics has proposed an implicit division of labor with organizational theory: you take care of what goes on inside the firm and we will take care of what goes on outside the firm. The outside was always bigger than the inside and the outside either looked like or should look like markets. Organization theorists were free to think of the internal information environment in whatever way they chose. Economists assumed that it was the external information environment that would actually shape the relevant strategic choices—'in the beginning there were markets', and that internal organization is an emergent consequence of market failure. In Boisot and Li (2005), we argued that the heterogeneity of organizations does not square with this assumption. In this chapter, we have challenged the information premises on which this assumption is built. In themselves, our conclusions are not new and have been 'in the air' for sometime. But they have been in need of some theoretical underpinning. Hopefully, our chapter has provided some of that underpinning.

Appendix

Shannon entropy or the information content of a perfectly codified message is given by the following equation:

$$H_s = -N \sum p_i \log p_i \tag{A.1}$$

where $i = 1, \ldots, n$ is a letter in some alphabet, N is the length of a message and where p_i is the probability that gives the frequency of i in some specific language (Shannon 1948). In Shannon's scheme, i is perfectly codified and thus exhibits no fuzziness. Under conditions of fuzziness, however, each member of the alphabet, that is, i is subject to a membership function $A_i \in (0, 1]$. A_i represents the degree of membership of the *sign i* in the *letter i* rather than in some alternative set, where $0 \le A_i \le 1$ (Pedricz and Gomide 1998). In any real-world act of communication, therefore, the likelihood of any i being identified as such without equivocation will therefore be a function of both the original probability p_i and the membership functions A_i of each of the symbols in the alphabet. For a defined alphabet of n letters, the degree of codification of the entire alphabet, C, equals the weighted average of the membership functions of each individual letter:

$$C = \sum_{i=1}^{n} A_i p_i \tag{A.2}$$

In a perfectly codified world each letter of the alphabet can be perfectly and unproblematically identified and distinguished from other alternatives, whether these reside inside the alphabet or outside it. Here the membership function is 1 and $C = 1$. In this perfectly codified world the information entropy, H_s, as defined by Shannon, is a function both of message length and of the frequency distribution of the alphabet in which the message is formulated. That is,

$$H_s = -N \sum_{i=1}^{n} p_i \log p_i \tag{A.3}$$

where

$$\sum_{i=1}^{n} p_i = 1 \tag{A.4}$$

If we now allow the degree of codification of the alphabet to *vary*, we effectively give each letter in the alphabet a membership function as in Figure 4A.1.

In this figure, we effectively 'digitize' the membership function of each letter of the alphabet so as to partition possible outcomes into two distinct states, one that will be deemed to be fully codified with $C = 1$, and the other fully uncodified with $C = 0$. Digitization will operate at a different threshold for each letter as a function

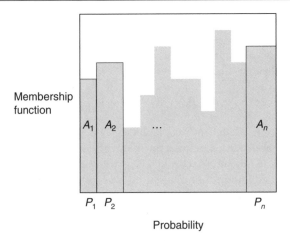

Figure 4A.1. Fuzziness versus Probabilities in an Alphabet (the unshaded area is a source of noise and entropy)

of its formal characteristics. Above a certain threshold, we can say that a letter's specific membership function acts like an attractor for the sign, constraining it to move toward $C = 1$. Below that threshold, by contrast, the sign remains unconstrained by a given letter's membership function and maintains a 0 value. In a fully codified state—now taken as the grey-shaded area in the figure—the alphabet is readily identifiable and is subject to a frequency distribution as indicated by the Shannon formula for entropy, H_s. In the unshaded and uncodified state, by contrast, chaos now rules in the sense that all signs fall below the membership threshold level at which they can be assigned to a particular alphabet or sign system. In this second world, all states—taken here as the set of all possible sign systems—are now undefined and thus taken to be equiprobable. The degree of codification of the alphabet a whole, then, corresponds to the grey-shaded area and is given by Adc (A.2)

The size of the uncodified world corresponds to the unshaded area and is given by $1 - C$. As we have already seen, in a perfectly codified world, the Shannon entropy formula applies. In an uncodifed world, however, where all states are equiprobable, the entropy of a message reaches its maximum

$$H_{\max} = -N \sum_{i=1}^{n} \left(\frac{1}{n}\right) \log \left(\frac{1}{n}\right) = N \log n \tag{A.5}$$

In a *perfectly uncodifiable* world, however—that is, a purely chaotic state—there will exist undefined states or sets, that is, forms or signs, which do not exist in the

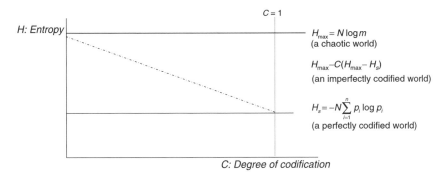

Figure 4A.2. Codified versus Chaotic Worlds

reference alphabet n and which must be added to n when computing H_{max}. In that case, the maximum entropy H_{max} of an uncodified message will be

$$H_{max} = -N \sum_{i=1}^{m} \left(\frac{1}{m}\right) \log\left(\frac{1}{m}\right) = N \log m \tag{A.6}$$

where m $(m > n)$ is the size of the enlarged alphabet. The total entropy of a message in an imperfectly codified world is then a weighted average of H_s and H_{max} with a weighting factor of $1-C$.

$$H = CH_S + (1 - C)H_{max} = H_{max} - C(H_{max} - H_S) \tag{A.7}$$

Graphically, we can represent the situation as in Figure 4A.2.

Adapting our equation to the structuring of knowledge, $i \ldots n$ can now be made to stand for the number of *categories* available in a given repertoire rather than for the number of symbols in an alphabet. The message length, N, will then reflect how many times different categories are actually drawn upon from the available repertoire in outputting a given message—this may or may not match the p_i. Just as with symbols in Shannon's use of the formula, the number of categories in the repertoire, n, can be judiciously reduced by applying Shannon's theory of efficient coding (Shannon 1948), that is, by exploiting the prior correlations that exist between categories to perform an act of *abstraction*. The more abstract a message, the fewer the categories required and therefore the smaller n can be.[7] This will

---

[7] When $n \to \infty$, then although the correlation or transitional probabilities between any two states may be quite high, the probability of appearance of such states in a message becomes so vanishingly small that no stable expectation can ever be built up from any frequency count of the states. In such a situation, since a convention cannot be developed *ex ante*, as in language, it must be developed *ex post* on the basis of empirical observations and inferences that gradually constrain the n to a manageable number. This is the situation in science.

have the effect of reducing message length and, by implication, H. In sum, the total entropy, H, of a given message, stands in an inverse relationship with its degree of codification and abstraction.

References

Arrow, K. (1984). *Information and Economic Behavior, the Economics of Information: Collected Papers of Kenneth J. Arrow*. Cambridge, MA: Belknap Press of Harvard University, pp. 136–52.

Arthur, B. W. (1989). 'Competing Technologies, Increasing Returns, and Lock-in by Historical Events', *Economic Journal*, 99: 116–31.

Barkow, J., Cosmides, L., and Tooby, J. (1992). *The Adapted Mind: Evolutionary Psychology and the Generation of Culture*. Oxford: Oxford University Press.

Bennett, C. (1999). 'Quantum Information Theory', in A. Hey (ed.), *Feynman and Computation: Exploring the Limits of Computers*. Reading, MA: Perseus Books, pp. 177–90.

Boisot, M. (1986). 'Markets and Hierarchies in Cultural Perspective', *Organization Studies*, 7(2): 135–58.

—— (1995). *Information Space: A Framework for Analyzing Organizations, Institutions and Cultures*. London: Routledge.

—— (1998). *Knowledge Assets—Securing Competitive Advantage in the Information Economy*. Oxford: Oxford University Press.

—— and Canals, A. (2004). 'Data, Information, and Knowledge: Have We Got It Right?', *Journal of Evolutionary Economics*, 14: 43–67.

—— and Child, J. (1988). 'The Iron Law of Fiefs: Bureaucratic Failure and the Problem of Governance in the Chinese Economic Reforms', *Administrative Science Quarterly*, 33: 507–27.

—— and Cohen, J. (2000). 'Shall I compare Thee to...An Organization?', *Emergence*, 2(4): 113–35.

—— and Li, Y. (2005). 'Codification, Abstraction, and Firm Differences: A Cognitive Information-Based Perspective', *Journal of Bioeconomics*, 7: 309–34.

—— and Sanchez, R. (2004). Economic Organization As a Nexus of Rules: Emergence and the Theory of the Firm. Unpublished Manuscript.

Bonner, J. (1980). *The Evolution of Culture in Animals*. Princeton, NJ: Princeton University Press.

Brannigan, M. L. (2002). 'There is No Spoon: A Buddhist Mirror', in W. Irwin (ed.), *The Matrix and Philosphy: Welcome to the Desert of the Real*. Chicago, IL: Open Court, pp. 101–10.

Casti, J. and DePauli, W. (2000). *Gödel: A Life of Logic*. Cambridge, MA: Perseus Books.

Chaitin, G. J. (1974). 'Information-Theoretic Computational Complexity', *IEEE Transactions on Information Theory*, IT-20: 10–15.

Cheung, S. (1983). 'The Contractual Nature of the Firm', *Journal of Law and Economics*, 3(1): 1–21.

Clark, A. (1997). *Being There: Putting Brain, Body, and World Together Again*. Cambridge, MA: MIT Press.

Coase, R. (1937). 'The Nature of the Firm', *Economica* NS, 4: 386–405.

Deacon, T. W. (1997). *The Symbolic Species*. New York: Norton.

Debreu, G. (1959). *Theory of Value*. New York: John Wiley & Sons.

Dretske, F. (1981). *Knowledge and the Flow of Information*. Cambridge, MA: MIT Press.

Dupuy, J. P. (1992). *Intoduction aux sciences sociales: logique des phenoménes collectifs*. Paris: Ellipses.

——(2004). 'Intersubjectivity and Embodiment', *Journal of Bioeconomics*, 6: 275–94.

Evans, P. and Wurster, T. (1997). 'Strategy and the New Economics of Information', *Harvard Business Review*, September–October: 71–82.

Fuller, S. (2002). *Social Epistemology*. Bloomington, IN: Indiana University Press.

Ghiselin, M. and Landa, J. (2005). 'The Economics and Bioeconomics of Folk and Scientific Classification', *Journal of Bioeconomics*, 7: 221–38.

Godel, K. (1962). *On Formally Undecidable Problems*. New York: Basic Books.

Hacking, I. (1983). *Representing and Intervening*. Cambridge: Cambridge University Press.

Hahn, U. and Chater, N. (1998). 'Similarity and Rules: Distinct? Exhaustive? Empirically Distinguishable?', in S. Sloman and L. Rips (eds.), *Similarity and Symbols in Human Thinking*. Cambridge, MA: MIT Press, pp. 111–44.

Hall, E. (1976). *Beyond Culture*. New York: Doubleday.

Hamilton, W. (1964). 'The Genetical Theory of Social Behavior, I, II', *Journal of Theoretical Biology*, 7: 1–52.

Hanson, N. (1965). *Patterns of Discovery*. Cambridge: Cambridge University Press.

Hart, O. (1989). 'An Economist's Perspective on the Theory of the Firm', *Columbia Law Review*, 89: 1756–74.

Haynie, D. (2001). *Biological Thermodynamics*. Cambridge: Cambridge University Press.

Hori, I. (1967). 'The Appearance of Individual Self-Consciousness in Japanese Religion and Its Historical Transformation', in C. Moore (ed.), *The Japanese Mind: Essentials of Japanese Philosophy and Culture*. Honolulu, HI: University of Hawaii Press, pp. 201–27.

Huang, Y. (2003). *Selling China: Foreign Direct Investment During the Reform Era*. Cambridge: Cambridge University Press.

Hurwicz, L. (1972). 'On Informationally Decentralized Systems', in C. McGuire and R. Radner (eds.), *Decisions and Organizations*. Amsterdam: North-Holland, pp. 297–336.

Johnson, M. (1987). *The Body in the Mind: The Bodily Basis of Meaning, Imagination, and Reason*. Chicago, IL: Chicago University Press.

Kishimoto, H. (1967). 'Some Japanese Cultural Traits and Religion', in C. Moore (ed.), *The Japanese Mind: Essentials of Japanese Philosophy and Culture*. Honolulu, HI: University of Hawaii Press, pp. 110–21.

Kornblith, H. (1994). 'Naturalism: Both Metaphysical and Epistemological', in P. A. French, T. E. J. Uehling, and H. K. Wettstein (eds.), *Midwest Studies in Philosophy*. Notre Dame, IN: University of Notre Dame Press, pp. 39–52.

Lakoff, G. and Johnson, M. (1999). *Philosophy in the Flesh: The Embodied Mind and Its Challenge to Western Thought*. New York: Basic Books.

Landa, J. (1981). A Theory of the Ethnically Homogenous Middleman Group: An Institutional Alternative to Contract Law', *The Journal of Legal Studies*, 10: 349–62.

—— (1999). 'Bioeconomics of Some Nonhuman and Human Societies: New Institutional Economics Approach', *Journal of Bioeconomics*, 1: 95–113.

Landauer, R. (1999). 'Information is Inevitably Physical', in A. Hey (ed.), *Feynman and Computation: Exploring the Limits of Computers*. Reading, MA: Perseus Books, pp. 77–92.

Lange, O. (1937). 'On the Economic Theory of Socialism', *Review of Economic Studies*, 4(1): 53–71, 4(2): 123–42.

Lerner, A. (1936). 'A Note on Socialist Economies', *Review of Economic Studies*, 4: 72–6.

Mac Cormac, E. L. (1985). *Cognitive Theory of Metaphor*. Cambridge, MA: MIT Press.

McQuade, T. and Butos, W. (2005). 'The Sensory Order and Other Adaptive Classifying Systems', *Journal of Bioeconomics*, 7: 335–58.

Marshall, A. (1920). *Principles of Economics*. London: MacMillan.

Maturana, H. and Varela, F. (1980). *Autopoiesis and Cognition: The Realization of the Living*. Boston, MA: D. Reidel.

Miller, G. (1956). 'The Magic Number Seven, Plus or Minus Two: Some Limits on Our Capacity for Processing Information', *Psychological Review*, 63: 81–107.

Mirowski, P. (1989). *More Heat than Light: Economics as Social Physics, Physics as Nature's Economics*. Cambridge: Cambridge University Press.

—— (2002). *Machine Dreams: How Economics Became a Cyborg Science*. Cambridge: Cambridge University Press.

Moles, A. (1968). *Information and Esthetic Perception*. Urbana, IL: University of Illinois Press.

Moore, C. (ed.) (1967). *The Japanese Mind: Essentials of Japanese Philosophy and Culture*. Honolulu, HI: University of Hawaii Press.

Nelson, R. and Winter, S. (1982). *An Evolutionary Theory of Economic Change*. Cambridge, MA: Harvard University Press.

Nonaka, I. and Takeuchi, H. (1994). *The Knowledge Creating Company: How Japanese Companies Create the Dynamics of Innovation*. New York: Oxford University Press.

Pedricz, W. and Gomide, F. (1998). *An Introduction to Fuzzy Sets*. Cambridge, MA: MIT Press.

Pinker, S. (1997). *How the Mind Works*. London: Penguin Books.

Polanyi, M. (1958). *Personal Knowledge: Towards a Post-Critical Philosophy*. London: Routledge & Kegan Paul.

Popper, K. R. (1972). *Objective Knowledge: An Evolutionary Approach*. Oxford: Clarendon Press.

Prietula, M., Carley, K., and Gasser, L. (1998). *Simulating Organizations: Computational Models of Institutions and Groups*. Cambridge, MA: MIT Press.

Pugh, D. S., Hickson, D. J., Hinings, C. R., and Turner, C. (1969). 'The Context of Organization Structures', *Administrative Science Quarterly*, 14(1): 91–114.

Quine, W. (1969). *Naturalized Epistemology in Ontological Relativity and Other Essays*. New York: Columbia University Press.

Rebber, A. (1993). *Implicit Learning and Tacit Knowledge: An Essay on the Cognitive Unconcious*. New York: Oxford University Press.

Ryle, G. (1949). *The Concept of Mind*, Harmondsworth. UK: Penguin Books.

Shannon, C. E. (1948). 'The Mathematical Theory of Communication', *Bell System Technical Journal*, 27: 379–423.

——and Weaver, W. (1949). *The Mathematical Theory of Communication*. Urbana, IL: University of Illinois Press.

Sipser, M. (1997). *Introduction to the Theory of Computation*. Boston, MA: PWS Publishing Company.

Smith, B. C. (1996). *On the Origins of Objects*. Cambridge, MA: MIT Press.

Spender, J. C. (2002). 'Knowledge, Uncertainty, and an Emergent Theory of the Firm', in C.W. Choo and N. Bontis (eds.), *The Strategic Management of Intellectual Capital and Organizational Knowledge*. Oxford: Oxford University Press, pp. 149–62.

Stewart, I. and Cohen, J. (1997). *Figments of Reality: The Evolution of the Curious Mind*. Cambridge: Cambridge University Press.

Suzuki, T. D. (1956). *Zen Buddhism: Selected Writings of T.D. Suzuki*. New York: Doubleday.

——(1967). 'Reason and Intuition in Buddhist Philosophy', in C. Moore (ed.), *The Japanese Mind: Essentials of Japanese Philosophy and Culture*. Honolulu, HI: University of Hawaii Press, pp. 122–42.

Teece, D. J. (1986). 'Profiting from Technological Innovation: Implications for Integration, Collaboration, Licensing, and Public Policy', *Research Policy*, 15(6): 285–305.

Thelen, E. and Smith, L. (1994). *A Dynamic Systems Approach to the Development of Cognition and Action*. Cambridge, MA: MIT Press.

Tönnies, F. (1955). *Community and Association*. London: Routledge & Kegan Paul.

Tsoukas, H. (1996). 'The Firm as a Distributed Knowledge System: A Constructionist Approach', *Strategic Management Journal*, 17: 11–25.

Weber, M. (1978). *Economy and Society*. Berkeley, CA: University of California Press.

Williamson, O. E. (1975). *Markets and Hierarchies: Analysis and Antitrust Implications*. Glencoe: Free Press.

Williamson, O. E. (1985). *The Economic Institutions of Capitalism: Firms, Markets, Rational Contracting*. New York: Free Press.

Wise, M. N. (1995*a*). *'Introduction'*, in M. N. Wise (ed.), *The Values of Precision*. Princeton, NJ: Princeton University Press, pp. 3–16.

——(1995*b*). 'Precision: Agent of Unity and Product of Agreement', in M. N. Wise (ed.), *The Values of Precision*. Princeton, NJ: Princeton University Press, pp. 92–100.

Ziman, J. (1968). *Public Knowledge: The Social Dimension of Science*. Cambridge: Cambridge University Press.

5

Moving to the Edge of Chaos: Bureaucracy, IT, and the Challenge of Complexity

Max H. Boisot

5.1. Introduction

How many of us have not yet encountered modern state or corporate bureaucracies, either through the taxes or the utility bills that we pay, the endless forms that we fill in, the laws or regulations that they impose on us or through any other of their myriad bureaucratic manifestations? For some this complex piece of administrative machinery constitutes an exhilarating manifestation of progress at work. For others, by contrast, its impersonal functioning seems to deny them their very claim to being a person. How did bureaucracies evolve?

The past 600 years have witnessed—first in Europe and increasingly in other parts of the world—what the late nineteenth-century sociologist, Ferdinand Tönnies, called the movement from *Gemeinschaft* toward *Gesellschaft*, the slow metamorphosis of small highly local and personalized communities characteristic of the Middle Ages into large, ubiquitous, and impersonal organizations (Tönnies 1955). Modern state bureaucracies, Gesellschaft structures par excellence, were built out of the interaction between the rapid spread of printing and literacy after Guttenberg on the one hand, and the scientific revolution that took place in Europe in the seventeenth century on the other (Eisenstein 1983; Goody 1986). These two developments, taken together, allowed the state to create a powerful administrative machine and to increase its spatiotemporal reach. Through its formal and increasingly rational bureaucracies, it could collect more taxes, more quickly and reliably, from more people, and from further away than had ever been possible under a fragmentary feudal regime. In return, it could offer its 'citizens'—at least in republican regimes or in constitutional monarchies—something approaching a uniform and reasonably predictable system of laws and justice. The result was the creation of a new political entity: the European nation-state.

The effectiveness of the state as an organization (*gesellschaft*), however, rested on the prior existence of the nation. Nations are built out of shared sentiments, either territorial or ethnic, to produce a community (*gemeinschaft*) of fate. States are built out of the rules of the game—that is, constitutions and institutions (North and Weingast 1989)—that such a community will subscribe to. In nation-states, the rules of the game reflect what these shared sentiments make possible. Yet, as a community, a nation far exceeds in size the parochial groupings that had characterized the Middle Ages. How was the enlargement of this new community of fate brought about? There were many factors involved, but an important part of the answer is that, through the rapid spread of the newly printed word, vernacular languages simultaneously replaced Latin and the local dialects that kept communities small and apart (Eisenstein 1983; Goody 1986). The first effect marked a power shift from a religious to a secular order; the second created the necessary binding agent for a larger community to come together.

Given the nation how was the state then built up? We can break down the process into two distinct components. First, the scientific revolution created a culture of meticulous and precise observations, written records, codification, and abstraction (Rusnock 1997). How many permanent inhabitants, for example, resided in the city of Tours in the year 1647? What did they possess that was taxable? What do the parish registers tell us about who migrated into the city and who migrated out of it in that year? How do the aggregate figures compare with those for the city of Nantes? What implications for French demographics and for the state budget? For answers to such questions, one could now consult and analyze the written records. The most immediate beneficiary of this development was the emerging state bureaucracy (Landes 1999).

Second, if the scientific revolution legitimated a culture of codification and abstraction—that is, of information structuring—the printing revolution provided a technology of information storage and diffusion. The rapid and extensive spread of the printed word—and printed in an accessible national language rather than in the more remote Latin—ushered in a period of mass literacy that gradually eroded the parochialism of the oral traditions that it displaced. In the space of a few years, for example, the very first scientific publications, in the form of letters, had woven together a scientific community that spread right across Europe (Hill 1968; Shapin 1994). Space and time shrunk simultaneously as a consequence.

Rational–legal bureaucracies, like the institutions of science—and in contrast to the 'patrimonial' type of bureaucracies through which Imperial China was governed until 1908 (Boisot and Child 1988; Weber 1951)—have a commitment to the codification and abstraction of knowledge. Structuring knowledge in this way is a source of data processing and communicative efficiencies that allows bureaucracies to extend their administrative reach. However, these do not necessarily share the commitment of scientific institutions to the free diffusion of knowledge. The kind of knowledge held by bureaucrats constitutes a source of power and influence that could be quickly eroded if it was openly and indiscriminately shared with outsiders. Bureaucratic culture, in effect, is a presumption in favor of *hoarding* knowledge, of diffusing it in a controlled manner to a limited number of selected recipients. The selective hoarding of knowledge generates a hierarchy in which those 'in the know' end up locating themselves authoritatively above those who are not. In the Middle Ages, such information asymmetries generated the patrimonial bureaucracies of the Catholic Church. From the sixteenth and seventeenth centuries onward, new rational–legal bureaucratic cultures formed natural complements to those of Europe's emerging absolutist states. Market culture, a competing presumption in favor of *sharing* knowledge and—by implication—of democracy, slowly emerged out of the Scottish and the Continental Enlightenments in Europe. It required the emergence and empowerment of an educated commercial class and took longer to get established (Himmelfarb 2004; Mokyr 2002).

When a sizable commercial class finally emerged, did bureaucratic culture thereby disappear? No, but it now had to share the stage with a powerful institutional alternative: the open market. In effect, over time, bureaucratic culture gradually penetrated the market itself to create the large modern corporation (Chandler 1977). As before, science and technology once again acted as a midwife to this development. In the late nineteenth century, the arrival of new transport and communications technologies—the railways and the telegraph—assisted by the new data-processing technologies of cost accounting, planning, and control (Pollard 1965) helped to integrate markets and to create the first giant corporations (Chandler 1962). Since these required tight managerial coordination over large distances, formal bureaucracies entered the world of business

149

to help organize the process efficiently and rationally. Just as 300 years before, the marriage between ICTs on the one hand, and organization on the other had successfully extended the spatiotemporal reach of the state, so now it was enhancing the territorial reach of commercial and industrial organizations. In both cases, the creation of a well-oiled bureaucratic machine proved to be the key to a successful expansion.

In this chapter, we ask two questions. Could the new ICTs that have appeared over the past twenty years have a similar impact on twenty-first-century organizations? And would such a development necessarily presage a further extension of either state or corporate bureaucracy? If not, what might it presage? Ever since Coase's seminal 1937 paper (Coase 1937), the options, whether applied at the level of the firm, or at the level of the state have tended to be framed exclusively as either bureau-cratic hierarchies or competitive markets (Williamson 1975; Williamson 1985). Are such institutional forms our only options? Might the clan-like networks that characterize China's social and economic evolution (Boisot and Child 1996), for example, point to possible alternatives? To answer these questions, we must first briefly consider how knowledge is structured and shared within and between organizations and how this might affect the way that such organizations get institutionalized. We can then explore the effect that ICTs might have on this process. The chapter is structured as follows. In Section 5.2, we present a simple conceptual framework, the Information-Space or *I-Space*, that relate the extent that knowledge is structured to the extent that it can be shared within and across groups of different sizes. The resulting knowledge flows, when recurrent, set the scene for the emergence or not of institutions. Section 5.3 examines the impact of ICTs on such knowledge flows. Apply-ing the I-Space, Section 5.4 discusses some of the implications of ICTs for the institutionalization process and, in particular, for the future of state and corporate bureaucracies. A conclusion follows in Section 5.5.

5.2. The Information Space

Things that can be articulated and written down travel further and faster than things that cannot. Unless captured on film, for example, a facial grimace does not travel much further than its author's immediate physical surroundings. A message typed up as an e-mail, by contrast, can travel around the globe in seconds. Structuring knowledge and information, then, facilitates and speeds up its diffusion. But what does structuring knowledge involve? Hahn and Chater have argued that in living systems, the structuring of knowledge is brought about by the twin activities of discrimination and association (Hahn and Chater 1997). Boisot as taken these as corresponding to the data-processing activities of *codification* and *abstraction* (Boisot 1995, 1998). Codification involves an ability to distinguish between the categories of experience in order to reliably assign phenomena to these. What is then known about the categories will have predictive value for dealing with phenomena so assigned. Abstraction minimizes the number of categories needed to deal with phenomena by establishing associations between categories that also have predictive value and allow one category to stand in for another. Both codification and abstraction save on data-processing energy and time, thus allowing a living system to respond to the complexities of its environment in a timely fashion and with a minimum of effort. Codification minimizes the amount of data processing required to assign events to categories; abstraction minimizes the number of categories that are actually needed (Bennett 1999; Chaitin 1974; Lloyd 2005). In this way, one progresses from the flux of immediate experience to what can be talked about—a move from *experiential knowledge* to *narrative knowledge*—and thence to those aspects of experience that exhibit sufficient regularities to yield predictions— *abstract symbolic knowledge* (Boisot and Li, 2006). The relationship between codification and abstraction on the one hand, and diffusion on the other, can be captured diagrammatically in an Information Space, or *I-Space* (Boisot 1995,1998) as shown in Figure 5.1

On the vertical scale of the diagram, we can locate an item of knowledge or information according to how far it has been codified, that is, compressed into codes that allow for speedy and reliable categorization. On one of the horizontal scales, the one labeled 'concrete' and 'abstract', we can trace how far the number of categories required to capture an item of knowledge or information have been minimized. Concrete experiences draw on a potentially infinite number of categories, whereas abstract representations draw on just a few. A discursive text, for example, is more codified and abstract—that is, compressed—than an image, and an algebraic formula, in turn, is more codified and abstract than a discursive text. On the other horizontal scale, the one labeled 'undiffused' and 'diffused', we can plot how far an item of knowledge or information can get diffused within a given population of agents per unit of time. The chosen agent population could be made up of individual human beings, but could also be made up of firms or other organizations that exhibit agency—whether through a legally constituted 'personality' or otherwise. Toward the left

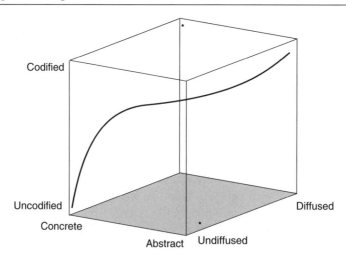

Figure 5.1. The I-Space

on the diffusion scale, knowledge and information do not diffuse beyond one or two agents—people or organizations. Toward the right, by contrast, they diffuse to the agent population as a whole.

The curve of Figure 5.1 then tells us that the more codified and abstract an item of information or knowledge, the more extensively it will diffuse within a target population within a given time frame. If one wants to reach a large agent population quickly, therefore, one tries to compress one's message as much as possible into concise, intelligible codes—something that advertisers learnt a long time ago. Of course, the convenience in speed and reach achieved by codification and abstraction carries a price: a loss of contextual richness. If my facial expression helps you to make sense of the words that I utter—it might, for example, tell you that I am in a blind fury and not in a joking mood—then, if you receive my words alone through some impersonal channel (e-mail, a letter, etc.) that fails to convey my facial expression, you cannot know whether your response to them will provoke me to further paroxysms of rage or to uncontrollable laughter. To gauge this, you would actually need to see me while I talk—something that is typically only possible in a face-to-face situation.

Codification and abstraction, in effect, trade off communicative *effectiveness* for communicative *efficiency* (Evans and Wuster 2000). The extent of the trade-off will vary according to circumstances, but where the need for a trade-off becomes recurrent, it may give rise to institutional

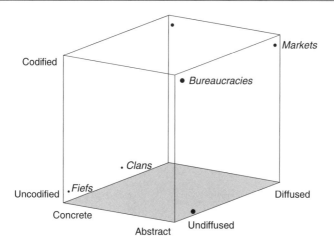

Figure 5.2. Four Institutional Structures in the I-Space

structures that will lower the cost of communicating each time such circumstances arise. Figure 5.2 locates four such institutional structures in the I-Space. Each operates in a distinct information environment whose codification, abstraction, and diffusion dynamics give rise to different social behaviors. Through recurrent interactions, these then get stabilized and institutionalized as norms and values that reflect the specificities of the information environment that gave rise to them. Distinctive cultures—national, regional, corporate, occupational, etc.—result from how these four institutional structures are mixed, matched, and configured within and across groups of different sizes. Briefly taking each institutional type in turn:

- *Markets* are built on the ready availability of well codified and abstract-symbolic price information within a given population
- *Bureaucracies* operate on a 'need-to-know' basis, that is, on the controlled diffusion of well-codified narrative and abstract-symbolic information to selected players within a given population
- *Clans* develop on the basis of concrete shared experiences and tacitly held values—which will often be derived from abstract principles—that arise within small groups in a given population. Since such sharing requires a face-to-face interaction, the diffusion of tacit (uncodified) knowledge is typically limited to a number of players that is small when compared to markets.

Table 5.1. Some Attributes of the Four Institutional Types in the I-Space

Bureaucracies
- Information diffusion limited and under central control
- Relationships impersonal and hierarchical
- Submission to superordinate goals
- Hierarchical coordination
- No necessity to share values and beliefs

Fiefs
- Information diffusion limited by lack of codification to face-to-face relationship
- Relationships personal and hierarchical (feudal/charismatic)
- Submission to superordinate goals
- Hierarchical coordination
- Necessity to share values and beliefs

Markets
- Information widely diffused, no control
- Relationships impersonal and competitive
- No superordinate goals—each one for himself
- Horizontal coordination through self-regulation
- No necessity to share values and beliefs

Clans
- Information is partially diffused but still limited by lack of codification to face-to-face relationships
- Relationships personal but nonhierarchical
- Goals are shared through a process of negotiation
- Horizontal coordination through negotiation
- Necessity to share values and beliefs

- *Fiefs* reflect the charismatic power granted to one or two individuals on the basis of unique situated—that is, concrete and uncodified—knowledge that they are deemed to possess but that is hard to articulate and share.

Table 5.1 briefly summarizes some of the distinctive characteristics of each institutional type.

The different information environments generated by the I-Space vary in their *complexity*. How might we characterize this? In spite of the growing popularity of complexity as a field of study, there is as yet no single agreed meaning of the term 'complexity' (Gell-Mann 1994). We take complexity to be either a property of the world itself—objective complexity—or of our response to the world—subjective complexity (Taylor 2001). Taken as a property of the world, complexity emerges from the nonlinear interaction of elements that make up some phenomenon under study (Cilliers 1998; Cowan 1994). Taken as a property of our response to the world, complexity measures the effort that we need to invest in to make sense of such a phenomenon—individually or collectively—given the information available to us (Freeman 2000). Clearly, as an information-based framework, the I-Space deals with the latter kind of complexity. Each of the I-Space's three dimensions deals with a different aspect of this kind of complexity:

Codification deals with *descriptive complexity*. In the tradition of algorithmic information complexity (AIC), descriptive complexity measures the amount of data processing that an agent must engage in either to assign phenomena to categories or to distinguish the categories relevant to the assignment task from each other (Chaitin 1974; Gell-Mann 1994; Kolgomorov 1965). Whereas the identification and classification of some phenomena will require very little data processing, others may require an almost infinite amount—that is, for all practical purposes, they may be indescribable.

Abstraction deals with *computational complexity*. Phenomena exhibit different degrees of freedom and their description is thus captured by different numbers of variables in interaction with each other. Computational complexity is a function both of the dimensionality of phenomena—that is, the number of variables required to apprehend their behavior—as well as of the nonlinearity of their interactions (Dooley and Van de Ven 1999; Lloyd 2005; Prigogine 1980; Sipser 1997; Zurek 1990). More variables require more categories, a move toward the concrete end of the abstraction dimension of the I-Space. Yet if the interaction of variables can be described by linear correlations, then one category can be made to stand for another (Dretske 1981)—a move toward the abstract end of the abstraction dimension. The question of abstraction can be reframed as: what is the minimum number of categories needed to capture some phenomenon given how its constituent variables are related to each other?

Diffusion deals with *relational complexity*. Agents in the I-Space process data *and* exchange data with other agents, receiving data as inputs from some and transmitting the outputs of their data-processing efforts to others. In this sense, the I-Space depicts social computational processes in which agents collectively try to make sense of the phenomena that confront them (Epstein and Axtell 1996; Prietula, Carley, and Gasser 1998). Locating phenomena along the codification and abstraction dimension establishes their *cognitive complexity* (Edelman and Tononi 2000) Locating them along the diffusion dimension indicates how many agents will be involved in making sense of them and establishes their *relational complexity*. This last kind of complexity will be partly a function of the nature of the interaction between agents as determined by the institutional structures available to support social computational processes in that region of the I-Space (see Figure 5.2).

In any attempt to apprehend phenomena, the codification, abstraction, and diffusion of the information that captures them interact to yield different 'complexity regimes' located in the I-Space as indicated in Figure 5.3: the chaotic, the complex, and the ordered (Boisot and Child

155

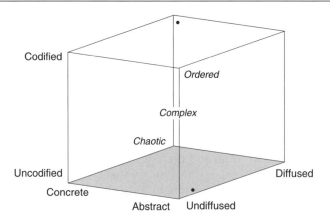

Figure 5.3. Ordered, Complex, and Chaotic Regimes in the I-Space

1999; Kauffman 1993; Langton 1992). Each regime reflects the descriptive and computational loads imposed on agents both by the phenomena that confront them and by the social need for achieving some consensus in interpreting and responding to them. Computational theory teaches us that problems whose size is exponential in the inputs will call for what for all practical purposes amounts to an infinite amount of data processing for their solution (Chaitin 1974; Sipser 1997). To an agent grappling with such problems, the inputs may then be experienced as random or chaotic. Whether they describe deterministic or stochastic processes, they defy meaningful interpretation. Problems whose size is polynomial in the inputs will strike an agent as highly complex—computationally tractable, but costly to deal with (Sipser 1997). Only problems whose size is linear in the inputs will register with an agent as ordered.

Boisot (1998) has shown that where in the I-Space the information environment is at its most concrete—that is, phenomena are characterized by numerous categories that resist abstraction—at its most uncodified—phenomena cannot be meaningfully categorized—and at its most diffused—the agent population that has access to such phenomena is too large to reach any consensus as to what they might mean—agents can extract no structure from it that would facilitate an adaptive interpretation and response. Agents will experience such an information environment as *chaotic*, one in which everything appears to be possible but nothing is sufficiently probable for a discernable structure to emerge, stabilize, and subsequently shape agent expectations. Note that since the I-Space deals with the data processing and transmission activities of agents, we are dealing with a subjective use of the term 'chaotic' that does not require us to distinguish, as would an objective use of the term, between deterministic and stochastic chaos (Freeman 2000). Whether the phenomena that are captured by an agent's data processing and transmission activities are themselves deterministically chaotic—as studied by the mathematical theory of chaos (Ott, Grebogi, and Yorke 1990)—or stochastically so, they will be experienced as random by an agent and thus will occupy similar locations in the I-Space.

At the other extreme, an information environment characterized in the I-Space by high levels of codification and abstraction and subject to highly controlled diffusion processes will be experienced by agents as *ordered*. Here, alternative possibilities have all been eliminated; phenomena appear to be unproblematically structured, so that only one interpretation and course of action commends itself. Somewhere in between these extremes, an information environment characterized by moderate levels of codification and abstraction and partial diffusibility of information will be experienced as *complex*. Here it is possible to extract meaningful structures from the information environment and to exercise strategic choices (Child 1972), but only through a process of reflection and deliberation— that is, greater data processing and communication efforts that would be required under an ordered regime, but less than what would be required under a chaotic regime.

As Figure 5.3 indicates, no institutional structure can be associated with the chaotic regime. It is beyond the reach of any effective data processing and transmission strategies. The ordered regime, by contrast, we can associate with bureaucratic institutions, with their emphasis on stability, repeatability, and the controlled diffusion of information to selected recipients. The three other institutional forms we associate with different mixes of cognitive and relational complexity. The complexity that we associate with fiefs, for example, emerges from the way in which cognitive, motivational, and affective processes interact within a single individual—the fief-holder—rendering his or her actions largely unpredictable except to those who are closely in contact with that individual. The complexity that characterizes clans, by contrast, is more reminiscent of the three-body problem in physics. It arises from the way that a small group of agents interact, bargain, and mutually adjust to each other's behavior on a recurrent basis. Here the cognitions and motivations that different participating agents bring to bear on these group processes reinforce and constrain each other in ways that are multidimensional and unpredictable to those outsiders who are unfamiliar with the dynamics of the group. Finally, as the number of interacting agents expands, the highly personalized forms of cognitive (descriptive and computational) and relational complexity that we associate with clans give way to the more impersonal relational complexity that we associate with markets, one in which cognitive complexity has been reduced. Here, multidimensional agent interactions have been replaced by two-dimensional concerns with prices and quantities. In sum, each institutional form blends cognitive and relational complexity in varying proportions, with cognitive complexity being at its highest in the case of fiefs, and relational complexity being dominant in the case of markets.

Too much time spent in the ordered regime eventually leads to fossilization due to an inability to respond to phenomena outside a very narrow range. At several points in its long history, for example, the Chinese bureaucracy, seeking to escape the ravages of the chaotic regime, stagnated in the ordered regime and blocked the country's evolution (Boisot and Child 1988, 1996)—it became, in effect, what Gouldner termed a 'mock bureaucracy'(Gouldner 1954). On the other hand, too much time spent in the chaotic regime leads to disintegration due to an inability to extract meaningful information structures from phenomena that one can adapt to—the situation that one encounters today in a number of failed states in which both cognitive and relational complexity are at their maximum. The challenge is to maintain the bulk of one's organizational capacities in the complex regime without spilling over into the chaotic regime. In effect, adaptive organizations live on the edge of chaos, a zone that varies in size and that lies between the complex and the chaotic regime (Kauffman 1993; Waldrop 1992).

The ordered regime fossilizes; the chaotic regime disintegrates. To avoid such outcomes one needs to broaden the scope of the complex regime. As already mentioned, driven by a strong belief in the power of hierarchy, China pushed too much in the direction of the ordered regime. Its traditional political and cultural structure was 'cellular', with little horizontal connectivity between different regions in the country (Donnithorne 1981). The creation of a command economy in the 1950s, following the communist takeover, reinforced rather than weakened this cellular structure (Boisot and Child 1988). The experience of other countries in managing complex horizontal interactions between different regions suggests that the 'divide and conquer' approach promoted by cellularization is not always desirable. The challenge for bureaucracies, then, is to expand into the complexity region of the I-Space without spilling over into the chaotic one. One is naturally led to ask: how wide is the complexity region and what determines this width? We hypothesize that building effective institutional structures in the market and clan regions of the I-Space widens the complexity region and helps to stabilize it while simultaneously reducing the size of the region in the I-Space from which the chaotic regime can 'attract' transactions—that is, its *basin of attraction.*

Bureaucracies have a deeply rooted tendency to pursue order through hierarchical command-and-control strategies. They shun the complexity region of the I-Space because they do not know how wide it is. China's bureaucratically inclined policymakers, for example, although tolerating market-oriented policies since 1978, continue to dichotomize the I-Space into an ordered region and a chaotic one in their policy pronouncements in order to justify confining themselves to the ordered region. For them, there is no complexity region. And for them, unless it is tightly controlled, decentralization leads straight to chaos (Boisot and Child 1988)—hence the constant and arbitrary interventions by government bureaucrats in market processes. The former Soviet Union pursued similar strategies (Nove 1977), adhering tenaciously to a bureaucratic order that, over time, became overloaded with transactions that should have been assigned elsewhere in the I-Space. Paradoxically, by denying the reality of the complex regime, communist countries deny themselves institutional responses that are adapted to the information environments that they find themselves in. They thus bring about the very chaos that they purport to flee. Large corporate bureaucracies, of course, are subject to a similar dynamic. The urge to monopoly, for example, is often little more than an attempt to live a quiet and comfortable life in an ordered regime and to escape the stressful complexities of the market process (Hicks 1939; Marris 1964).

5.3. The Influence of ICTs

How does the emergence of ICTs modify the dynamics of information flows in the I-Space that we have described and the institutionalization that results from these?

The development story of the Western world—initially Europe and the United States—can be interpreted as a slow move toward increasing codification and abstraction in the I-Space, from the oral to the written and the quantitative and from the 'enchanted' to the rational and the abstract

(Goody 1986; Weber, 1951). Both the advent of printing and the scientific revolution contributed to this move (Cohen 1985). Through the spread of literacy and education, the upward move was then accompanied—to be sure, with a lag—by a gradual diffusion of codified knowledge to ever-larger populations. This process of decentralization, over time, fostered both the spread of democracy and the emergence of markets. The creation of appropriate infrastructures—essentially bureaucratic and market institutions—facilitated both the moves up the I-Space and along the diffusion curve of Figure 5.1. The trajectory thus originated in fiefs, moved toward ordered bureaucratic regimes and then toward a self-regulating market order bounded by bureaucratic regulations (Boisot and Child 1996).

In those parts of the world where such institutions are either absent or malfunctioning—today, mostly in emerging and less-developed economies—the institutional environment still remains heavily oriented toward the lower regions of the I-space, namely, toward fiefs and clans. Here personal power and particularistic ties of loyalty rather than impersonal rule continue to characterize the social order. Here, given the inability to reduce cognitive complexity by articulating robust institutional structures, the prizes go to those who can manage relational complexity. The tension between the globalizing dynamics that drive cultures and institutions located in the upper regions of the I-Space and the local dynamics that animate those in the lower regions are none other than those first noticed by Tönnies (1955). They reflect some of the oppositions between *Gemeinschaft* and *Gesellschaft*.

Will ICTs further increase the tensions that are already evident between the global and the local? With ever-increasing bandwidth available to all at an ever-lower cost, we can assume that, at any given level of codification and abstraction, more information will reach more people per unit of time along the diffusion scale than hitherto. We call this the *diffusion effect* and interpret this as a rightward shift in the diffusion curve as indicated by the horizontal arrow in Figure 5.4. The downward-pointing arrow in Figure 5.4 also indicates that any given proportion of a population located at some point along the diffusion scale can be reached at a lower level of codification and abstraction—that is, at a higher bandwidth—than hitherto. Thus, for example, today low-cost telephony and video conferencing replaces what thirty years ago would have had to be dealt with through a few laconic telegrams or telexes, we call this the *bandwidth effect*. The implication here is that recent developments in ICTs, in contrast to earlier ones, do not systematically move one up the codification

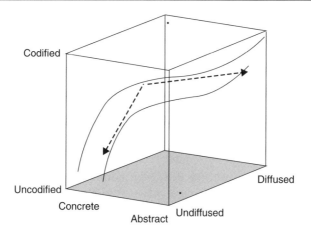

Figure 5.4. An ICT-induced shift in the diffusion curve

and abstraction scales of the I-Space. If anything, in the contest between a personal and an impersonal transactional order, the new ICTs favor a re-personalization of communication in the lower regions of the I-Space.

The rightward shift in the diffusion curve appears to privilege both market institutions over bureaucratic ones and clan-like institutions over fiefs. Evidence for the first kind of institutional change is to be found in the increasing use of outsourcing in markets by large firms. Far from getting larger—and hence more bureaucratic—the average size of firm in the United States has actually been falling over the past thirty years. Evidence for the second kind of institutional change has been the emergence of interpersonal networks and relational contracting between firms (Williamson 1985).

Increasing bandwidth does not eliminate the tensions between the local and the global, but it modifies the terms of the trade-off between them. In both the state and the corporate sector, there has taken place, to be sure, a further move away from bureaucratic institutions and toward market institutions—a product of the diffusion effect that is in line with the most popular interpretation of the globalization thesis. But, under the influence of the bandwidth effect, this is now accompanied by a parallel movement from fiefs to clans. Thus, whereas earlier ICTs had the effect of favoring institutional developments up the codification scale of the I-Space and toward greater abstraction, current trends in ICTs—that is, increasing bandwidth and decreasing costs—favor institutional developments to the right along the diffusion scale as well as some move back down the space toward more personalized transactional forms. If earlier ICTs privileged the development of bureaucracies and markets over fiefs and clans, the ones under development encourage the development of markets and clans over that of bureaucracies and fiefs. The earlier ICTs of the twentieth century helped to fuel an ideological tug-of-war in the upper regions and toward the front of the I-Space between a Marxist-Leninist bureaucratic order located on the left in the space and a capitalist market order located on the right. Can we expect a similar ideological struggle in the twenty-first century between the capitalist institutions of a global market order and the more communitarian institutions of local clan-like networks—that is, between a high-tech *Gesellschaft* and a high-tech *Gemeinschaft*? And does the rightward shift of the diffusion curve in Figure 5.4 imply that both corporate and state bureaucracies are about to disappear under the impact of the current generation of ICTs?

The downward arrow of Figure 5.4—the one that describes the bandwidth effect—effectively brings one closer to the chaotic regime in the I-Space. Now fear of chaos or an excessive preoccupation with order could keep one tethered to bureaucratic institutions that are ill-adapted to the social and economic opportunities opened up by the new ICTs—a challenge for both the current Chinese and Russian leadership. But is this fear of chaos justified? Much will depend on the properties of the edge-of-chaos, that is, on how large the complexity regime turns out to be. As we suggested earlier, effective fief, clan, and market institutions have the effect of stabilizing and extending the dominion of the complexity regime in the I-Space. Within that regime, the rightward shift of the diffusion curve in the I-Space provoked by the new ICTs is likely to lower both the costs of transacting in markets and clans and the risks of doing so. At the same time, the more effective fief, clan, and market institutions turn out to be, the wider their respective basins of attraction in the I-Space—that is, the broader the regions in the space from which they can 'attract' uncommitted transactions. By lowering the costs of transacting in clan and market institutions, the new ICTs will disproportionately extend their respective basins of attraction, thus bringing them into more intensive competition, not only with each other, but also with other transactional options in the I-Space. This would lead us to expect more frequent phase transitions between the different institutional orders in the I-Space as corporations and state bureaucracies find their uncommitted transactions oscillating between competing basins of attraction.

5.4. Implications

The upshot of the preceding analysis is that the benefit–cost ratio of transacting in bureaucracies and fiefs is likely to drop under the impact of the new ICTs and the shift of the diffusion curve that these will bring about in the I-Space, whereas the benefit–cost ratio of transacting in either markets or clans is likely to rise. Are bureaucracies and fiefs condemned to disappear then? No. Fiefs did not exactly disappear when modernizing European monarchies built the first state bureaucracies or when the first giant corporations entered the scene—indeed, they still thrive today in those niches of the information environment where valuable tacit knowledge remains the property of one or two individuals. On this argument, there is no reason to suppose that either bureaucracies or fiefs are going to be wiped out by any ICT-induced shift in the diffusion curve. But the curve shift does suggest that increased transparency is now both expected and possible, and that the information asymmetries that were until now the main source of bureaucratic and fief-like authority and power, are about to be further eroded—witness the impact of 'embedded reporting' on Western public perceptions of the Iraq War, or the impact that Internet websites such as netdoctor and webMD are already having on the expert power of doctors relative to that of their patients.

Just as the move of information and knowledge up the codification and abstraction dimensions of the I-Space transformed individuals from 'subjects' with obligations into 'citizens' with rights, so an increase in ICT-induced flows of information and knowledge to the right along the diffusion dimension in the space will transform them from being citizens into becoming *customers* of the state—a status that they now already enjoy with the corporate sector. And, just like the corporations that only survive by operating competitively in the market region of the I-Space, so the state will then only retain its popular legitimacy by satisfying its customers. These, however, do not like to think of themselves as belonging to an impersonal order, whether of the bureaucratic or of the market variety. Recall that moves up the codification and abstraction scales of the I-Space typically sacrifice to the needs of efficiency the very contextual richness that is a source of meaning for individuals. The anti-globalization movement is at least in part about the restoration of personhood, of community values associated with clan forms of governance.

A credible customer-centricity in both the state and the corporate sector, therefore, will move transactions both to the right and further down the I-Space, toward lower levels of codification and abstraction, but toward higher levels of diffusion. As a consequence, task complexity will increase and so will the challenges of managerial coordination. Effective coordination of complex processes will need to rely more on principles of self-organization bounded by regulation than on the more traditional command-and-control approaches that we associate with bureaucratic governance. In the future, corporate and state bureaucracies will be increasingly limited to managing boundary conditions—as regulators do in markets when they focus on zones of discontinuity in the behavior of selected variables—and, under the dynamic pull of overlapping and competing basins of attraction, these will be constantly shifting. What we need are institutions capable of managing complexity, either by *reducing* it through effective cognitive strategies—a move up the I-Space traditionally pursued by those who favor efficient markets and bureaucracies—or by *absorbing* it through effective relational strategies—a downward movement in the I-Space preferred by fiefs and clans (Boisot and Child 1999).

The new ICTs call for a paradigm shift in the way we conceive of organizations, a change that in many places confronts deeply rooted ideological commitment to the impartial—read impersonal—values of bureaucracy. As Marx would have put it, the relations of production are once more lagging behind the forces of production. By implication we also face a paradigm shift in our conception of both the state and the corporation. In the future political and managerial structures will be less unitary and more of a multilevel entangled set of hierarchies displaying emergent properties (Dupuy 1992; Thomas Kaminska-Labbé, and McKelvey 2005). Different levels in this hierarchy will compete with each other for voice and for resources. In some parts of the system, one level will predominate, in other parts, another level will. In both the state and the corporation, clan-like processes of political give-and-take will appear at many levels—regional, national, and supranational—and new rules-of-the-game will be needed to regulate what promises to be a messy process. The deeply rooted belief in a stable rational order amenable to the joint exercise of bureaucratic and market control is thus likely to be severely tested.

How will today's corporate and state bureaucracies be affected? Policymakers who confront this challenge could usefully heed some of the lessons on offer in the Chinese economic and institutional reforms, perhaps the most massive exercise in organizational change ever deliberately undertaken. Can the I-Space as a framework and the ICT-induced shift in the diffusion curve within it help to make sense of what happened to the country over the past twenty-eight years?

In its long history, China has always faced a trade-off between order and stagnation on the one hand, and disorder and dynamic growth on the other (Goodman 1994). In 1949, China attempted to create a Marxist-Leninist order located in bureaucracies in the I-Space, but, given the irrationalities of the command economy—one in which the corporate bureaucracies of state-owned enterprises (SOEs) imperceptibly shade off into those of the state—it got sucked back in fiefs by individuals who could only survive through the use of personal power rather than impersonal rules (Boisot and Child 1988).

The rightward shift of the diffusion curve brought about by the new ICTs in the past few years—the diffusion effect—is forcing a degree of decentralization on economic and social activity that exceeds the ability of China's central bureaucracy to control things. There is little indication that Chinese SOEs are adapting to the new order of things. They remain for the most part loss-making and hence dependent on the benevolence of a government that struggles to keep them competitive in China's emerging market environment (Steinfeld 1998).

However, mainly through benign neglect—after all, the attention of Chinese policymakers was focused primarily on salvaging SOEs—China has allowed a private sector to blossom into regional networks of small- and medium-sized enterprises that are based on personal relations of trust and prior familiarity (*guanxi*) and that collaborate and compete on an informal basis in clans (Boisot and Child 1996).

Because of their particularistic traditions and the ambiguities of their language, Chinese people exhibit a strong preference for the personal over the impersonal, and for the informal over the formal (Boisot and Child, 1988). This preference is particularly evident in the functioning of the overseas Chinese networks (Redding 1990). China has developed both cultural and institutional competences in the lower part of the I-Space and is thus well placed to take advantage of what we have called the bandwidth effect.

What we thus see in China is that the diffusion effect brought about a considerable weakening of bureaucratic institutions that maintained order but that allowed the State-run economy to stagnate. On the other hand, the bandwidth effect has allowed a considerable strengthening of clan-like networks that are hard for outsiders to penetrate and control, but that exhibit dynamism and adaptability when faced with the rapid changes that are taking place in the country (Boisot and Child 1996).

We have already suggested that the main challenge for China's state and corporate bureaucracies will be to move into the complex regime without spilling over into chaos. How can they do this? By incorporating into their structures, cultures, and processes two new institutional forms, one of which pursues cognitive strategies that reduce complexity, and the other of which pursues relational strategies that absorb it—respectively, markets and clans. The above analysis points to a massive challenge of organizational and cultural change. Are the country's state and corporate bureaucracies up to the task? Arguably many are not, and some are probably destined to disappear.

To summarize. By any standard, the results of China's reforms have been impressive. Over twenty-eight years, the country has changed beyond recognition—and for the better. Yet, surprisingly, the reforms were implemented with comparatively little coercion. The Chinese leadership merely allowed a measure of *organizational and institutional competition* that allowed new structures—many of them private, and hence small and fragile—to grow up alongside existing ones. The latter were then invited to adapt or die. Some adapted; many more died. Considering the sheer scale of the undertaking these massive changes took place with remarkably little conflict or resistance—the tragedy of Tiananmen Square of June 1989 notwithstanding. How so? Boisot and Child (1996) have argued that, although they never developed much competence in rational–legal bureaucracies and efficient markets—that is, in the upper regions of the I-Space—throughout its reforms, both the Chinese state and Chinese firms retained strong cultural and institutional competences in fiefs and clans—that is, in the lower regions of the I-Space. China thus appears to be well placed to exploit the organizational potential of the new ICTs in those regions.

5.5. Conclusion

In 1956, the cybernetician, William Ross Ashby formulated a *law of requisite variety.*. This held that a system, living or otherwise, survives by drawing on its internal resources to match the variety that impinges on it from its external environment. The variety that confronts corporate, national, and supranational bureaucracies has dramatically increased in the past decades, and, with scientific and technical progress accelerating, it is set to go on doing so. There is a general consensus that organizations and institutions are once more about to become transformed by the ICTs that are either already available or under development. Our analysis suggests that the centripetal forces that helped to build the modern nation-state are weakening while centrifugal ones are growing. The sciences of complexity teach us that new order can emerge out of chaos, but that this outcome is not guaranteed. The problem is that human beings have a deep need for a familiar order and for stable organizations to underpin it—one possible reason why so many older people in the former Soviet Union continue to pine for the impoverishing yet predictable stability of the planned economy. Chaos as such generates anxiety. Until now for many people, state and corporate bureaucracies, with their predictable rules and routines, constituted major sources of stability. With any move toward market and clan forms of governance, however, rules and routines are likely to become more transient and open to renegotiation. The prizes will then go to those with the ability to change the rules rather than to follow them. Bureaucratic organizations will thus lose much of their 'givenness' and will become more contingent, both for those who operate them and for those who are either served or controlled by them. The transformation will favor 'hunter-gatherers' rather than 'farmers' (Hurst 1995). The time for policymakers and corporate executives to ponder the nature of the challenge this transformation presents them with is now upon them.

References

Ashby, R. W. (1956). *An Introduction to Cybernetics*. London: Methuen.

Bennett, C. (1999). 'Quantum Information Theory', in A. Hey (ed.), *Feynman and Computation: Exploring the Limits of Computers*. Cambridge, MA: Perseus Books, pp. 177–90.

Boisot, M. (1995). *Information Space: A Framework for Learning in Organizations, Institutions and Culture*. London: Routledge.

—— (1998). *Knowledge Assets. Securing Competitive Advantage in the Information Economy*. New York: Oxford University Press.

—— and Child, J. (1988). 'The Iron Law of Fiefs: Bureaucratic Failure and the Problem of Governance in the Chinese Economic Reforms', *Administrative Science Quarterly*, 33: 507–27.

—— —— (1996). 'From Fiefs to Clans: Explaining China's Emerging Economic Order', *Administrative Science Quarterly*, 41(4): 600–28.

—— —— (1999). 'Organizations as Adaptive Systems in Complex Organizations: The Case of China', *Organization Science*, 10(3): 237–52.

—— and Li, Y. (2006). 'Organizational versus Market Knowledge: From Concrete Embodiment to Abstract Representation', *Journal of Bioeconomics*, 8: 219–51.

Chaitin, G. J. (1974). 'Information-Theoretic Computational Complexity', *IEEE Transactions, Information Theory*, 20(10).

Chandler, A. (1962). *Strategy and Structure: Chapters in the History of the American Industrial Enterprise*. Cambridge, MA: MIT Press.

Chandler, A. D. (1977). *The Visible Hand: The Managerial Revolution in American Business*. Cambridge, MA: Belknap Press at Harvard University Press.

Child, J. (1972). 'Organizational Structure, Environment and Performance: The Role of Strategic Choice', *Sociology*, 6: 1–22.

Cilliers, P. (1998). *Complexity and Postmodernism: Understanding Complex Systems*. London: Routledge.

Coase, R. (1937). 'The Nature of the Firm', *Economica* N.S. 4: 386–405.

Cohen, I. B. (1985). *Revolution of Science*. Cambridge, MA: Belknap Press at Harvard University Press.

Cowan, G. (1994). 'Conference Opening Remarks', in G. Cowan, D. Pines, and D. Meltzer (eds.), *Complexity: Metaphors, Models, and Reality*. Reading, MA: Addison-Wesley.

Donnithorne, A. (1981). *China's Economic System*. London: Hurst.

Dooley, K. and van de ven, A. (1999). 'Explaining Complex Organizational Dynamics', *Organization Science*, 10 (Number 3 May–June): 358–72.

Dretske, F. (1981). *Knowledge and the Flow of Information*. Cambridge, MA: MIT Press.

Dupuy, J. P. (1992). *Intoduction aux Sciences Sociales: Logique des Phenoménes Collectifs*. Paris: Ellipses.

Edelman, G. and Tononi, G. (2000). *A Universe of Consciousness: How Matter Becomes Imagination*. New York: Basic Books.

Eisenstein, E. (1983). *The Printing Revolution in Early Modern Europe*. Cambridge: Cambridge University Press.

Epstein, J. and Axtell, R. (1996). *Growing Artificial Societies: Social Sciences from the Bottom Up*. Cambridge, MA: MIT Press.

Evans, P. and Wuster, T. S. (2000). *Blown to Bits: How the New Economics of Information Transforms Strategy*. Boston, MA: Havard Business School Press.

Freeman, W. (2000). *Neurodynamics: An Exploration of Mesoscopic Brain Dynamics*. London: Springer-Verlag.

Gell-Mann, M. (1994). 'Complex Adaptive Systems', in G. Cowan, D. Pines, and D. Meltzer (eds.), *Complexity: Metaphors, Models, and Reality*. Reading, MA: Addison-Wesley.

Goodman, D. (1994). 'The Politics of Regionalism: Economic Development, Conflict and Negotiation', in D. Goodman and G. Segal (eds.), *China Deconstructs: Politics, Trade and Regionalism*. London: Routledge.

Goody, J. (1986). *The Logic of Writing and the Organization of Society*. Cambridge: Cambridge University Press.

Gouldner, A. (1954). *Patterns of Industrial Bureaucracy*. Gencoe, IL: Free Press.

Hahn, V. and Chater, N. (1997). 'Knowledge, Concepts and Categories', in K. Lambert and D. Shanks (eds.), *Concepts and Similarity*. Cambridge, MA: MIT Press.

Hicks, J. (1939). *Value and Capital: An Inquiry into Some Fundamental Principles of Economic Theory*. Oxford: Oxford University Press.

Hill, C. (1968). 'The Intellectual Origins of the Royal Society—London or Oxford', *Notes and Records of the Royal Society of London*, 23: 144–56.

Himmelfarb, G. (2004). *The Roads to Modernity: The British, French, and American Enlightenments*. New York: Vintage Books.

Hurst, D. (1995). *Crisis and Renewal: Meeting the Challeng of Organizational Change*. Boston, MA: Harvard Business School Press.

Kauffman, S. (1993). *The Origins of Order*. Oxford, UK: Oxford University Press.

Kolgomorov, A. (1965). 'Three Approaches for Defining the Concept of Information', *Information Transmission*, 1: 3–11.

Landes, D. (1999). *The Wealth and Poverty of Nations: Why Some Are so Rich and Some Are so Poor*: New York: W.W. Norton.

Langton, C. (1992). *Artificial Life*. Reading, MA: Addison-Wesley.

Lloyd, S. (2005). *Programming the Universe: A Quantum Computer Scientist Takes on the Cosmos*. London: Jonathan Cape.

Marris, R. (1964). *The Economic Theory of 'Managerial' Capitalism*: London: MacMillan.

Mokyr, J. (2002). *The Gifts of Athena: Historical Origins of the Knowledge Economy*. Princeton, NJ: Princeton University Press.

North, D. and Weingast, B. (1989). 'The Evolution of Institutions Governing Public Choice in 17th Century England', *Journal of Economic History*, 4: 803–32.

Nove, A. (1977). *The Soviet Economic System*. London: Allen & Unwin.

Ott, E., Grebogi, J., and Yorke, J. (1990). 'Controlling Chaos', *Physical Review Letters*, 64: 2296–99.

Pollard, S. (1965). *The Genesis of Modern Management: A Study of the Industrial Revolution in Great Britain*. Middlesex, UK: Penguin Books.

Prietula, M., Carley, K., and Gasser, L. (1998). *Simulating Organizations: Computational Models of Institutions and Groups*. Cambridge, MA: MIT Press.

Prigogine, I. (1980). *From Being to Becoming: Time and Complexity in the Physical Sciences*. New York: W.H. Freeman.

Redding, S. G. (1990). *The Spirit of Chinese Capitalism*. Berlin: Walter de Gruyter.

Rusnock, A. (1997). 'Quantification, Precision and Accuracy: Determinations of Populations in the Ancien Regime', in M. N. Wise (ed.), *The Values of Precision*. Princeton, NJ: Princeton University Press.

Shapin, S. (1994). *A Social History of Truth: Civility and Science in Seventeenth Century England*. Chicago, IL: University of Chicago Press.

Sipser, M. (1997). *Introduction to the Theory of Computation*. Boston, MA: PWS.

Steinfeld, E. S. (1998). *Forging Reform in China: The Fate on State-Owned Industry*. Cambridge Modern China Series. Cambridge: Cambridge University Press.

Taylor, M. (2001). *The Moment of Complexity: Emerging Network Culture*. Chicago, IL: University of Chicago Press.

Thomas, C., Kaminska-Labbé, R., and McKelvey, B. (2005). 'Managing the MNC and the Exploration/Exploitation Dilema: From Static Balance to Dynamic Oscillation', in G. Szulanski, Y. Doz, and J. Porac (eds.), *Advances in Strategic Management: Expanding Perspectives on the Strategy Process* (22: Elsevier).

Tönnies, F. (1955). *Community and Association*. London: Routledge & Kegan Paul.

Waldrop, M. M. (1992). *Complexity: The Emerging Science at the Edge of Order and Chaos*. Harmondsworth, UK: Penguin Books.

Weber, M. (1951). *The Religion of China: Confucianism and Taoism*. New York: Free Press.

Williamson, O. (1975). *Markets and Hierarchies: Analysis and Antitrust Implications*. New York: Free Press.

Williamson, O. E. (1985). *The Economic Institutions of Capitalism: Firms, Markets, Rational Contracting*. New York: Free Press.

Zurek, W. (1990). 'Algorithmic Information Content, Church-Turing Thesis, Physical Entropy, and Maxwell's Demon', in W. Zurek (ed.), *Complexity, Entropy and the Physics of Information*. Redwood City, CA: Addison-Wesley.

6

Property Rights and Information Flows: A Simulation Approach

Max H. Boisot, Ian C. MacMillan, and Kyeong Seok Han

6.1. Introduction

6.1.1. *The Issue Defined*

Two 'hot topics' are currently much discussed in the business world:

- Devin Leonard, writing in *The Business* of the 4/6th of May, 2003 wrote: 'If ever there was an industry in need of transformation, it's the music business. US music sales plunged 8.2% last year, largely because songs are being distributed free on the internet through illicit file-sharing destinations like KaZaA.... Unlike Napster, KaZaA and its brethren have no central servers, making them tougher to shut down. The majors have tried to come up with legal alternatives. But none of those ventures has taken off because they are too pricey and user-hostile... the five major record companies have had to slash costs in the face of declining sales. BMG laid off 1,400 people, EMI shed 1,800 and Sony Music recently announced it was reducing headcount by 1,000... Even with those cuts, average profit margins for the five majors have slipped to 5%, compared with 15% to 20% in the late 1980s when the CD came into vogue'.

- Millions of poor Africans are dying of AIDS. Pharmaceutical products exist to treat the condition and to prolong human life. People are coming to the view that these pharmaceutical products should be available for free or for a much-reduced price. Pharmaceutical

companies are in the dock for what are considered immoral monopolistic practices.

What do the two issues have in common? The answer is: intellectual
property rights (IPRs). The message of both vignettes is that if you relax
IPRs you lose money. The modern economy is a knowledge-based economy and its key resource is knowledge. Nakamura has shown that private
US firms, for example, currently invest at least US$1 trillion a year in
intangible assets and that the market value of the United States's capital stock of intangible assets is at least US$5 trillion (Nakamura 2003).
Intangible assets, however, remain hard to identify and to measure. As
a result, their management and valuation remain haphazard (Hands and
Lev 2003). Property rights on these kinds of assets cannot be fully secured;
as economists put it, they are only 'partially excludable'. Although the
knowledge economy needs a properly worked out set of IPRs, it turns out
that property rights in intangible assets can only take us a small part of
the way. The issue is partly a question of understanding and partly one of
fairness.

Understanding: Knowledge itself is not subject to the natural scarcities
of physical objects (Arrow 1962; Parker 1978). If you have the candy
then I cannot have the same candy. If you have the knowledge, by
contrast, then if you transfer it to me you still have the knowledge. Where
knowledge can be readily transferred from one party to another in this
way, it escapes the condition of natural scarcity that forms the physical
basis of our current understanding of property rights, namely, that a
physical object cannot be in two places at the same time. Consumption
of a knowledge good under certain circumstances is thus *non-rivalrous*
(Grant 1996). Since the main purpose of property rights is to establish an
acceptable procedure for the allocation of resources under conditions of
natural scarcity and of rivalry—they entitle the owner of a good to exclude
other from the consumption of that good where this would diminish the
utility that he or she would derive from it—why, some have argued, do
we need property rights for knowledge goods where these lack natural
scarcity?

Fairness: The issue of fairness is linked to that of understanding. Those
who argue that IPRs are an artificial restriction on the supply of what
should be a free good, focus on the marginal cost of supplying them.
If we take a pharmaceutical product as an example, the marginal cost
of supplying its physical content may be trivial—sometimes just a few
cents—and the marginal cost of supplying its information content *once*

this has been created—that is, its formulation, the process for making its active ingredients, etc.—may be little more than the cost of photocopying it (Shapiro and Varian 1999). Such an argument has been put forward by those who believe that, given the trivial costs of reproducing it, music should be freely downloadable on the Internet.

The counter-arguments have stressed a knowledge good's conditions of *production* rather than the conditions of its reproduction. The knowledge embedded in a pharmaceutical product, for example, may cost a few pennies to reproduce, but its initial development might have involved an expenditure of hundreds of millions of dollars of research and testing over several years with little or no guarantee that the money would ever be recovered. After all, they can be rendered obsolete by competing alternatives shortly after they have been launched. In the absence of secure IPRs, what incentive would there be to engage in the costly and risky production of knowledge goods?

The question, of course, is how robust do such rights need to be in order to elicit the required production and distribution of knowledge goods (Gilfillan 1964; Mansfield 1968; Penrose 1959). Make them too weak and spillovers will deprive knowledge creators of a fair reward for their efforts; knowledge goods will then be undersupplied. On the other hand, make them too strong and you end up with monopolistic regimes, and quite possibly once more with an undersupply of knowledge goods. At the policy level, the issue is one of balancing out the competing claims of producers and consumers so as to maximize total welfare. Lessig, for one, has argued that IPRs have now become too favorable to existing producers and that their 'winner-take-all' characteristics are constraining the creators of tomorrow (Lessig 2001). Where analytical schemes are available to do the balancing out, the problem can be considered a purely economic one. Where no such scheme is available, the balancing out will require a mixture of politics and economics, that is, it becomes a problem in political economy. Boisot has argued that the production and distribution of information and knowledge goods is not yet amenable to treatment by economics alone (Boisot 1998). Indeed, it may never be. What we therefore need is a political economy of information.

A workable set of IPRs requires a credible political economy of information and knowledge. This, in turn, can only be built on some understanding of how the emergence, development, and flow of knowledge within a population is stimulated or restricted by selective controls over its sharing and diffusion.

With the growth of the information economy, the proportion of knowledge-intensive goods to total goods is constantly increasing. Yet, are the terms on which the increase is being achieved, considered fair by the different stakeholders? Could such terms undermine the incentive to create future flows, as they now appear to be doing in the music industry? Getting IPRs 'right' is becoming a pressing requirement. Some of these goods will have their knowledge content deeply embedded in the physical product and will not be easy to copy—they exhibit a natural scarcity. Such will be the case, for example, with much of the 'architectural knowledge' that underpins the creation of complex pieces of machinery (Henderson and Clark 1990). Others, by contrast—clothes or furniture designs—will readily lend themselves to imitation by those with the necessary technical skills. Finally, a third group of goods—pure information goods such as books, music, or films—will be easy to copy directly and on a large scale. In all the above cases, the challenge will not just be one of striking some acceptable balance between the competing claims of producers and consumers; it will also involve finding a point of balance that is stable over time as well as being technically and legally enforceable.

6.1.2. *The Structure of the Chapter*

In this chapter, we look at how variations in IPRs regimes might affect the flow of new knowledge in an economic system. The relation between IPRs and knowledge creation has been the subject of extensive empirical investigations (Arrow 1962; Mansfield 1968). What has been less emphasized is the way that knowledge flow dynamics as a whole might be affected by variations in the strength of the property rights regime. In what follows we adopt a simulation approach to the issue. We take the ability to control knowledge spillovers as a proxy measure for an ability to establish property rights in such knowledge and hence to extract rents from it. We take the rate of obsolescence of knowledge as a proxy measure for the degree of turbulence induced by different regimes of technical change. The higher the rate of technical change, the higher the rate at which certain types of knowledge become obsolete and hence erode in value. We are interested in how the interaction of spillovers and obsolescence affect the value of knowledge.

We proceed as follows. In Section 6.2, we discuss the nature of property rights in more detail. Section 6.3 presents a conceptual framework, the Information Space, or *I-Space*, which relates the diffusion of knowledge to how far it has been structured (Boisot 1995, 1998). In Section 6.4, we briefly describe a simulation model, SimISpace, that implements the concepts of the I-Space. In Section 6.5, we describe some simulation runs and discuss them in Section 6.6. A conclusion follows in Section 6.7.

6.2. Property Rights

6.2.1. *What Are Property Rights?*

The seventeenth century theories of possessive individualism defined human society in terms of market relations, expressed in terms of contracts (Macpherson 1962). In his *Two Treatises on Government*, Locke made the preservation of property rights the centerpiece of his theory of civil society and government (Locke 1964; Macpherson 1962). The primary function of the state, according to Locke, is to enforce property rights and to arbitrate competing claims. In Section 173, Locke explains that: 'By Property I must be understood here, as in other places, to mean that Property which Men have in their Persons as well as Goods' (Locke 1964). Here was an indication that if we take ideas to 'reside' in persons, then ideas too could be subject to a property rights regime.

North and Thomas have claimed that the preeminence of the West owes a great deal to the quality of its institutional arrangements, foremost among these being those concerning property rights. As they put it: 'Efficient organization entails the establishment of institutional arrangements and property rights that create an incentive to channel individual economic effort into activities that bring the private rate of return close to the social rate of return' (North and Thomas 1973: 1). The modern corporation could not exist without a robust set of property rights (Liebeskind 1996). Where these are poorly defined, or where the private costs of defining and enforcing them exceed the private benefits or doing so, individuals will not normally undertake a given activity even if it is profitable (Barzel 1989; Demsetz 1967; Field 1989).

Barzel takes the property rights of individuals over assets to consist of the rights—or the power—to consume, to obtain income from, and to alienate those assets (Barzel 1989). Such rights are neither absolute—they have always been subject to some restrictions—nor constant. Property rights are an institution and hence a human construct. Although we find property *claims* in Nature—manifest in the defensive territorial behavior of different species—we find no property *rights* there except in the sense of might-is-right: the stronger will secure possession at the expense of the weaker (Maynard-Smith 1982). Whether brought about by the tribe or by the state, only collective action can legitimately replace might with right (Henriques 1983; Olson 1971).

Where states are weak, however, this does not happen. De Soto claims that it is the failure of a large proportion of a given population to achieve equitable access to property rights, and their consequent inability to convert their personal assets—often not inconsiderable—into capital, which explains the underdeveloped state of many economies—most specifically those of Latin America (De Soto 2000). In many third world countries, for example, people may possess land, but they cannot establish legal ownership of it. Property rights require a clear delimitation and establishment of title. De Soto argues that it is the difficulty of establishing unambiguous claims to property that prevents it from becoming capital in the hands of its possessor and hence of contributing to the process of wealth creation.

In sum, property rights clearly matter. But some property rights are easier to deal with than others. Some are easily aligned with our intuitive sense of natural justice. The enduring appeal of Marxism, for example, resides in the simplicity of Marx's labor theory of value:[1] each worker is entitled to the fruits of his own labor. The capitalist appropriates for himself part of that fruit and is therefore stealing what should naturally be regarded as the worker's property. The Marxist concept of property rights applies to the output of a physical process that can be measured in terms of time and effort expended. The labor theory of value derives the value of the output from the value of the input, which in turn is measured in terms of the socially necessary labor time[2] required to produce the input. Value, in effect, derives from labor costs incurred, and for that reason looks to a frozen past rather than to uncertain flows of future benefits (Dobb 1973; Marx 1972).

---

[1] The origins of the labor theory of value can be traced back to Aristotle. Its core tenets can be found in economic thinking from St Thomas Aquinas right down to Adam Smith and David Ricardo (Dobb 1973).

[2] Marx recognized that different levels of skill might command a different price. But this price was also set by the inputs that went into creating the skill, namely the time taken to acquire the skill.

6.2.2. *IPRs*

Rights in intellectual property differ in significant ways from those in physical property. The two we need to note here are that they are often hard to define and hard to enforce.

Defining them: Patents protect the principle that underpins a novel idea. It requires the citation of prior art and journal publications in order to clearly delineate the property rights or claims of the patent (Lanjouw and Schankerman 1997). Copyright, by contrast, protects the concrete form or expression rather than the abstract principle of an idea. In both cases, the process is more effective in the case of simple rather than complex ideas since the former are easier to describe unambiguously. But then, for the same reason, simple ideas are easier to 'invent around' than complex ones (Mansfield 1985).

Enforcing them: IPRs are much more difficult—and hence costly—to enforce than physical ones (Besen and Raskind 1991; Cheung 1982; Friedman, Landes, and Posner 1991; Liebeskind 1996). Even well-delineated patents give rise to ambiguous interpretations and, partly for that reason, the violation of property rights can remain undetected for a long time.

The US Constitution imposes on Congress an explicit obligation 'to promote the progress of science and useful arts, by securing for limited times to authors and inventors, the exclusive right to their respective writings and discoveries' (Shapiro and Varian 1999: 4). Where such rights cannot be secured, innovation may not take place. Countries that offer little protection for intellectual property see less innovation and more diversification across industries than those that do offer protection. In the former case, intellectual property is kept inside the firm as a 'secret' rather than externally traded (Khanna and Palepu 1997). Unfortunately, IPRs lack the intuitive appeal of property rights in tangible goods. They often challenge our notions of fairness and, as the music industry has discovered to its cost, do not always mobilize much popular support in their defense.

Why is it so much more difficult to come to grips with property rights in knowledge and ideas than with property rights in physical things? The history of science is replete with examples of major discoveries that were made quite casually or accidentally (Root-Bernstein 1989). The relationship between inputs (search) and outputs (discovery) is more often than not nonlinear and this nonlinearity can work both ways. Years of arduous intellectual search can yield pitifully modest results—and typically does. On the other hand, a casual observation can yield a discovery that can literally change the world. Although, as Louis Pasteur put it: 'luck favors the prepared mind', in the realm of the intellect, the labor theory of value has little or no purchase. A strict application of its tenets—that is, that value can be derived from effort alone—would lead to absurd results.

The linear logic of effort that underpins traditional concepts of property—we worked for it, therefore we own it—is by itself sufficient to call forth a labor supply provided that such labor is rewarded at least at its marginal rate of productivity. The nonlinear logic of luck and talent that underpins our concepts of intellectual property, however—a winner-take-all logic based on priority claims—will not necessarily call forth a supply of innovations if such property rights fail to secure an adequate reward (Mansfield 1968). Here, in contrast to more traditional property rights concepts, the rewards are for talented risk-taking under conditions of uncertainty rather than for efforts expended.

If the man in the street is guided by a logic of effort—and, by implication, by an intuitive and simple approach to property rights—the new economy, by contrast, is guided by a logic that is a mixture talent and luck as well as of effort. People have little difficulty identifying what constitutes fairness in a logic of effort. The process is linear. People also have little difficulty identifying what constitutes fairness in a logic of talent and luck where all possible outcomes can be specified *ex ante* and risks can be computed. Risks may be high, but uncertainty need not be and the process remains essentially linear. They thus have little difficulty understanding lotteries, gambling wagers, and can often identify with the winners.

People do have difficulty, however, with the concept of IPRs. The reason for this is that IPRs are often granted in return for reducing uncertainty rather than for bearing risk. As Frank Knight pointed out, whereas risk can be measured—that is, the probability calculus can be applied—uncertainty cannot (Knight 1921). The nonlinear nature of both knowledge creation and of the returns to knowledge creation in an IPRs system often makes these noncomputable. A lottery offers computable risks as do a horserace or a baseball game—the number of possible outcomes can be identified and assessed. Innovation on the other hand is characterized as much by uncertainty as by risk. The range of possible outcomes cannot be fully identified *ex ante* and neither can the probabilities that attach to such outcomes. Because the system is essentially noncomputable, it is hard to specify what fairness is, either *ex ante* or *ex post*.[3]

The rate of technical change has been increasing in the new economy. Rapidly diffusing new knowledge is making existing knowledge obsolete at a higher rate than ever before and levels of turbulence are high. We are living in a Schumpeterian environment subject to ever increasing 'gales of creative destruction' (Schumpeter 1934). With a properly functioning set of property rights institutions, such turbulence might be perceived as a source of opportunity for wealth creation. Absent such institutions, however, and the result could easily be a loss of competitiveness and a consequent loss of wealth.

The concept of fairness that underpins the institution of IPRs is at least in part culture-specific (Douglas 1986). The flow of knowledge across cultural boundaries is therefore likely to be different from what it is within them. According to Stan Shih, the CEO and founder of the Taiwanese group Acer, IPRs are a relatively new concept in Asian societies. Traditionally, it was assumed that innovations and intellectual property belonged to society and not to the individual or company that discovered them. And without proper legal protection, secrecy was the only way to benefit from a new idea (Romer 1998). The view of intellectual property in mainland China prior to the economic reforms illustrates this point. It was only in the 1980s that the People's Republic of China began to set up a patent system. Until then, locally generated scientific discoveries were freely available to all. The problems that this created were exacerbated by the idea—originating in the labor theory of value—that value resided in physical assets created by physical labor. In order to maintain the value of physical assets, therefore, one depreciated them very slowly. Inevitably, the intellectual property embodied in machinery also got replaced very slowly. Because of such sluggish depreciation schedules, China's pre-reform rate of technical change was very slow and little new knowledge accumulated in the system (Boisot and Child 1988). The labor theory of value clouded the understanding of IPRs, slowed down the rate at which one could obsolete old machinery, and undermined the country's technological evolution.

Lawrence Lessig, in his book *The Future of Ideas*, has argued that in the New Economy, we need a rebalancing of the competing claims of

---

[3] It thus escapes John Rawls's solution that specifies some original position under conditions of ignorance (Rawls 1971).

producers and consumers of intellectual property (Lessig 2001). In contrast to the case of property rights in physical goods, however, we may not be able to compute what constitutes a fair reward in an IPRs system—the granting of a temporary monopoly to inventors through the patent system merely highlights the problem rather than resolving it—but we may nonetheless be able to understand the issue better if we can identify how such rewards are likely to get distributed under different conditions of turbulence. We want to know how strong an IPR system should be, and under what circumstances.

> *How Strong?* Romer claims that it is possible to have a property rights system that gives too much protection. As he points out: 'If we had given AT&T an infinite-lived patent on the transistor, everybody in the world who wanted to do something new with the transistor would have had to negotiate a contract with the people at AT&T first. This could have significantly slowed down the development of the whole digital electronics industry' (Romer 1998).

> *Under what circumstances?* Schumpeter pointed out that at times, innovation unleashes 'gales of creative destruction' rendering much existing knowledge and techniques obsolete. Does the value of having IPRs vary with the degree of turbulence in the technological environment and the rate of knowledge obsolescence?

In what follows, we shall focus on two features of knowledge assets that are affected by the strength—or lack of it—of an IPRs regime: (*a*) the rate at which they spillover; (*b*) the rate at which they become obsolete. We first present a conceptual framework, the I-Space, which will help us to explore these two features.

6.3. The I-Space

As a conceptual framework, the I-Space is built on a simple and intuitively plausible premise: structured knowledge flows more readily and extensively than unstructured knowledge. While the concrete and tacit knowledge of the Zen master, for example, is only accessible to a small number of disciples through prolonged face-to-face interactions, the abstract, symbolic knowledge of prices and quantities manipulated by a bond trader is often available to a global market in a matter of seconds. Human knowledge is built up through the twin processes of discrimination and association (Thelen and Smith 1994). Framing these as information processes, the I-Space takes information structuring as being achieved through two cognitive activities: codification and abstraction.

6.3.1. *Codification, Abstraction, and Diffusion*

Codification articulates and helps to distinguish from each other the categories that we draw upon to make sense of our world. The degree to which any given phenomenon is codified can be measured by the amount of data processing required to categorize it. Generally speaking, the more complex or the vaguer a phenomenon or the categories that we draw upon to apprehend it—that is, the less codified it is—the greater the data-processing effort that we will be called upon to make.[4]

Abstraction, by treating things that are different as if they were the same (Dretske 1981), reduces the number of categories that we need to draw upon in order to apprehend a phenomenon. Concrete experiences offer a potentially infinite number of categories to draw upon. This increases our data-processing load. When two categories exhibit a high degree of association, however—that is, they are highly correlated—one can stand in lieu of the other. The fewer the categories that we need to draw upon to make sense of phenomena, the more abstract our experience of them.

Codification and abstraction work in tandem. Codification facilitates the associations required to achieve abstraction, and abstraction, in turn, by keeping the number of categories needed down to a minimum, reduces the data-processing load associated with the act of categorization. Taken together, they constitute joint cognitive strategies for economizing on data processing. The result is more and usually better structured data. Better-structured data, in turn, by reducing encoding, transmission, and decoding efforts, facilitates and speeds up the diffusion of knowledge within a given population of agents while economizing on communicative resources.

The relationship between the codification, abstraction, and diffusion of knowledge is illustrated by the diffusion curve of Figure 6.1. The figure tells us that the more codified and abstract a given message, the larger the population of data-processing agents that it can be diffused to in a given time period. Such agents might be individual human beings, but they might also be aggregates of these such as small groups, departments, or whole organizations, such as firms. All that is required to establish the candidacy of an agent is firstly, an ability to receive, process, and transmit

---

[4] The way that we measure codification bears more than a passing ressemblance to the way that Kolmogorov or Chaitin measure complexity (Chaitin 1974; Kolmogorov 1965).

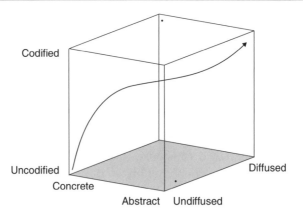

Figure 6.1. The Diffusion Curve in the I-Space

data to other agents within a population, and secondly, a capacity for unified agency.

6.3.2. *Value in the I-Space*

In moving information and knowledge around the space, an agent incurs both costs and risks. There is no guarantee that a learning cycle can be completed. How, then, does an agent extract enough value from its learning processes to compensate for the efforts and risks incurred? If we take the term value in its economic sense, then it must involve a mixture of utility and scarcity (Walras 1926). The utility of knowledge is a function of both its content and its form. The I-Space says nothing about the content of knowledge.

Codification and abstraction relate only to the form that knowledge can take, whatever its content. In the I-Space, utility of form is achieved by moving information up the space toward higher levels of codification and abstraction. Codification and abstraction together economize on data processing and transmission resources while increasing the reliability and generalizability of information so created. Codification and abstraction also make it easier to build robust and durable linkages between different items of knowledge, thus reducing their vulnerability to obsolescence and further enhancing their utility. Moving up toward greater codification and abstraction thus facilitates the linking together of knowledge assets into more sophisticated and complex networks. Scarcity, by contrast, is achieved by keeping the knowledge assets created located toward the left hand side of the diffusion curve—clearly, the scarcity of information will

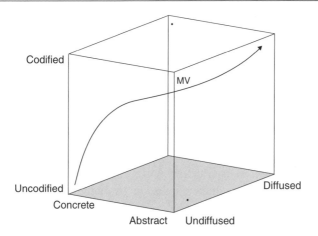

Figure 6.2. Maximum Value (MV) in the I-Space

be inversely related to the number of people who possess it. Here we encounter a difficulty that is unique to knowledge goods. As indicated in Figure 6.2, maximum value is achieved in the I-Space at point MV, that is, at the point where codification and abstraction are at a maximum and where diffusion is at a minimum. Yet, as can be seen from the diffusion curve, this is a point at which, on account of its high degree of codification and abstraction, the *diffusibility* of knowledge goods is also at a maximum. The point is therefore unstable and a cost must therefore be incurred—in patenting, in secrecy, etc.—to prevent diffusion taking place.

With a knowledge good, then, and in contrast to the case of a purely physical good, utility and scarcity are inversely related. The greater the utility achieved, the more difficult it becomes to secure the scarcity necessary to extract full value from the good in question. The paradoxical nature of value in the case of an information good can be dealt with in two ways:

By hoarding—this strategy builds upon the diffusion dynamics suggested by Figure 6.1. It is assumed that all the potential economic returns offered by a given knowledge asset over and above a normal accounting rate of return—that is, its *rent*—will be exhausted by the time it has diffused to the population as a whole. The strategy then consists of reducing its tendency to spillover in order to maintain its rent at some positive level.

By sharing—It is assumed that the creation of new knowledge assets is in some way dependent on the knowledge assets currently being diffused, and that the value of these new knowledge assets will be greater than that lost through the erosion of scarcity brought about by diffusion of existing knowledge assets. The strategy then consists of learning faster than competitors in order to secure first-mover advantages in the creation of new knowledge and the destruction of existing knowledge.

6.3.3. *Property Rights Implications of the Paradox of Value*

Hoarding strategies focus on preserving and exploiting existing knowledge whereas sharing strategies focus on challenging or destroying such knowledge through new knowledge creation—that is, through exploration and innovation (Nelson and Winter 1982, March 1991). The value of existing knowledge is thus precarious on two accounts:

1. Through spillovers it loses its *scarcity*. On account of its greater proneness to rapid diffusion, the loss of scarcity will erode the value of well codified and abstract knowledge more rapidly and more powerfully than it will that of uncodified and concrete knowledge. Where codified and abstract knowledge—the kind of knowledge that we typically associate with science and technology—gives rise to IPRs, it is often protected by *patents*.

2. New knowledge, by rendering existing knowledge obsolescent, destroys its *utility*. Such destruction will erode the value of uncodified and concrete knowledge more rapidly and more powerfully than that of codified and abstract knowledge. Knowledge that is uncodified and concrete lacks stability and is thus costly to store and preserve. It is typically highly 'situated' and hence only of local utility. Where it remains uncodified and concrete—one aims to formalize scientific and technical knowledge (Nonaka and Takeuchi 1995)—it is the kind of knowledge that we typically associate with arts and literature. Where it gives rise to IPRs, it does so through *copyright*.

We locate the knowledge associated respectively with patents and copyrights in the I-Space in Figure 6.3.

An IPR regime, by affecting both the rate at which knowledge diffuses out and the rate at which it is rendered obsolete, has a significant impact on its value (Lessig 2001). Make the regime too strong, and society ends up paying too much for its existing stock of intellectual property. New knowledge creators then also find it difficult to displace incumbents. Make

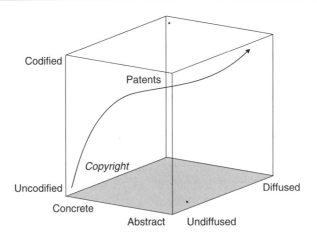

Figure 6.3. Patents versus Copyright Knowledge in the I-Space

it too weak, and you deprive would-be innovators of any incentive to contribute new value-adding knowledge to the social stock.

Creative destruction is a complex phenomenon that does not lend itself to easy theorizing or predictions. For this reason we will approach it using simulation rather than analytical methods. Our aim is to use a simulation model as a support to our theorizing activities (Carley 1999; Carley and Lee 1998). The model will help us to generate empirically testable hypotheses concerning the relationship between different kinds of property rights regime and the phenomenon of creative destruction. In Section 6.4 we present in outline form an agent-based simulation model—SimISpace—that will be used to explore the issue.

6.4. SimISpace: An Agent-based Simulation Model

6.4.1. *Model Architecture*

SimISpace is a multiagent simulation characterized by mixture of competition and collaboration; it implements some of the main features of the I-Space as a conceptual model.[5] SimISpace has two model components:

1. *Agents*—In SimISpace, individual agents aim at surviving and maximizing their wealth. Although at this stage in the simulation's

---

[5] A more detailed description of SimISpace can be found at http://www.wep.wharton.upenn.edu/Research/SimISpace20031021.pdf

development they have no individual learning capacity—that is, they have no memory—the game as a whole displays elements of evolutionary behavior. Profits, the difference between the rents that agents earn and the costs that they incur in doing so, offer agents a means of survival and if they run out of profits they are 'cropped' from the simulation—that is, they are selected out. Agents, however, also have the option of exiting the simulation while they are still ahead.

2. *Knowledge Assets*—SimISpace is populated by agents each of which carries an endowment of knowledge assets in its head. A knowledge asset has a location in the I-Space and takes the form a node or a link between nodes.[6] The location of each node and link in the I-Space determines its revenue-generating potential and hence the price an agent can charge for it. The more codified and abstract a knowledge asset the greater its utility and hence the greater its price. Likewise, the less diffused a knowledge asset, the scarcer it is and hence, again, the greater its price. The different locations in the I-Space thus have different price multipliers applied to them to reflect their different degrees of utility and scarcity. Agents can enhance the prices their knowledge assets command—and hence their rent-generating potential—in two ways: *(a)* by investments in the codification, abstraction, absorption, and internalization phases of a Social Learning Cycle (SLC) (Boisot, 1998) that offer the possibility of creating new knowledge assets in the I-Space; *(b)* by combining nodes and links into networks that under certain circumstances can be *nested* and in this way building up more complex knowledge assets.

Knowledge assets are not fully under the control of the agents who possess them. First, they are subject to diffusion forces, either through the deliberate exchange of assets between agents, or through unintended spillovers. Through spillovers, knowledge can diffuse unpredictably to other agents or to a population located beyond the diffusion scale and hence located outside the simulation. Such spillovers constitute a social externality that can arise from the expiry of a patent, from inventing around a patent, from inadequate protection of one's intellectual property, and so forth. Second, knowledge assets can also grow obsolete over time as new and more effective knowledge replaces the

---

[6] Here we follow Henderson and Clark (1990) by distinguishing between knowledge residing in components (nodes) and knowledge residing in the architecture (links).

existing stock—a process that Schumpeter labeled creative destruction (Schumpeter 1934). The proneness of the asset to spillover or to obsolescence also varies with its location in the I-Space. Both spillover and obsolescence in the simulation—have the effect of eroding the economic rents that an agent can earn from a given stock of knowledge assets. As would be predicted by the I-Space—and as was discussed in Section 6.3—the spillover rate is higher when a knowledge asset is codified and abstract since it can travel more easily. By contrast, the obsolescence rate is higher when a knowledge asset is uncodified and concrete—that is, it has not been articulated enough to get stabilized, registered, stored, and protected. The degree of codification and abstraction of knowledge assets thus affects their proneness to spillovers (their diffusibility) and their proneness to obsolescence in opposite ways. Spillovers and obsolescence will be the focus of the simulation runs that we present in Section 6.5.

Natural selection is at work in SimISpace at two levels. Agents survive by making good use of their knowledge assets, either directly to earn revenue—rents[7]—or indirectly by entering into trades with other agents who will then themselves use them directly. Agents that fail to make direct or indirect use of their knowledge assets in a timely fashion are eventually likely to get selected out of the simulation—that is, to get 'cropped'. Existing agents, however, have the option of quitting the game while they are ahead and before they are cropped. Conversely, new agents can be drawn into the game if the environment becomes sufficiently rich in opportunities, that is, if the rental potential of the knowledge assets currently in play across all agents is high enough. The rate of new agent entries is based on total mean rents generated by the game in any given period. Both entry and exit rates are based on the difference in total mean rents between two periods.

In what follows, we first briefly explore how well SimISpace implements the basic assumptions that underpin our conceptual framework, the I-Space—that is, we validate the simulation (Gilbert and Troitzsch 1999). The number of SimISpace parameters—sixty-five variables can be parametized in the model—makes it possible to fine-tune the simulation in order to model a variety of diverse situations with a considerable degree of flexibility, thus improving its grounding in the real world. In the following sections we focus primarily on the parameters that shape

---

[7] SimISpace only models the *economic rental* component of agent revenue. Agents get cropped not because they have gone bankrupt, but because they fail to earn the minimum level of rents that allow them to stay in the game.

the 'creative destruction' environment that agents find themselves in, namely, spillover and obsolescence rates. Specifically, we are interested in the extent to which two different types of IPRs regimes that can be found in the real world, patents, and copyright, can modify the impact that spillovers and obsolescence have on rents. The tightness of a given property rights regime is indexed by the constraints that it imposes on the diffusibility of knowledge. We can thus simulate such tightness through an appropriate setting of the spillover parameter. Whether we are dealing with the kind of knowledge that would be subject to patents or to copyright can be established through a setting of the obsolescence parameter— low obsolescence corresponding to a patent regime and high obsolescence corresponding to a copyright regime.

Through such parameter settings we can explore the two questions posed at the end of Section 6.2: how strong should an IPRs regime be and under what circumstances? We do so by looking firstly at how much total knowledge (total nodes and links) is present at the end of the simulation under different conditions of spillover and obsolescence as compared with the beginning. This gives us the gross benefit to society offered by a given regime of IPRs. The benefit includes both the creation of new knowledge— that is, *invention*—and its embodiment in 'new combinations' and its spread from one agent to another—that is, *innovation* (Schumpeter 1934). We then assess how much total rent was captured by all agents in the course of the simulation under different conditions of spillover and obsolescence. Total rent paid to agents measures the gross costs to society offered by the regime. Finally we look at the rental cost to society per unit of knowledge created by all agents under different conditions of spillover and obsolescence.

6.5. Knowledge Creation Under Different Regimes: A Simulation

To explore the influence of property rights under different conditions of knowledge flows we carried out a set of simulations in which we systematically varied the rates, respectively, of obsolescence and spillover. Recall that obsolescence measures the speed at which the utility of knowledge assets erodes, and that spillover measures the speed at which knowledge flows from agents inside the simulation either to other agents or to the general population—both erode the price that an agent can charge for the use of a knowledge asset. We take obsolescence as a proxy measure of creative destruction taking place in a given industry or economy. We take spillover as a proxy measure of the solidity of the property rights regime available to protect agent rents. A study of both will thus help us to address the two questions posed at the end of Section 6.2.

We ran multiple sets of simulations, each set with a different combination of obsolescence and spillover. Both obsolescence and spillover conditions were set at five levels: very low, low, average, high, and very high. This gave twenty-five sets of simulation conditions, with the combinations ranging from very high obsolescence with very high spillover to very low obsolescence with very low spillover. 200 simulations were run for each combination of conditions, resulting in 5,000 individual simulations (25 × 200) in total. The data analyzes were carried out using the average scores (with their standard deviations) of the 200 simulations for each condition.

In each individual simulation study we allowed the simulation to run for eighty periods, then determined the mean and standard deviation for the periods 41 to 80 for the following variables:

- The average of the maximum codification, abstraction, and diffusion knowledge attained by agents in each simulation condition. This taps the extent to which the structure of knowledge evolves and gets distributed under different obsolescence and spillover conditions.
- Total number of knowledge assets—nodes and links together— created from period 41 to period 80.
- Total cumulative economic rent earned by all agents from their knowledge assets (including agents that exited or were cropped) from period 41 to period 80.
- The average economic rent captured per unit of knowledge asset (total cumulative economic rents/total cumulative knowledge) between period 41 and period 80.

The reason that we focused on periods 41 to 80 is that after 40 periods the simulation's relatively unstable 'start-up' conditions began to settle down and the simulation then evinces relatively steady trends in the key variables.[8]

---

[8] When the results for the entire number of periods 1 to 80 are compared we get essentially the same results, but with much higher standard deviations for each combination of decay conditions.

The data are reported in seven tables in the Appendix, they show the means and standard deviations of the key variables of interest for each combination of conditions simulated. We conducted comparison of means tests for 'corner conditions' (namely highest obsolescence/highest spillover, highest obsolescence/lowest spillover, lowest obsolescence/highest spillover, and lowest obsolescence/lowest spillover). With one exception we universally found statistically significant differences between means. The tables provided the base data for the graphs presented below.

6.5.1. *Validating the Baseline Model*

The results, plotted in Figures 6.4 to 6.6, display evidence that validates the baseline model. Figure 6.4 plots the maximum codification of knowledge that is achieved by agents in the simulations against the spillover rate under different obsolescence conditions. For each simulation we recorded the maximum level of codification of knowledge that was reached. For each spillover/obsolescence condition, we then calculated the average of these maximum codifications achieved for the 200 simulations that we ran. These average maxima are plotted against spillover rate in Figure 6.4, which shows that increasing the spillover rate causes an increase in the level of codification attained for all obsolescence conditions. It also shows that as the rate of obsolescence of knowledge decreases from very high (the bottom, 0.02 line) to very low (the top, 0.01 line), the codification attained by knowledge increases. The simulation model thus implements the key causal relationships between spillover rate, obsolescence rate and codification specified by the I-Space framework as discussed in Section 6.4.

Figure 6.5 plots different maximum levels of abstraction for knowledge assets against their spillover rate under different obsolescence conditions. This result also validates one of the key causal relationships specified by the I-Space and discussed in Section 6.4, namely, that increasing spillover increases the level of abstraction attained and decreasing obsolescence also increases it.

We also tracked the diffusion of knowledge assets to other agents in the course of the simulation. For each spillover/obsolescence combination in the simulation we determined the maximum diffusion that occurred and calculated the average maximum diffusion score for the 200 runs in each set. Figure 6.6 plots maximum level of diffusion attained by knowledge assets against their spillover rate for different rates of obsolescence. It shows that for all levels of obsolescence the spillover rate causes an

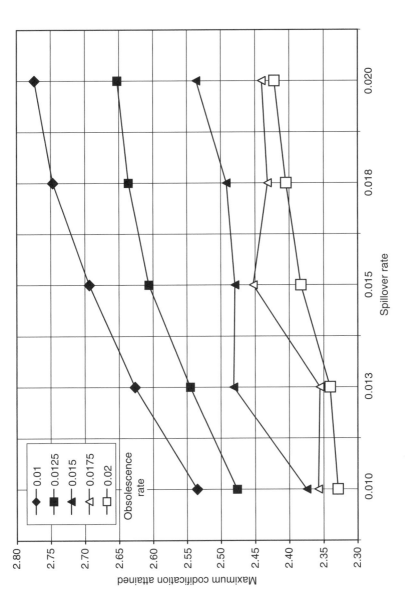

Figure 6.4. Maximum Codification Attained vs. Spillover Rate for Different Obsolescence Rates

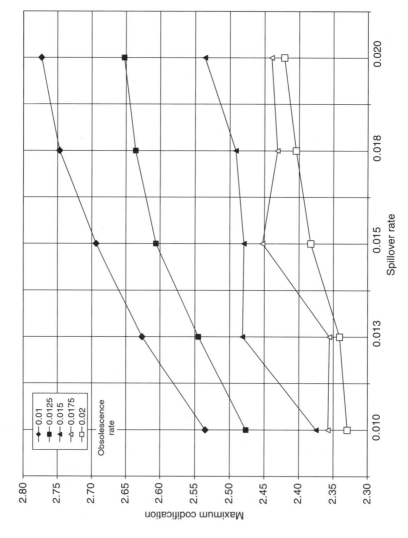

Figure 6.5. Maximum Codification Attained vs. Spillover Rate for Different Obsolescence Rates

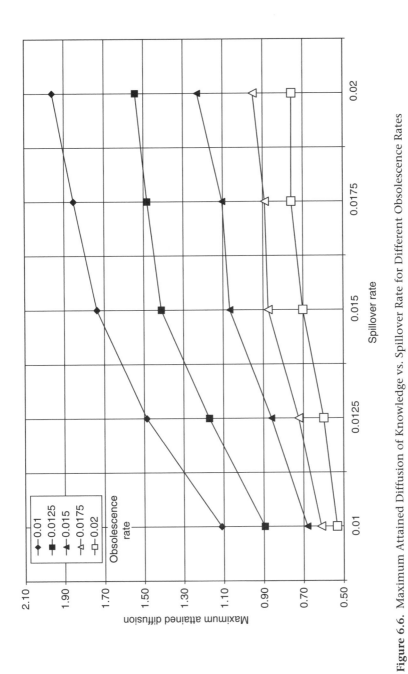

Figure 6.6. Maximum Attained Diffusion of Knowledge *vs.* Spillover Rate for Different Obsolescence Rates

increase in the level of diffusion attained and. As obsolescence increases from 0.01 (the top line) to 0.02 (the bottom line), however, the maximum diffusion attained decreases. This validates the model's treatment of the third key causal relationship specified by the I-Space: increasing spillover increases the level of diffusion attained; increasing obsolescence inhibits diffusion.

The similarity of our results for abstraction and codification justifies reducing the structuring of knowledge to a single measure we called knowledge structuring, which simplifies the discussion below. For each simulation we counted up all the rents captured by all agents from period 41 to 80, including rents of agents who exited or were cropped. Then we calculated the average of these total rents per knowledge asset for the 200 simulations of each spillover/obsolescence combination. Figure 6.7 plots the total economic rents extracted by agents per knowledge asset against the degree of structure of the knowledge assets—a measure created by adding together the scores for abstraction and codification. We see from the figure that increases in knowledge structuring causes increases in rent per knowledge asset for all levels of obsolescence, further validating the simulation model.

6.5.2. *Experimental Findings*

Figures 6.8 to 6.11 move us beyond validation with respect to the I-Space and allow us to explore the impact of changing spillover and obsolescence rates on knowledge creation and on the resultant rent generation—that is, on its cost to society. In the simulation we took knowledge generation as stemming from two sources identified by Schumpeter (1934): from *invention*, the creation of entirely new knowledge by an agent; and from *innovation*, the subsequent embodiment of that knowledge in 'new combinations' and its spread from one agent to another. Knowledge generation combines these into a single measure. For each run we determined the total amount of knowledge (new nodes and links) generated in the population of agents during that run. We then calculated the average of these totals for the 200 simulations done for each spillover/obsolescence combination. Figure 6.8 plots total knowledge generated against the structure of that knowledge for different spillover and obsolescence rates.

Figure 6.8 shows that for all levels of obsolescence, increasing spillover rates increases total knowledge generation. Furthermore decreases in obsolescence cause increases in the total knowledge created. Since our definition of total knowledge generated includes innovation—that is, the

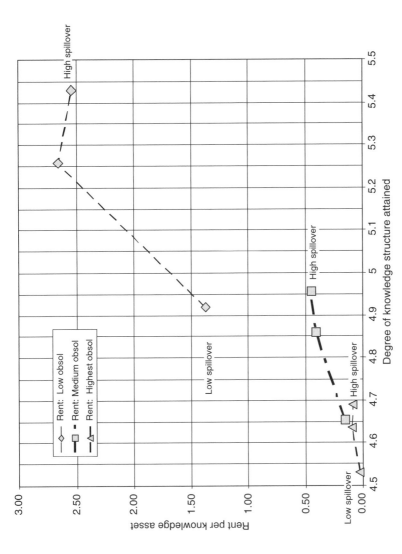

Figure 6.7. Degree of Knowledge Structure Attained vs. Rent per Knowledge Asset Generated

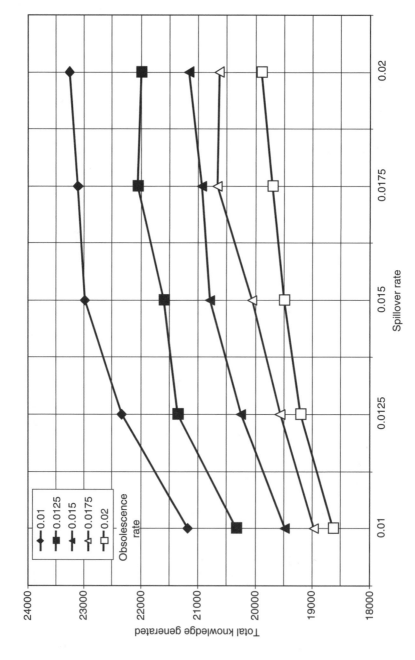

Figure 6.8. Total Knowledge Generated vs. Spillover Rate for Different Obsolescence Rates

rate at which knowledge is adopted within the agent community—the positive association with spillover is hardly a cause for surprise. Note, however, that for all obsolescence conditions, the slope of the curve showing *rate* of knowledge generation increases faster at lower rates of spillover and flattens off at high rates of spillover. Thus increasing the spillover rate pays off via rate of increase in total knowledge generation (slope of the lines in Figure 6.8) whatever the obsolescence rate. Knowledge generation also increases as the rate of obsolescence decreases from 0.02 to 0.01, and the effect is significantly greater at high spillover rates. Finally, knowledge generation is much more sensitive to changes in obsolescence rates than spillover rates, especially when spillover rates are low. Thus, increasing spillover rate pays off most when both spillover and obsolescence are low, and least when they are both high.

But at what cost to society (or rewards to the agents)? Economic rents measure both the gross benefits received by the population of agents for the creation and exploitation of knowledge as well as the gross costs to society of having agents create knowledge of a given degree of structure. Figure 6.9 presents the total rent paid to agents at different levels of spillover and obsolescence. The figure shows that increasing the spillover rate generates little cost for society when obsolescence is high (0.02 line), but increasing spillover begins to markedly increase total rents paid by society as the obsolescence rate decreases (0.01 line).

The prospects of securing rents affect an agents' motivation to create new knowledge. Since the total amounts of knowledge generated reflect the total rents paid in each regime, we were also interested in the total economic rent captured from society per knowledge asset created. Figure 6.10 plots the total rent generated per knowledge asset against the total amount of knowledge created in the simulation, for different obsolescence and spillover conditions. The total amount of knowledge created measures the level of innovation achieved by the population of agents, while the rent per knowledge asset captures the level of reward agents receive for achieving it. The figure shows that as the rate of obsolescence decreases from 0.02 (bottom curve) to 0.01 (top curve), the *amount* of knowledge created increases, but that this increase is accompanied by a very substantial increase in the total rent per knowledge asset paid by society to the agents creating it.

The graphs also show that at high obsolescence rates (0.02, bottom curve), increasing the spillover rate (i.e. relaxing property rights) causes the amount of knowledge created to increase—from 18,500 to 20,000 knowledge assets—but has little effect on the total rent paid

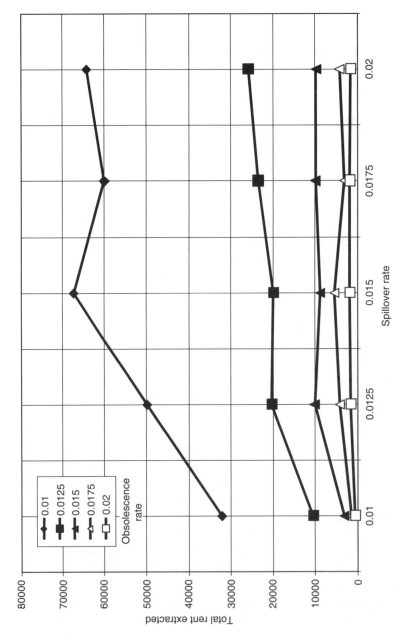

Figure 6.9. Total Rent Extracted by Agents vs. Spillover Rate for Different Obsolescence Rates

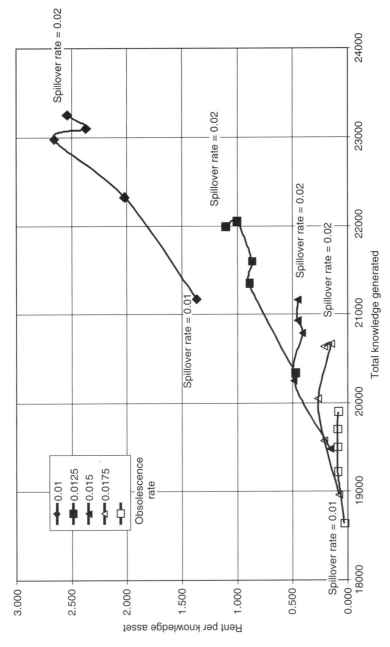

Figure 6.10. Total Knowledge Generated *vs.* Rent per Unit Knowledge for Different Spillover/Obsolescence Rates

per knowledge asset. However at low obsolescence rates (top curve), increasing the spillover rate (i.e. relaxing property rights) also increases knowledge creation (from just over 21,000 to 23,000) but this increase in spillover rate significantly increases the total rents per knowledge asset paid by society to agents in the simulation newly in possession of the knowledge—from less than 1.5 to over 2.5 per knowledge asset. Increasing spillover thus causes increases in the supply of knowledge created at little cost to society under high obsolescence conditions, but it does so at a substantial cost to society under low obsolescence conditions. At high levels of spillover particularly for low obsolescence, the graphs tend to be less stable, resulting in wavy lines. Our summary interpretation of this graph is that under low obsolescence conditions, increasing property rights—and thereby reducing spillover rates—offers huge benefits in terms of rent per knowledge asset paid by society to possessors of knowledge, provided a reduction in the amount of knowledge generated is acceptable. However at high obsolescence rates increasing property rights (reducing spillover rate) reduces the amount of knowledge generated *without* much benefit in terms of reduced cost per knowledge asset to society.

Figure 6.10 provides further validation of SimISpace. Recall from Section 6.4 that under conditions of high spillover and low obsolescence the levels of both codification and abstraction of knowledge will be at their highest. Since we stipulated that rents are a positive function of the degree of knowledge structuring, the unit value of such knowledge should also be at its highest.

What we see is that with decreasing obsolescence rates, we move up and toward the right of the diagram, and this upward right shift is accentuated the greater the spillover rate. So, as the obsolescence rate decreases—reflecting higher levels of codification and abstraction—relaxing property rights (increasing spillover rates) increases the total supply of generated knowledge. But since decreasing obsolescence rates also increases the average durability of this knowledge, it has the effect of increasing the total rents earned by the agent population over the life of a given knowledge asset.

6.6. Interpretation

In Section 6.2 we asked how strong an IPR regime should be and under what circumstances. In exploring these questions under different spillover and obsolescence conditions, we saw that by varying the parameter setting for diffusion and for obsolescence, we got very different results for knowledge structuring, knowledge creation and knowledge cost to society. Since the purpose of such modeling is to generate rather than test hypotheses, what hypotheses does our simulation suggest?

6.6.1. *Different Property Rights Regimes*

First, what hypotheses do these results suggest for policy decisions regarding property rights? The overall message of Figure 6.10 is that at high rates of obsolescence (bottom curve in Figure 6.10), tightening up property rights (i.e. reducing spillover) reduces knowledge supply by 1,260 knowledge assets but achieves little reduction in total cost to society per knowledge asset generated. In contrast, under low obsolescence conditions (the topmost curve in Figure 6.10), tightening up property rights leads to a somewhat greater reduction in total knowledge produced than for high obsolescence conditions, but the reduction in total rent generated per knowledge asset is now substantial. This suggests that the strength of a property rights regime should take into account the obsolescence rate. Furthermore, as indicated in Figure 6.10, for moderate obsolescence rates there are indications of a nonlinear effect associated with a relaxation of property rights—total rents per knowledge asset first rise then fall off as spillover rates increase.

Irrespective of spillover levels, the low-obsolescence conditions in the simulation typically have higher levels of abstraction (Figure 6.5), of codification (Figure 6.6), and of total rent generate per knowledge asset (Figure 6.7). As we suggested in Section 6.3, low obsolescence conditions represent the more cumulative, durable, science-based knowledge associated with patenting and scientific publication. The high obsolescence condition, by contrast—characterized by lower total rents generated per knowledge asset and lower degrees of codification and abstraction—represents the more transient and noncumulative type of knowledge associated with copyright, the media and entertainment.

Under this interpretation we could hypothesize that, given the nonlinear relationship between total rent generated per knowledge asset and total knowledge created that obtains under high obsolescence conditions (see Figure 6.10), relaxing property rights (spillover from 0.015 to 0.02) leads to a small reduction in total rents paid to the agents creating knowledge while also increasing the amount of knowledge created. It is here that Lessig's arguments in favor of a greater leakiness of property rights finds support (Lessig 2001). Indeed, his book, *The Future of Ideas*, focuses almost exclusively on issues of knowledge subject to copyright, that is, knowledge that is comparatively low in codification and abstraction. In the case of patented knowledge, by contrast, our simulation results suggest that the relaxation of property rights may actually incur a substantial cost for society in terms of total rents paid to possessors of knowledge. Here, tightening property rights may well allow society to get better value for money from knowledge creation than relaxing them.

We summarize our findings in the following propositions:

Proposition 1: Increases in spillover rate and deceases in obsolescence rates cause the average level of codification and abstraction (structuring) of knowledge assets held by agents to go up.

Proposition 1.1: In setting the appropriate spillover rate of a property rights regime, the obsolescence rate of the relevant knowledge assets frames the trade off between the production of new knowledge assets and the costs to society in rents paid to agents.

Proposition 1.2: When the degree of knowledge structuring is low (associated with high obsolescence and low spillover) relaxing property rights (copyright protection) beyond a certain point moderately reduces total rents earned per knowledge asset while increasing the amount knowledge produced more substantially. When the degree of knowledge structuring is high (associated with low obsolescence and high diffusion), relaxing property rights (patent protection)—that is, increasing spillover—increases knowledge production substantially while increasing the total rental cost of such knowledge to society very substantially.

Proposition 2: Low rates of obsolescence increase the importance of the overall rent-enhancing effects of high rates of spillover, whereas high rates of obsolescence undermine whatever rent-enhancing effects high rates of spillover might have.

Increases in economic rents associated with decreasing obsolescence are unmatched by concomitant increases in knowledge created. However, as indicated by Table 6.A.7 in the Appendix, whatever knowledge is created now resides in the heads of—and is therefore used by—more agents than under high obsolescence conditions. How might we interpret this? Let us speculate a little. Recall that low levels of obsolescence correspond to patented knowledge, a kind of knowledge that may be much more valuable to society than most copyrighted knowledge. Patented knowledge has to be *novel*, *useful*, and *nonobvious*—that is, penicillin as opposed to the local newspaper's gossip column. From a societal perspective, however, the key issue is still whether society is paying too much for this low-obsolescence knowledge. If policies could increase the rate of obsolescence from a minimum to something more than the minimum—thus increasing the system's rate of creative destruction and innovation—society would pay significantly less economic rent for this knowledge. Patenting, per se, does not entirely determine whether such knowledge is cumulative or not, although by helping to get it institutionalized and embedded in social and technical practices (Bowker 1992) patenting can be one source of the 'lock-in' effects that will slow down its obsolescence rate (Arthur 1989; David 1985).

The practices of the scientific community, by legitimating and institutionalizing what counts as abstract 'law-like' and knowledge, also contribute to its durability and thus help to reduce its obsolescence rate. Scientists and scientific institutions, like all organizations, operate according to a dominant logic, one that exhibits inertia (Prahalad and Bettis 1986). Here, obsolescence or the lack of it resides more in the mind of the agent than in the outside world. Knowledge that has been scientifically mandated, through repeated use, over time becomes unconscious and taken-for-granted (Knorr Cetina 1991). Like patenting, therefore, the practices of the scientific community help to institutionalize abstract knowledge thus embedding it in the fabric of society.

Proposition 3: Abstract knowledge creates powerful 'lock-in' effects that are paid for by society in the form of economic rents. The institutional conditions under which society 'recognizes' codified and abstract knowledge—patenting practices and those of the scientific community—will therefore significantly affect the total economic rents paid for by society.

6.7. Policy Implications

What are the policy implications of the propositions that we have put forward? Utility and scarcity jointly determine the value of a knowledge asset. It follows that this value can be eroded by the loss of utility, either in the content or the form of the knowledge asset, or by the loss of scarcity—brought about by the diffusion of the asset. Loss of utility is brought about in SimISpace by obsolescence. Loss of scarcity is brought about by spillover. Each of these can be partly affected by policy variables.

Obsolescence refers to decreases in the utility of knowledge relative to alternatives. Effectively it measures the rate at which new knowledge replaces old knowledge. In the case of copyrighted knowledge such as newspapers, yesterday's news is, well, yesterday's news. In the case of patented knowledge, by contrast, obsolescence can be taken more as a measure of the rate of innovation—that is, the rate at which creative destruction is at work. The rate of obsolescence of a firm's knowledge base can be affected by depreciation schedules, the investment incentives available to other firms to create either substitute or complementary knowledge, official standards setting, new regulations, etc.

Spillover refers to the involuntary diffusion of knowledge assets to competitors who are then in a legal position to use them. Taking out a patent, for example, is an invitation to competitors to 'invent around the patent', to challenge it in court, or to devise alternative yet legal ways of using the knowledge on which the patent was built. Copyright invites rephrasing, stylistic imitation, etc. Spillovers can be affected by property rights legislation, ease of patenting, the effectiveness of trade secrets, the mobility of qualified labor, legal enforcement practices, the regulation of media behavior, of education, demand, etc.

While policy variables do not actually determine the rate of obsolescence and of spillover in a given industry they may significantly influence them. However, policymakers must take into account the fact that different industries will naturally enjoy different rates of obsolescence and spillover and tailor their prescriptions accordingly. In industries subject primarily to copyright protection—such as in the fashion or music industries—the natural rate of obsolescence of knowledge is likely to be much higher than in industries protected by patents.

What we learn from Figure 6.10 is that the total rents paid per knowledge asset by society begins to level off or decline when the rate of spillovers crosses a certain threshold and property rights become leaky, and particularly so when obsolescence is low yet increasing. Yet high-obsolescence (copyright) regimes do not generate much new knowledge as compared with low-obsolescence (patenting) regimes. Even at the lowest level of spillover, the low-obsolescence regime generates much more new knowledge than the high-obsolescence regime. And up to some threshold the rate increases as spillover increases. Does society then pay a price in knowledge foregone at high rates of obsolescence? The answer may well be, yes, *unless the society in question is populated by fast learners* capable of profiting from a regime of creative destruction, and *no* if it is populated by slow learners (see the discussion in Section 6.3).

Proposition 4: Societies populated by fast learners can afford to operate in regimes where the rate of obsolescence is high whereas those that are populated by slow learners cannot.

The general message of our simulation results is that, if society is to get value-for-money from the management of its knowledge base, the strength of its property rights regime and the policy measures that speed up or slow down the rate of obsolescence of knowledge—that is, *that affect society's rate of innovation*—must be considered jointly. But is this not also a workable prescription for innovation policies *inside* entrepreneurial firms? A fast-learning firm, for example, might well prefer an open-source approach to software development—a relaxation of property rights—rather than a patenting approach—a tightening of property rights. The question clearly has policy implications for topical issues such as software patenting.

So what are IPRs worth to society? Our application of SimISpace suggests, unsurprisingly, that there is no single answer. Having IPRs and not having them both carry a cost and a benefit, but these costs and a benefits are often borne by different stakeholders and these will vary from society to society. What emerges from our analysis is that, given that patented and copyrighted knowledge are each naturally subject to different rates of obsolescence and, by implication, are subject to different rates of spillover, they require different property rights regimes. Different societies will want to 'mix' these two regimes in different ways adapted to their institutional structures and learning capacities.

Matching the benefits of IPRs to their costs is a key challenge of effective policymaking since unless knowledge creation is paid for according to its marginal productivity—like other factors of production—society's scarce resources will be misallocated. Our simulation exercise suggests a contingency approach to the problem, one that would take into account the dynamics of knowledge flows in a given industry and that would relate the degree of IPRs protection on offer—the ability to block diffusion—to the degree of turbulence prevailing in that industry—that is, to its rate of obsolescence. Our results, modest as they are, point to the possibility of, as well as the need for, a more dynamic theory of IPRs in the new economy.

6.8. Conclusions

In this chapter, we first presented a conceptual model, the I-Space, that highlighted the paradoxical nature of value when it resides in information rather than physical objects, and then, through agent-based simulation modeling, we showed how we could derive a number of insights relevant for policymaking in the new economy. We believe that this approach has potential for addressing the complex issues that confront policymakers in this new environment. But we are also aware that we have only scratched the surface of the challenging subject of IPRs.

As a simulation model, SimISpace is still under development and at this stage must be considered more of a 'proof-of-concept' model rather than a robust and usable piece of simulation equipment. The Propositions that we derive from our simulation results are thus developed for illustrative purposes only rather than for systematic testing. Nevertheless, they should allow the reader to assess the usefulness of this kind of simulation model for generating policy-relevant hypotheses. The model still has many gaps that need to be filled. Society, for example, one of the key beneficiaries of our property rights analysis, remains located outside the model. This will need to be rectified in further research if a more discriminating analysis is required. Also, further research should deliver: (*a*) a more articulated way of representing the intensity of creative destruction within a given industry; (*b*) metrics for examining the different knowledge structures that arise in the course of the simulation; (*c*) metrics for analyzing the structure of agent interactions; and (*d*) agents with some memory.

The new economy is characterized by the rapid growth of intangible assets relative to tangible assets. Since many of these intangible assets are built on intellectual property foundations, their value is highly sensitive to the nature and functioning of the IPRs regime in place. The stakes are high and increasing (Nakamura 2003). As the recent DotCom debacle has shown, the stock market valuation of firms operating mainly with intangible assets displays increasing volatility—what we have called obsolescence. Yet it turns out that we do not as yet much understand intangible assets. The best we have been able to do so far is to come up with IPRs regimes that mimic the more traditional ones based on tangible assets. The complexity of the relationships between the creation, diffusion, and obsolescence of knowledge, however, make this approach increasingly problematic. Our chapter set out to explore how variations in IPRs regimes affect the flow of knowledge in an economic system. Our analysis points to the need for a contingency approach to these rights, one that openly recognize the differences between those of a material-based society and those of an information-based society.

Appendix: Statistical Results

This appendix reports the means, standard deviations, and comparison between means tests for the data that were used in Figures 6.2 through 6.12.

Table 6A.1. Maximum Codification of Agents' Knowledge

Spillover	Obsolescence				
	0.01	0.0125	0.015	0.0175	0.02
0.01					
Mean	2.54	2.48	2.37	2.36	2.33
Std Dev	0.25	0.23	0.21	0.22	0.23
0.0125					
Mean	2.63	2.55	2.48	2.36	2.34
Std Dev	0.28	0.25	0.22	0.24	0.22
0.015					
Mean	2.69	2.61	2.48	2.45	2.38
Std Dev	0.27	0.26	0.24	0.24	0.22
0.0175					
Mean	2.75	2.64	2.49	2.43	2.40
Std Dev	0.30	0.26	0.24	0.23	0.20
0.02					
Mean	2.77	2.65	2.54	2.44	2.42
Std Dev	0.28	0.27	0.25	0.21	0.21

Note: There are significant differences between means for all corner conditions, and between the midpoint condition and all corner conditions.

Table 6A.2. Maximum Abstraction of Agents' Knowledge

Spillover	Obsolescence				
	0.01	0.0125	0.015	0.0175	0.02
0.01					
Mean	2.39	2.36	2.28	2.25	2.20
Std Dev	0.25	0.27	0.23	0.26	0.23
0.0125					
Mean	2.52	2.42	2.31	2.27	2.24
Std Dev	0.31	0.28	0.24	0.27	0.24
0.015					
Mean	2.57	2.48	2.38	2.32	2.25
Std Dev	0.31	0.27	0.27	0.26	0.23
0.0175					
Mean	2.60	2.49	2.39	2.30	2.29
Std Dev	0.32	0.29	0.28	0.26	0.24
0.02					
Mean	2.66	2.49	2.42	2.33	2.27
Std Dev	0.31	0.30	0.28	0.24	0.21

Note: There are significant differences between means for all corner conditions, and between the midpoint condition and all corner conditions except low/low.

Table 6A.3. Maximum Diffusion of Knowledge to Agents

Spillover	Obsolescence				
	0.01	0.0125	0.015	0.0175	0.02
0.02					
Mean	1.96	1.54	1.23	0.95	0.76
Std Dev	0.54	0.58	0.58	0.46	0.35
0.0175					
Mean	1.85	1.48	1.10	0.87	0.76
Std Dev	0.59	0.60	0.51	0.45	0.37
0.015					
Mean	1.74	1.41	1.07	0.87	0.70
Std Dev	0.53	0.57	0.49	0.46	0.34
0.0125					
Mean	1.49	1.17	0.86	0.72	0.60
Std Dev	0.58	0.55	0.42	0.38	0.28
0.01					
Mean	1.11	0.89	0.68	0.61	0.53
Std Dev	0.51	0.45	0.30	0.33	0.29

Note: There are significant differences between means for all corner conditions, and between the midpoint condition and all corner conditions.

Table 6A.4. Total Knowledge Generated

Spillover	Obsolescence				
	0.01	0.0125	0.015	0.0175	0.02
0.01					
Mean	21177	20336	19481	18964	18637
Std Dev	2373	2047	2115	2496	1510
0.0125					
Mean	22326	21346	20249	19269	19216
Std Dev	2288	2335	1928	2088	1889
0.015					
Mean	22980	21596	20791	20051	19499
Std Dev	2217	2070	2077	2147	5338
0.0175					
Mean	23104	22050	20934	20669	19702
Std Dev	2685	2001	1965	2517	1682
0.02					
Mean	23252	21988	21164	20637	19897
Std Dev	2246	2047	2048	2217	2142

Note: There are significant differences between means for all corner conditions, and between the midpoint condition and all corner conditions.

Table 6A.5. Total Economic Rent Generated

Spillover	Obsolescence				
	0.01	0.0125	0.015	0.0175	0.02
0.01					
Mean	32,143	10,431	3,196	1,456	556
Std Dev	72,692	24,304	9,142	4,240	1,587
0.0,125					
Mean	49,854	20,315	10,214	4,186	1,644
Std Dev	75,500	39,349	25,312	11,289	7,092
0.015					
Mean	67,307	19,917	8,784	5,468	1,865
Std Dev	88,652	29,909	16,777	17,506	4,681
0.0,175					
Mean	59,835	23,649	9,975	3,222	1,856
Std Dev	87,743	34,536	15,119	5,948	3,696
0.02					
Mean	64,194	25,964	9,807	4,308	1,682
Std Dev	71,524	33,423	15,559	7,674	5,338

Note: Since the distributions of results are highly right-skewed, we performed comparisons of log means. There are significant differences between log means for all corner conditions, and also between the midpoint condition and all corner conditions except high obsolescence/high spillover.

Table 6A.6. Economic Rent Generated per Knowledge Asset

Spillover	Obsolescence				
	0.01	0.0125	0.015	0.0175	0.02
0.01					
Mean	1.367	0.475	0.157	0.078	0.032
Std Dev	1.322	0.365	0.104	0.047	0.018
0.0125					
Mean	2.018	0.890	0.486	0.212	0.092
Std Dev	1.802	0.709	0.368	0.139	0.048
0.015					
Mean	2.654	0.864	0.407	0.267	0.096
Std Dev	2.274	0.642	0.258	0.188	0.053
0.0175					
Mean	2.367	1.002	0.453	0.153	0.097
Std Dev	1.991	0.727	0.302	0.095	0.046
0.02					
Mean	2.539	1.107	0.451	0.211	0.088
Std Dev	2.051	0.798	0.300	0.124	0.046

Note: Since the distributions of results are highly right-skewed, we performed comparisons of log means. There are significant differences between log means for all corner conditions, and between the midpoint condition and all corner conditions.

Table 6A.7. Number of Agents Surviving

Spillover	Obsolescence				
	0.01	0.0125	0.015	0.0175	0.02
0.01					
Mean	12.6	8.3	6.3	4.8	3.6
Std Dev	8.9	5.6	4.1	3.2	2.8
0.0125					
Mean	18.8	12.5	9.4	6.7	5.0
Std Dev	12.0	9.2	7.6	4.7	3.3
0.015					
Mean	24.8	15.7	10.1	7.7	5.9
Std Dev	11.9	8.6	6.9	6.3	3.9
0.0175					
Mean	26.5	17.2	12.3	7.6	6.4
Std Dev	13.3	11.1	7.7	5.1	4.1
0.02					
Mean	29.6	19.6	12.6	9.2	6.3
Std Dev	15.4	10.4	8.3	6.5	3.9

Note: There are significant differences between log means for all corner conditions, and between the midpoint condition and all corner conditions.

References

Arrow, K. J. (1962). 'The Economic Implications of Learning by Doing', *Review of Economic Studies*, 29: 155–73.

Arthur, B. (1989). 'Competing Technologies, Increasing Returns, and Lock-in by Historical Events', *The Economic Journal*, 99 (394 March): 116–31.

Barzel, Y. (1989). *Economic Analysis of Property Rights*. Cambridge: Cambridge University Press.

Besen, S. and Raskind, L. (1991). 'An Introduction to the Law and Economics of Intellectual Property', *Journal of Economic Perspectives*, 5: 3–27.

Boisot, M. (1995). *Information Space: A Framework for Learning in Organizations, Institutions and Culture*. London: Routledge.

—— (1998). *Knowledge Assets. Securing Competitive Advantage in the Information Economy*. Oxford: Oxford University Press.

—— and Child, J. (1988). 'The Iron Law of Fiefs: Bureaucratic Failure and the Problem of Governance in the Chinese Economic Reforms', *Administrative Science Quarterly*, 33: 507–27.

Bowker, G. (1992). 'Whats in a Patent?', in W. Bijker and J. Law (eds.), *Shaping Technology/Building Society*. Cambridge, MA: MIT Press.

Carley, K. (1999). 'On Generating Hypotheses Using Computer Simulations', *Systems Engineering*, 2(2): 69–77.

Carley, K. and Lee, J. (1998). 'Dynamic Organizations: Organizational Adaptations in a Changing Environment', in J. Baum (ed.), *Advances in Strategic Management 15*. Stamford, CT: JAI Press.

Chaitin, G. J. (1974). 'Information-Theoretic Computational Complexity IEEE Transactions', *Information Theory*, 20: 10.

Cheung, S. (1982). 'Property Rights in Trade Secrets', *Economic Inquiry*, 20: 40–53.

David, P. (1985). 'Clio and the Economics of QWERTY', *American Economic Review Proceedings*, 75: 332–7.

Demsetz, H. (1967). 'Towards a Theory of Property Rights', *American Economic Review*, 57: 347–59.

De Soto, H. (2000). *The Mystery of Capital: Why Capitalism Triumphs in the West and Fails Everywhere Else*. London: Bantam Press.

Dobb, M. (1973). *Theories of Value and Distribution: Ideology and Economic Theory*. Cambridge: Cambridge University Press.

Douglas, M. (1986). *How Institutions Think*. Syracuse, NY: Syracuse University Press.

Dretske, F. (1981). *Knowledge and the Flow of Information*. Cambridge, MA: MIT Press.

Field, B. (1989). 'The Evolution of Property Rights', *Kylos*, 42: 319–45.

Friedman, D., Landes, W., and Posner, R. (1991). 'Some Economics of Trade Secret Law', *Journal of Economic Perspectives*, 5: 61–72.

Gilbert, G. and Troitzsch, V. (1999). *Simulation for the Social Scientist*. London: Open University Press.

Gilfillan, S. (1964). Invention and the Patent System. A study for the US Congress Joint Economic Committee, 88th Congress, 2nd Session, US Government Printing Office.

Grant, R. (1996). 'Toward a Knowledge-Based Theory of the Firm', *Strategic Management Journal*, 17 (Winter Special Issue): 109–22.

Hands, J. and Lev, B. (2003). *Intangible Assets: Values, Measures, and Risks*. Oxford: Oxford University Press.

Henderson, R. M. and Clark, K. B. (1990). 'Architectural Innovation: The Reconfiguring of Existing Product Technologies and the Failure of Established Firms', *Administrative Science Quarterly*, 35: 9–30.

Henriques, E. (1983). *De la Horde a L'Etat: Essai de Psychanalyze du lieu Social*. Paris: Editions Gallinard.

Khanna, T. and Palepu, K. (1997). 'Why Focused Strategies May Be Wrong for Emerging Markets', *Harvard Business Review*, 74(4): 41–51.

Knight, F. (1921). *Risk, Uncertainty, and Profit*. New York: Harper & Row.

Knorr Cetina, K. (1991). 'Epistemic Cultures: Forms of Reason in Science', *History of Political Economy*, 21(1): 105–22.

Kolmogorov, A. (1965). 'Three Approaches to the Quantitive Definition of Information', *Problems in Inform. Transmissions*, 1: 3–11.

Lanjouw, J. and Schankerman, M. (1997). 'Stylized Facts on Patent Litigation: Value, Scope and Ownership', Working Paper No. 6297. National Bureau of Economic Research.

Leonard, D. (2003). 'Apple Enters Contentious World of Online Music', *The Business*, 12: 4–6.

Lessig, L. (2001). *The Future of Ideas: The Fate of the Commons in a Connected World*. New York: Vintage.

Liebeskind, J. (1996). 'Knowledge, Strategy, and the Theory of the Firm', *Strategic Management Journal*, 17 (December winter special issue): 93–107.

Locke, J. (1964). *An Essay Concerning Human Understanding*. London: Collins.

Macpherson, C. (1962). *The Political Theory of Possessive Individualism: Hobbes to Locke*. Oxford: Oxford University Press.

Mansfield, E. (1968). *Industrial Research and Technological Progress*. New York: W.W. Norton.

—— (1985). 'How Rapidly Does New Technology Leak Out?', *Journal of Industrial Economics*, 34: 217–24.

March, J. (1991). 'Exploration and Exploitation in Organizational Learning', *Organization Science*, 2.

Marx, K. (1972). *Capital: A Critique of Political Economy*. London: Lawrence & Wishart.

Maynard-Smith, J. (1982). *Evolution and the Theory of Games*. Cambridge: Cambridge University Press.

Nakamura, L. (2003). 'Trillion Dollars a Year in Intangible Investments and the New Economy', in J. Hands and B. Lev (eds.), *Intangible Assets: Values, Measures, and Risks*. Oxford: Oxford University Press.

Nelson, R. and Winter, S. (1982). *An Evolutionary Theory of Economic Change*. Cambridge, MA: Belknap Press of Harvard University Press.

Nonaka, I. and Takeuchi, H. (1995). *The Knowledge-Creating Company: How Japanese Companies Create the Dynamics of Innovation*. New York: Oxford University Press.

North, D. and Thomas, R. (1973). *The Rise of the Western World: An Economic History*. Cambridge: Cambridge University Press.

Olson, M. (1971). *The Logic of Collective Action: Public Goods and the Theory of Groups*. Cambridge, MA: Harvard University Press.

Parker, J. (1978). *The Economics of Innovation: The Natinal and Multinational Enterprise in Technological Change*. London: Longman.

Penrose, E. (1959). *The Theory of the Growth of the Firm*. New York: John Wiley & Sons.

Piaget, J. (1967). *Biologie et Connaissance: Essai sur les Relations entre les Regulations Organiques et les Processus Cognitifs*. Paris: Gallimard.

Prahalad, C. and Bettis, R. A. (1986). 'The Dominant Logic: A New Linkage between Diversity and Performance', *Strategic Management Journal*, 7: 485–501.

Prusak, L. (1996). 'The Knowledge Advantage', *Strategy and Leadership*, March/April 24: 6–8.

Rawls, J. (1971). *A Theory of Justice*. Oxford: Oxford University Press.

Romer, P. (1998). 'The Social Revolution: Achieving Growth by Managing Intangibles', *Journal of Applied Corporate Finance*, 11(2): 8–14.

Root-Bernstein, R. (1989). *Discovering: Inventing and Solving Problems at the Frontiers of Scientific Knowledge*. Cambridge, MA: Harvard University Press.

Schumpeter, J. (1934). *The Theory of Economic Development: An Inquiry into Profits, Capital, Credit, Interest and the Business Cycle.* London: Oxford University Press.

Shapiro, C. and Varian, H. (1999). *Information Rules: A Strategic Guide to the Network Economy.* Boston, MA: Harvard Business School Press.

Thelen, E. and Smith, L. (1994). *A Dynamic Systems Approach to the Development of Cognition and Action.* Cambridge, MA: MIT Press.

Utterback, J. (1994). *Mastering the Dynamics of Innovation: How Companies Can Seize Opportunities in the Face of Technological Change.* Boston, MA: Harvard Business School Press.

Walras, L. (1926). *Elements of Pure Economics or the Theory of Social Wealth.* Philadelphia, PA: Orion Editions.

7

Conclusion

Max H. Boisot

In this book, we have sought to do two things. First, through a series of thematically linked chapters, to build up the theoretical foundations for a conceptual framework centered on knowledge flows, the I-Space. This was the job of the first five chapters. Second, in Chapter 6, to open up a window on the kind of research that the I-Space lends itself to. Taking each in turn.

7.1. Recapitulation

Clarifying the way knowledge differs from information and data and exploring some of the implications of the differences was the task of Chapter 1. Although one frequently encounters attempts to draw a distinction between these concepts, such attempts are but weakly grounded in theory and often smack of ad hockery. We argued in this chapter that information mediates the relationship between the stimuli of the world that reach an agent and register with her as data—as Landauer (1999) put it, these are inevitably *physical*[1]—and an agent's prior knowledge, taken as a set of expectations that dispose her both to filter incoming stimuli and to act in particular ways. Information can be deemed meaningful to the extent that it modifies in some way these expectations, whether this is by shifting them or by actually reinforcing them. These are shaped firstly by

[1] The title of one of Landauer's papers 'Information is Inevitably Physical' makes no mention of data as such. Yet, as he observes in the paper, 'It was known in 1961 that it takes $kT\ln2$ to ship a bit, and in a computer we do lots of bit transmission, *even when we do not discard information*' (Landauer 1999: 79—italics added). Like most scholars working on the physics of information, Landauer does not distinguish between data and information in his terminology. But it is clear from his argument that he is referring to the processing of *data* which may or may not be information-bearing.

the need to economize on scarce energetic and data-processing resources and secondly by the historically unique situation of the agent. The historical uniqueness of agents, *pace* much economic theory to the contrary, makes it difficult to infer that because they can be subjected to identical stimuli—say, those emanating from the market—they necessarily register the same data from these, extract identical information from the data, and end up with identical knowledge with respect to external conditions.

Does our approach not effectively reduce all knowledge to a subjective experience as argued by the radical constructivists (von Glasersfeld 1995)? Not if, in Popper's memorable phrase, reality keeps 'kicking back' and nudging us gradually in the right direction (Popper 1983). Yet who is to say whether the direction that we are being nudged toward is the 'right' one? How can we know that we are not in fact being nudged in the wrong direction? Adopting an evolutionary perspective, the answer is that we never really know, but that to the extent that 'reality' sooner or later selects out those who take the wrong direction, the 'right' direction has survival value—or, as William James put it, it has 'cash value' (James 2000). As Chapter 1 argues, while this knowledge will vary across individual agents, the possibilities for objectivity will gradually emerge from overlaps in the respective situations and data-processing strategies of different agents. In this interpretation, objective knowledge becomes the intersubjective knowledge of the survivors. There is nothing, however, that guarantees that this kind of objective knowledge necessarily converges on something called 'the truth'. The assumption that knowledge that has survival value is somehow closer to some impersonal truth than knowledge that does not is a metaphysical one. You either buy it or you don't.

Chapter 2 further explored the different ways that we can be said to know things. We based our conceptualization of knowledge on an agent's effective willingness to act rather than on the degree of certainty that underpins that willingness—that is, on a pragmatic rather than a Platonic view of knowledge. We then argued that managers and entrepreneurs will differ with respect to both how strongly they need to hold a belief and how rigorously they need to justify holding it before acting. Evolving such belief involves what Gladwell (2005) labels *thin slicing*: finding patterns in experience on the basis of very narrow 'slices' of experience. But what minimal thickness will the slices need to have for an entrepreneur to discern some pattern in her experiences? How much thicker will the slices then have to be before the entrepreneur is actually willing to *act* on the pattern so discerned? Will a manager require thicker or thinner slices than the entrepreneur? And what minimal thickness will the manager require before committing to action? We have argued that entrepreneurs will act on the basis of plausible patterns and that managers will act on the basis of probable ones. The plausibility of a pattern can be established with thinner slices than its probability, leading to quite distinct epistemologies and, by implication, to quite distinct behaviors. Simply put, an entrepreneur will act sooner, and on the basis of more shaky experiential data than a manager will. Our arguments, if accepted, have both theoretical and practical implications. Our institutions and their governance structures are strongly biased in favor of managerial epistemologies, often at the expense of entrepreneurial ones. Managerial epistemologies are conservative, something which makes sense under conditions of stability. When innovation is called for, however, it makes less sense. We need to be aware of our options.

Chapter 3 investigated the nature of epistemic differences between agents. We saw in Chapter 1 that living systems with a capacity to learn and evolve are constantly substituting data for energy in their quest for economic forms of adaptation. In Chapter 3, we argued that they then attempt to economize on data processing and transmission through acts of *codification* and *abstraction* that allow them to judiciously extract information from the data. We then explored the implications of this conclusion for the way that we think about that class of agents that we call firms. Again we came up against established economic assumptions that firms could be assumed to be identical in knowledge and/or technologies. Such an assumption is required to make markets function 'efficiently'. Arrow and Debreu's celebrated first welfare theorem of economics assumes that all economic agents have the same information. Uncertainty, to be sure, may be present, but it will be present for all agents to the same extent and in the same way (Arrow and Debreu 1954; Postlewaite 1987). Although few economists actually believe the realization of such information symmetry to be feasible, it sets up an implicit default assumption that it is the differences between firms that need explanation rather than their similarities. In the chapter, we further developed the argument for agent heterogeneity that we presented in Chapter 1 and showed how epistemic differences can arise between firms both from the way that their respective codification and abstraction strategies operate as well as from their particular circumstances. Differences as such do not need explaining; similarities do. What does need explaining, however, is how, when such differences give rise to identifiable competitive advantages, they become *sustainable*—that is, they generate similarities in the performance of a given agent across different time periods. After all, efficient market processes should be competing these advantages away. What is it, specifically, that prevents this from happening?

Chapter 4 explored the organizational dimension of the issue to give us the glimmer of an answer. If we accept Williamson's starting assumption that 'in the beginning there were markets'[2] then we are left with the task of explaining the emergence of organization. But markets rely for their efficiency on the ready availability of well-codified and abstract information—that is, prices and quantities—to all players in the market. Was such information actually available to all players 'in the beginning'? We argue that if 'in the beginning' such information was neither codified nor abstract, then it follows that it could not have been readily available to all players. To develop this argument, we develop a conceptual framework, the I-Space, that relates the structuring of information through acts of codification and abstraction to its diffusibility. What does the framework suggest? The simple idea that historically *organization must have preceded markets as a way of organizing economic activity.* Face-to-face exchanges *within* structured kinship groups, for example, would have preceded impersonal exchange *between* such groups. The local comes first; the nonlocal has to be built up over time. The concept of market failure, therefore, being an implicit presumption in favor of efficient markets in which the nonlocal predominates, can be misleading.

In Chapter 5, we further developed the arguments presented in Chapter 4 and applied them to the emergence of cultures and institutions. Certain types of information flow give rise to recurrent interactions between agents. As initially demonstrated by Coase and further developed by North, the economic efficiency of these can be enhanced by the formation of stable institutional structures (Coase 1937; North 1990). In this chapter, we located these in different regions of the I-Space according to their information characteristics and labeled them markets, bureaucracies, clans and fiefs. We argued that over time, the institutional evolution that has characterized Western cultures has favored moving toward higher levels of codification and abstraction—a move from personal and particularistic community (*gemeinschaft*) to impersonal and universalistic organization (*gesellschaft*) (Tönnies 1955)—thus increasing the

---

[2] Thomas Hobbes, in *Leviathan*, likewise had to assume an initial state of nature that he characterized as 'a war of all against all' in order to account for the bottom-up contractual processes by which the modern state is created. Williamsom stresses that his starting assumption is an expositional convenience. Yet over time, expositional conveniences tend to evolve into default assumptions.

transactional scope and reach of both bureaucratic and market processes at the expense of fief and clan ones.

Recent developments in information and communication technologies, however, by massively increasing the bandwidth available to all, are making it possible to maintain the quality of face-to-face relationships at a distance, thus increasing the scope once more for fief- and clan-like relationships, albeit now more widely spread out in time and space. Our analysis somewhat challenges the widespread assumption that the phenomenon of globabalization reduces to a universal extension of market processes.

How does one demonstrate the utility of a conceptual framework such as the I-Space? Being constructed out of a network of interrelated theories rather than a single theory, it does not easily lend itself to direct empirical testing. This is hardly a new problem. In what became known as the Duhem–Quine thesis, both Duhem and Quine independently observed that one never tests theories individually, anyway, but in clusters (Duhem 1914; Quine 1951), one reason that crucial experiments are rarely conclusive. One measure of a framework's utility is its ability to give rise to testable new hypotheses and theories. In Chapter 6, we made a small step in the direction of demonstrating the I-Space's potential utility. We showed how simulation modeling could contribute to further theory development by generating empirically testable hypotheses derivable from the I-Space in nonobvious ways. Here we introduced an agent-based model, *SimISpace*, by means of which we explored an issue that naturally lends itself to I-Space theorizing: that of intellectual property rights. We showed that the I-Space could help to frame the issue as one of optimal diffusion, but one in which what is optimal differs depending on whether we are talking of knowledge that lends itself to patenting or to copyrighting. These two kinds of knowledge have different locations in the I-Space and require different types of IPR treatment.

What other kinds of research might the I-Space be applied to? We briefly present other possibilities in the closing section of the book.

7.2. A Research Agenda

The I-Space and the concepts on which it builds have been used on numerous occasions as conceptual aids both in research and in consulting interventions. The framework has proven its worth as a sense-making device in complex situations. But does it have any predictive value? The simulation model, SimISpace, described in Chapter 6, is one attempt to answer this. In what follows, we briefly examine a number of other research avenues along which the answer can be sought.

Mapping Knowledge assets: An organization's critical knowledge assets could be identified empirically and then mapped into the I-Space as a function of how codified, abstract, and diffused each of them is, and of how they are configured together into networks.[3] The organization could then assess the strategic value of its knowledge assets in terms of their attractiveness and the competitive position they yield for the organization. The resulting knowledge map would be valuable in its own right as a tool of strategic analysis, but it could then also be used as an input into a number of simulations that pit the organization against others with differing knowledge profiles. What knowledge asset configuration suggests a competitive relationship with other agents, and what configuration suggests a more collaborative stance? Under what conditions would the organization benefit from sharing critical knowledge assets in order to expand its knowledge base through joint learning? Under what conditions would it be better off hoarding them?

Mapping Cultural and Institutional Structures: As discussed in Chapter 5, repeated agent interactions give rise to emergent structures that reflect either an increasing or a decreasing propensity of these agents to do business with each other. We identified four generic interaction structures that reflected the nature of the information environment that either facilitated or impeded agent interaction: (*a*) Markets; (*b*) Bureaucracies; (*c*) Clans; and (*d*) fiefs. When these interaction structures rest on a cultural substrate of shared values and preferences and are consciously sought after and constructed, we can talk of institutionalization. It would be possible to empirically describe either whole organizations or parts of organizations according to how far they exhibit such interaction structures in their internal or their external processes. Such empirically derived cultural and institutional maps constitute valuable diagnostic tools, and, like knowledge maps, they could act as inputs into simulations. We could then explore the way that the interaction propensities imputed to different agents—the cultural substrates of values and preferences that give rise to institutional structures—both shape and are shaped by knowledge flows.

A further simulation possibility would be to prestructure the relationship between the agents located along the diffusion dimension according

---

[3] For an example of such mapping, see Max Boisot's book *Knowledge Assets: Securing Competitive Advantage in the Information Economy* (Oxford: Oxford University Press, 1998).

to the four generic interaction structures identified in Chapter 5. Thus instead of having such structures emerge in a bottom-up fashion from the initially random interaction of individual agents, a particular interaction propensity is imputed to such agents in a top-down manner at the beginning of the simulation and thus treated as a parameter of the simulation. The strength of the interaction between agents could also be specified *ex ante* along with the interaction preference, allowing us to model the differences between strong and weak ties (Granovetter 1985). We could then explore and compare how far given cultural preferences facilitate or impede knowledge flows—and by implication, social learning processes—and under what circumstances they do so.

Mapping Learning Processes: We saw in Chapter 6 that new knowledge emerges in the I-Space through a process of social learning by agents that we label the Social Learning Cycle or *SLC*. The SLC consists of scanning for opportunities and threats, articulating some insightful response to these through processes of codification and abstraction, sharing the insights—selectively or otherwise—with a wider population of agents, and the getting those newly created insights internalized and applied in new situations. Agents differ in their learning propensities and skills, some displaying greater mastery in some steps of the SLC than in others. The different learning skills possessed by an organization could be captured empirically and mapped onto a variety of SLCs. They could then serve as inputs into simulations that explore the different types of knowledge assets that these give rise to, the type of agent interactions that they enable or impede—and hence the kind of cultural and institutional dispositions that they engender.

The ability to map an organization's knowledge assets, its different cultures and institutional structures, and its learning processes would, we believe, be of considerable value in its own right, whether such mappings were then subsequently to yield inputs for further simulation work. Much work, however, remains to be done in and around the simulation model itself.

Further Development of the Simulation Model, SimISpace: One avenue of development involves the creation of new modules for the simulation itself. For example, one of our colleagues, Agusti Canals, coauthor of Chapter 1 of this book, has been working with us on the spatial modeling of knowledge flows. How are knowledge flows affected by the physical distance that separates agents from each other? When does the inability to interact face to face trigger increases in the level of codification and abstraction of knowledge exchanges between spatially separated agents and when does it block such exchanges? Because I-Space concepts are scalable, this work has implications that range from the layout of a research laboratory (Allen 1977) to the growth and development of geographic clusters, cities, regions, etc.

The scalability of the I-Space extends the range of phenomena that can be simulated. The only restrictions that we place upon the agents in *SimISpace* is that they should be capable of receiving data, processing it, and transmitting it. Given such restriction a population of agents can represent a population of countries (each one taken to be an 'actor' on the international scene), a population of firms representing an industry or a strategic alliance, a population of employees inside a single firm, or even a population of neurons in a single head! Currently under discussion are simulations of international security challenges, scientific discovery processes, knowledge-based regional development, migration and educational issues, industrial location, corporate strategy, and so on. The research agenda keeps growing. To engage with it in 2006, we created an organization, the *I-Space Institute*, whose mission is to carry out I-Space-related research and consulting—for us a form of results-oriented research. We welcome collaborators who share our interest in the nature of knowledge flows and the information economy.

References

Allen, T. J. (1977). *Managing the Flow of Technology: Technology Transfer and the Dissemination of Technological Information within the R&D Organization*. Cambridge, MA: MIT Press.

Arrow, K. and Debreu, G. (1954). 'Existence of an Equilibrium for a Competitive economy', *Econometrica*, 22: 265–90.

Coase, R. (1937). 'The Nature of the Firm', *Economica, NS* 4: 386–405.

Duhem, P. (1914). *La Théorie Physique: Son Objet, sa Structure*. Paris: Rivière et Cie. (Translated 1953 by Philip Weiner as The Aim and Structure of Physical Theory, Princeton, NY: Princeton University Press. Reprinted 1962, New York: Atheneum.)

Gladwell, M. (2005). *Blink: The Power of Thinking Without Thinking*. New York: Little, Brown.

Grannoveter, M. (1973). 'The Strength of Weak Ties' *American Journal of Sociology*, 78(6): 1360–80.

Landauer, R. (1999). *Information is Inevitably Physical. Feynman and Computation: Exploring the Limits of Computers*. Reading, MA: Perseus Books.

North, D. (1990). *Institutions, Institutional Change and Economic Performance.* Cambridge: Cambridge University Press.

Popper, K. R. (1983). *Realism and the Aim of Science.* London: Hutchinson.

Postlewaite, A. (1987). 'Asymmetric Information', in J. Eatwell, M. Milgate, and P. Newman (eds.), *Allocation, Information and Markets, The New Palgrave.* London: MacMillan.

Quine, W. V. (1951). 'Two Dogmas of Empiricism', *The Philosophical Review*, 60: 20–43.

Tönnies, F. (1955). *Community and Association.* London: Routledge & Kegan Paul.

Von Glasersfeld, E. (1995). *Radical Constructivism: A Way of Knowing and Learning.* London: Routledge-Falmer.

Index

Index